Subtropical Plants

A Practical Gardening Guide

Jacqueline Sparrow & Gil Hanly

Timber Press
Portland, Oregon

First published in North America in 2002 by
Timber Press, Inc.
The Haseltine Building
133 S.W. Second Avenue, Suite 450
Portland, Oregon 97204, USA
tel 1-800-327-5680 or 1-503-227-2878
fax 1-503-227-3070
www.timberpress.com

and distributed in the United Kingdom by
Timber Press
2 Station Road
Swavesey, Cambridge CB4 5QJ
tel (01954) 232959
fax (01954) 206040

ISBN 0-88192-544-6

A CIP record for this book is available from the Library of Congress

Cover photograph Gloriosa superba
Typesetting and production: Kate Greenaway
Printed in Hong Kong

Contents

Introduction 7

Trees 11

Shrubs 37

Palms and Cycads 71

Fruit 86

Climbers 98

Perennials and Bulbs 122

Cacti and Other Succulents 150

Bromeliads 159

Orchids 166

Index 173

Introduction

North and south of the tropics are the regions known as the subtropics, where a huge range of plants can be cultivated. Blessed with a benevolent climate, the gardener here has limitless scope. Bold colourful foliage plants, almost defying description, vie with vivid flowers at every season of the year. Gardeners in these areas can choose from a wide variety of subjects, from those thriving in warm temperate zones to many from the true tropics, which are often well adapted to semi-tropical conditions, although ultra-tropical plants may need extra care to really thrive. The tropical and subtropical zones contain the greatest variety of plants in the world, with an estimated minimum of 200,000 species.

Climatic conditions vary considerably in these regions, from dry and sunny to moist and steamy, with many microclimates in between. Roughly speaking, areas of successful

Ferns and tree ferns are well suited to subtropical gardens but can be temperamental.

Opposite: Gardeners in subtropical areas can choose from a variety of colourful foliage plants and vivid flowers.

Bird's nest ferns (foreground) and epiphytic staghorn ferns add to the lushness of a shady area in this subtropical garden.

orange growing mark the limit of the subtropics, and as a general rule the climate is frost free. Rapid growth is synonymous with the subtropics, where plants will romp away and mature precociously. In no time at all the exuberant growth will probably need to be curtailed, and unfortunately some plants enjoy the lifestyle so much they colonise, becoming a threat to the environment. Conversely, many species are disappearing from the wild and only survive by cultivation. Others are still being discovered.

Early explorers brought back fantastic plants from faraway places to their cooler homelands, but it was the 18th- and 19th- century plant-hunters and botanists who successfully established tender exotic plants in Europe. England, with its vast empire, was the forerunner, and plant exotica became a fad, a must for the wealthy seeking to fill their newly built, heated, iron-framed glasshouses with treasures. Kew Gardens were established and opened to the public in 1841, and the Palm House was built a few years later. It is still world renowned, home to a panoply of palms and other horticultural wonders.

In the 20th century, probably nobody made more of an impact on the availability of tropical and semitropical garden plants and their use in contemporary landscape design than Roberto Burle Marx, who died in 1994. He introduced 13 species to horticulture, most from his native, adored Brazil, and 11 species of plants are named after him. Burle Marx was as exuberant and flamboyant as his gardens, and passionate about nature and the environment, with a love of art and beauty. His creativity is celebrated throughout much of the world, and he lives on in more than 1500 public and private gardens. His Brazilian property, given to the government, contains one of the world's richest collections of tropical and semitropical plants, and is a centre for botanical research.

This book concentrates on plants suitable for gardens in warm climates: trees (apart from tree ferns), shrubs, palms and cycads, fruit, climbers, perennials and bulbs, cacti and succulents, bromeliads and orchids. Choices will depend on the gardener's own particular conditions: aspect, sunshine hours, soil type, available water and shelter. Tree ferns, usually more successful in their natural environment, are possible features for certain sites, but are difficult to establish and succumb quickly if stressed. Other ferns, beautiful but sometimes temperamental, need cossetting in bush houses or shady dells. Apart from a few hardy species, they are best left to specialist growers.

Palms provide a vertical element in the garden.

The flowers on some bromeliads can be quite outstanding, while the leaves provide year-round interest.

Bamboo provide structure and filtered light, making a good backdrop for other subtropical plants.

The design of subtropical gardens is a subject covered in many other publications by authors expert in landscape architecture or with hands-on experience. And as every garden design is different, dictated by site, size, its microclimate and the preferences of its creator, the topic is really outside the scope of this book. Suffice to say that the lush, colourful, constantly growing plants in the subtropical garden frequently dominate the landscape in a fashion which demands good basic design and constant monitoring to maintain the essential elements.

Whatever design you favour, the subtropical garden should be enhanced and complemented by suitable structures and accessories. These could include walls, steps and sculptures of stone, Oriental or Western ceramics, Polynesian wood and tree-fern carvings and many other artworks indigenous to the regions of the world from which the plants originated. Pools, fountains, pergolas and pavilions are integral to the style. Versatile bamboo and cane are ideal materials for all types of furniture, gates, screens, fences and other outdoor structures. Hammocks, umbrellas, banners and brilliantly coloured cushions complement the natural flamboyance of the flora.

Trees

Trees are the most important plants in the landscape, and noble trees dominate parks, large gardens and rural areas. Whatever their size, trees are cultivated for their many benefits of foliage, flowers, berries and fruit, ornamental bark and trunks. Quite apart from their aesthetic appeal, trees give shelter to birds and animals, as well as people, offer cool shade and privacy, control pollution, conserve water, provide oxygen and prevent erosion — all necessary for our wellbeing.

Tree growth varies considerably in all climate zones, and the ultimate height and width of most species is difficult to predict, with climate and soil the arbiters to a great extent. In the main, trees are columnar, rounded, pyramidal, oval, spreading or pendulous, although a few are not so easily defined. Choose carefully for the courtyard, terrace or smaller garden. Size at maturity, root space and growth pattern, shade and leaf drop must all be considered, as well as proximity to swimming pools, buildings and neighbours. The length of shade varies with the seasons; patterns of shade are never stationary, and it is surprising just how far shade lengthens in winter months.

Being permanent plants, trees, with their imperialist roots and longevity, deserve proper soil preparation, and the old French adage is particularly applicable: 'Spend three sous on the plant and 30 sous on the planting.' Newly planted trees are vulnerable for the first year or so and frequently require staking. It is wise to protect many species with shadecloth if they are in exposed positions.

In subtropical regions trees often grow particularly fast, so do select carefully. It can be expensive to get trees removed if they prove unsuitable for the site. However, every garden should contain at least one tree. In tiny areas a potted topiary or bonsai example may fit the bill.

Trees can be the most satisfying plants in a garden, supplying our spiritual needs and personal pleasures as well as providing a solid basis on which to build good design. Grow them in small groups in contemplative corners and secret bowers, perhaps placed at a sufficient distance from one another to accommodate a hammock. Site them to make a bold statement year round in large gardens, singly or massed for best effect. Use them to shelter smaller plants, create a vista, enhance a view or screen off undesirable features. In the following selection will be found species both attractive and practical for any of the above purposes in the subtropical garden.

Acacia
Fabaceae

With some 1200 species, acacias are a genus of shrubs and trees, some deciduous, others evergreen, differing in their foliage, form, flowers and cultural requirements. Australian species (there are over 900) are evergreens and range all over the country. Icons with their

Alberta magna

Albizia julibrissin

showy, brilliant flowers, they are collectively called wattles and are Australia's national floral emblem. Wattles grow rapidly but are not generally long lived, although there are exceptions. Within their lifetime they give their all, exploding annually into bright, fluffy, fragrant balls of bloom, many in the dull days of winter. Their foliage is often silvery and always attractive.

Open, sunny positions with sharp drainage ensure successful cultivation. If in doubt, plant your acacias on mounds. Small plants do best as they dislike having their roots disturbed. Give these youngsters some support till they grow. You can raise acacias easily from seed. The most popular species is *Acacia baileyana*, Cootamundra wattle, but it does better in cooler climates. The following are just a very few species of this spectacular genus to suit warmer areas.

A. fimbriata, Brisbane golden wattle, is a small tree, precocious even for a wattle, sometimes producing its sunshine-yellow balls of fluffy flowers when only a year old. Spectacular and showy, compact in growth, this is a good species for the garden. Alas, it only lasts for a few years, but seedlings should spread around it, ready to take over and shine.

A. pendula, weeping myall, is a desirable tree for dry areas, having a delightful arching habit,

silvery foliage and characteristic yellow flowers.

A. podalyriifolia, Queensland silver wattle, flowers in early spring as a rule and is a tough plant for warm areas.

Many more acacia trees are available, and small species of shrubs and even prostrate types can be found.

Another Australian with glorious golden flowers is the slow-growing but long-lived *Barklya syringifolia*, sometimes commonly called the gold blossom tree, a medium-sized rainforest species with handsome foliage. Often used in street plantings, it erupts into bloom in early summer. You will have to wait ten years for the pleasure.

Alberta
Rubiaceae

Subtropical evergreen trees, albertas are indigenous to South Africa and Madagascar, with just three species. The small South African tree is the one cultivated for its splendid flowers and bracts. Slow growing, neat and pleasingly rounded, albertas are ideal for the smaller garden and can be planted right by the house. They thrive at the coast, away from the worst winds, and relish humidity. Give them plenty of compost and mulch. Forget about propagating albertas; it is most difficult.

Alberta magna, Natal flame bush, displays bright scarlet flowers followed by clusters of vivid red bracts, which are even more brilliant than the blossoms and are retained for months on end. This alberta has deep green, glossy leaves, a perfect foil for the flowers. And you can cut the bracts for indoor decoration.

Albizia
Fabaceae

Although albizias number many species, only a few trees are thought to be worthy of cultivation. These are from the subtropics and tropics, and are quick growing, with a spreading habit, ferny leaves and fluffy, powderpuff flowers atop the branches. Albizias will tolerate some wind and salt spray, but need regular watering. Deciduous or semi-evergreen, they have seeds that germinate readily, and pests do not trouble them.

Albizia julibrissin, silk tree, is native to Asia, from China and Japan to Iran, and will grow rapidly into an elegantly shaped, spreading tree, wider than tall. In summer, fluffy, rosy pink flowers bedeck the top of the branches, and it is wise to site your albizia where you can look down upon it, as a specimen. Butterflies and birds are attracted to the blossoms. The width of the tree also makes it an ideal canopy for a terrace or

Alectryon excelsus

shady alfresco dining. Sometimes the flowers disappoint, as some trees carry blooms of a slightly faded pink. It may be wise to procure *A. julibrissin* var. *rosea*.

A. saman, monkey pod, dominates many areas in Hawaii with its umbrella-like shade and distinct structure. The pink flowers and ferny foliage are typical of the species.

Alectryon
Sapindaceae

Evergreen trees from Australia, New Zealand and the Pacific Islands, alectryons are respected for their structure and ornamental foliage. They have modest flowers followed by seeds enclosed in attractive coverings, and are best used as specimen trees in lawns and borders. Strong salt winds harm alectryons. They prefer a good, friable soil. Propagate from seed; you may find seedlings near the parent tree.

Alectryon excelsus, titoki, is one of two New Zealand species and grows into a handsome, medium-sized tree. Its pinnate leaves are brightly green and glossy; the tiny cream flowers hang in long panicles. The berries are a shiny black, embedded in a vivid red thick coating, and seeds and fruit are often found together on the tree. Other species are seldom seen in cultivation.

Araucaria
Araucariaceae

Sturdy giant conifers make up this genUnited States, and they originate in South America, Australia, Norfolk Island and New Caledonia. Although they grow very large, araucarias are an ideal choice for bigger gardens, seaside areas and parks. They reach an enormous height as a rule, and amaze with their straight, round trunks, distinctive foliage and arresting silhouettes. Araucarias appreciate good, rich friable soil, moisture and full sun, and will grow rapidly.

Araucaria heterophylla, Norfolk Island pine, from that island, and also north-eastern parts of Australia, is the type easily recognised by its affinity with the seaside and its stately structure,

especially when silhouetted against the sky. Salt-resistant, the foliage is protected by a waxy coating. Many warm beaches have been planted with a formal row of Norfolk pines, which are a great help in controlling erosion. You need a large garden to grow these colossal trees, but for the first few years they can be kept in containers and make a most acceptable Christmas tree.

Another araucaria for the seaside, and a feature of many Queensland beaches, is the hoop pine (*A. cunninghamii*), a fascinating, fast-growing conifer most suitable for the wild garden, but making a delightful container plant in its youth.

Artocarpus
Moraceae

Several species of *Artocarpus* are cultivated. This is a large genus of tropical evergreen trees from Asia, among which the jackfruit belongs, but it is the breadfruit that is the most well known.

Araucaria heterophylla

Artocarpus altilis

The tree probably started life in Malaysia and arrived in Polynesia in prehistoric times. The breadfruit tree has an intriguing history, quite apart from its beauty and fruit. Its very presence has caused chaos. The *Bounty* has an infamous reputation, and breadfruit plays no mean part in the mutiny on this ship. Valuable water was lavished on the tiny plants at the expense of the crew.

The genus is closely related to figs and shares many characteristics, such as the way they exude a milky sap, and a similarity in leaf patterns. Rich soil is needed, heat and ample water, also a generous mulch. Although these trees are tropical, they can be nurtured in the subtropics for the sheer majesty of their foliage; forget about the fruit.

Artocarpus altilis, breadfruit, boasts heavily indented leaves, large and luxuriant, up to 75 cm long, of a fresh glossy green, on an attractively shaped medium-sized tree. This grows quickly at first but takes many years to reach maturity. A breadfruit tree is best placed in the garden as a specimen, or where its outstanding foliage can be appreciated — a living sculpture.

Bauhinia
Fabaceae

Easy-care, popular small trees, shrubs and climbers from many parts of the subtropics and tropics, bauhinias have enchanting orchid-like, fragrant flowers and pleasant foliage, usually of a satisfying sea green. Some species are fast growing, others not, and their cultural require-ments differ too, but they are adaptable. All need a warm climate, protection from the strongest winds, sunlight, and a friable, open soil. After flowering, orchid trees develop long, flat pods that hang on the tree for a long time. They are increased from seed. Diseases are not a problem.

Bauhinia x *blakeana*, Hong Kong orchid tree, is fast growing and precocious. It is Hong Kong's floral emblem. This bauhinia will flower a year after planting. The large, orchid-like, fragrant blossoms are a deep wine to purple, and stay in

Bauhinia purpurea

bloom for many months amidst the pretty, butterfly-like foliage.

B. galpinii, red bauhinia or nasturtium bauhinia, from South Africa, has glowing, flame-to brick-red flowers that come in clusters, nasturtium shaped and sized. It is really a scrambling shrub, but will ramble to tree size in warm climates and needs to be clipped back to maintain its shape. In Kirstenbosch Gardens at Cape Town, red bauhinia is grown as a hedge. You can also train these amenable plants to grow over rocks or down a bank.

B. variegata, orchid tree, from India, usually flowers in early spring, and is an arresting sight with its shapely blooms of white, delicately veined in green, against the blue-green, double-lobed foliage. 'Candida' flaunts flowers of white, marked chartreuse. And there is a warm pink form with one petal stained a darker hue.

Many more bauhinias are to be seen in the subtropics, lending elegance and grace to gardens, and these are just a small selection from this outstanding genus.

Beaucarnea
Nolinaceae

Beaucarneas are natives of Mexico. There are over 20 species of these strange tree-like plants, but only one is highly regarded for ornamentation. Beaucarneas prefer full sun, gravelly soil and consistently warm conditions. They are related to yuccas and come from the same areas, but are not lookalikes. Water young plants to get them established, but only occasionally after that. They are slow growing; to speed them up, give them doses of a good palm fertiliser. You can use a gravel mulch or surround your beaucarneas with small stones and groundcovers. Mealy bugs may be a problem.

Beaucarnea recurvata, ponytail palm or elephant-foot tree, eventually develops a long, straight, thin trunk topped with a fountain of grass-like leaves that reach a metre and cascade down past the rounded, swollen base. It is thought the bulbous root stores water, camel-like, in times of drought. When plants are small, the base looks not unlike a big onion, and appears incongruous with its topknot of leaves. Young plants are best kept in pots for a few years until they develop. On a mature tree, the base can expand into a woody mass, a metre across, and will grow more branches, complete with arching, drooping leaves. Old plants will produce clusters of little white flowers.

Beaucarnea recurvata

Bixa
Bixaceae

One of a kind, a family all to itself, which gives it a certain status, quite apart from its decorative appeal, the sole genus of this small evergreen tree originates in tropical America. It is now seen in all parts of the world endowed with a genial climate. Full sun is needed for bixas, which like a fertile soil. You can make a hedge from them, as they take kindly to clipping. Propagate from cuttings.

Bixa orellana, annatto or lipstick tree, grows rounded and bushy, shrub-like, with handsome red-flushed, heart-shaped leaves. The pretty pink flowers arrive on the tree when it is only two years old, and are held high above the foliage. They give way to flame-coloured spiny pods which contain a profusion of orange seeds — the origin of annatto dye once used for colouring butter, margarine and cheese. The pods last on the tree for some time, well after the seeds have gone, and dry well. Both flowers and pods are useful in floral arrangements. The annatto is instantly recognisable by its curious pods — altogether a unique tree.

Brachychiton
Sterculiaceae

At least 12 species of *Brachychiton* are endemic to Australia, with a couple coming from New Guinea. Some are deciduous, others evergreen. A few hail from drier regions; others are large forest trees, but slow growing, and amenable to pruning, so still suitable for home gardens. Brachychitons have decorative foliage and bright flowers. They flourish in dry conditions once they get going, but need nurturing for the first few years. While differing in their requirements because their natural habitats are so diverse, most do like very well-drained soil, sun and shelter from strong winds. You can increase trees from seed.

Brachychiton acerifolius, Illawarra flame tree, prefers a good, deep, well-drained soil. It grows

Opposite: *Brachychiton acerifolius*

into a cone-shaped tree, and takes a fair while to do so; after 20 years it will be about 7 m tall. The large leaves usually drop before flowering, and then the tree is an explosion of fiery red, bell-shaped blooms, so that it quite dominates the landscape. However, this does not happen every year, and the flame tree is probably at its best in five-year cycles. Try to get a grafted variety, as it will then flower in three years instead of up to 10 when grown from seed.

B. discolor, kurrajong or pink lacebark, is from rainforests, and in time grows into a giant tree. It sports maple-shaped leaves, which drop at flowering, and blooms in spring with an extravaganza of appealing pink, starry flowers. When these fall, they form a rosy carpet around the tree.

Other brachychitons are cultivated, and the bottle tree (*B. rupestris*) is much used for fodder in the outback. Look out for a near relation, the Mexican hand plant (*Chiranthodendron pentadactylon*), a small to medium-sized tree grown mainly for its conspicuous foliage and strange-looking flowers. They do resemble a hand, with long, furry, dull red 'fingers'. These unusual flowers are filled with nectar. Star-shaped, very tough but attractive seed pods follow. A sunny site and protection from wind is required for this tree.

Callistemon
Myrtaceae

With 30 species, native to Australia, callistemons are a mix of small evergreen trees and shrubs noted for their bottlebrush bright red flowers, which provide food for nectar-eating birds. Adaptable, easy to grow, not particular about soil, stalwart at the beach or inland, callistemons are most useful. They are fairly drought resistant; you need only water to get a plant established. Pests pass them by, and you can increase from tip cuttings. The following are just two of the many available to try. They are much hybridised, too.

Callistemon citrinus, scarlet bottlebrush, from southeastern coastal areas, is a sturdy, quick-growing small tree, profuse with bright red

Chiranthodendron pentadactylon

flowers, although there can be differing colours, also cultivars in pinks and white. You can train scarlet bottlebrushes into shelter hedges, or use as specimens.

C. viminalis, weeping bottlebrush, from warmer eastern coastal areas, is perhaps the most handsome of the species, with its graceful, weeping structure and pretty young foliage of bronze. Deep crimson brushes appear several times a year. Always attractive, it is a tree to grow as a specimen, and a popular choice for street plantings, too.

Cassia
Fabaceae

Fast-growing tropical and subtropical evergreen and deciduous trees from many areas of the world, cassias include over 100 species. They have attractive foliage, divided into leaflets, and an abundance of bloom. As a rule, the flowers are yellow to apricot in colour, pea-shaped and outstandingly showy. What's more, they perform for months. Easy to please and almost pest free, cassias will grow in poor or rich soil as long as it is well drained, and some types do well at the seaside. There are plenty to choose from, and only the most favoured are listed here. You can propagate cassias from seed, which should be soaked overnight.

Cassia fistula, golden shower tree or Indian laburnum, is a tropical tree, but will shine in the subtropics, too. It is usually deciduous, and dazzles with its hanging trusses of fragrant buttercup-yellow flowers; long, round seed pods containing cascara-like seeds form later. It prefers full sun.

C. grandis, pink shower tree, from Central America, enjoys the heat, is semi-deciduous and lives up to its name of 'grand'. Best for the larger garden as a shade tree, or for street planting, this cassia is festooned with bold clusters of flesh-pink flowers with a golden throat.

C. javanica, pink shower tree, from Southeast Asia, is a high performer, and most decorative with its giant clusters of pretty pink flowers. *C.* 'Rainbow Shower' is an aptly named hybrid, and can be seen to perfection in Hawaii, where it puts on an enchanting display for many months, with a profusion of blooms in assorted shades of soft pink, rose, cream, gold, apricot and a warm bronze — a wondrous mix. Not only that, every tree is different, owing to its hybrid beginnings. No wonder it is Honolulu's official tree.

Unrelated, but slightly similar, are the three *Koelreuteria* species, from Asia. They are deciduous, spreading trees of medium size, and boast ferny foliage which changes to buttercup yellow in autumn, but before that they are adorned with clusters of yellow flowers through summer.

Another deciduous tree to try is *Melia azedarach*, a variable species roaming over many countries, from Asia down to Australia. The pretty foliage arrives in spring, followed by panicles of small lilac flowers. Clusters of cream or pale orange bead-like berries persist on the tree for some time, hence its common name of bead or rosary tree. Small, neat trees, melias are to be seen lining streets or gracing malls in urban areas.

Cassia fistula

Chorisia
Bombaceae

South American deciduous trees, with five species, chorisias are notable, not only for their entrancing flowers but also for their lethal-looking, heavily studded, spiked, round grey trunks. Treat them with respect, and plant away from pathways and where children play. Chorisias can be forgiven their ominous looks when they flower with an abundance of bloom; white, creamy or pink, large and showy. They do so just before the arrival of the new season's leaves, which are divided into leaflets. Give chorisias full sun, and they will flourish when put in rich, moist soil, albeit well drained. Seeds and cuttings should take.

Chorisia insignis, white floss-silk tree, boasts a cylindrical, rounded trunk, liberally studded with spikes, and grows quickly to a fair size. The flowers are white to soft yellow, with narrow petals, vaguely hibiscus-like.

C. speciosa, floss-silk tree, is the species most favoured, and grows at a fast rate for the first few years, and then slows down before reaching its large size. The bold, rounded flowers float like a rose-pink to deep wine-red haze above the branches. Several selections in warm pinks and rich dark red have been developed.

Another member of the family with brilliant flowers is *Bombax ceiba*, red silk-cotton tree or red kapok. Also displaying spiked trunks, these semi-deciduous trees are for large gardens as they grow very tall. The waxy, flame-red flowers are followed by conspicuous woody seed pods. Fluffy fibres are produced in the seed pods, hence one of its common names. It is easily propagated from seed.

Cordia
Boraginaceae

From subtropical and tropical parts of the world, cordias are deciduous and evergreen trees and shrubs, numbering about 300 species. Cordias are used as timber trees, and some species are made into canoes, bowls, trays, calabashes and containers, while others are cherished for their charming good looks. These smallish trees have trumpet-shaped flowers in hot colours, are not difficult to grow, and make fine landscaping subjects. Cordias like a balmy climate and a free-draining soil, and are easily increased by seed or cuttings.

Cordia sebestena, geiger tree or scarlet cordia, is a small evergreen species very popular in many

Chorisia speciosa

Chorisia speciosa

20

Cordia sebestena

Cordyline fruticosa

warm areas of the world. It carries oval leaves of a sandpapery texture, and luxuriant clusters of tangerine to scarlet flowers, followed by creamy white edible fruit.

C. subcordata, kou, is similar, and is to be seen in islands of the Pacific, where it blooms off and on all year round, when clusters of small orange flowers light up the dark green, glossy leaves.

Cordyline
Lomandraceae

A genus of some 15 species, evergreen shrubs and small trees, cordylines are mainly from the South Pacific region. Noted for their tropical appearance, lush and exotic, they are often mistaken for palms. Most are subtropical or tropical in origin. The New Zealand species, small trees, with many hybrids and cultivars, are quite hardy. The shrubby cordylines are amenable to a life in containers, and prefer a rich soil, plenty of moisture, and sun or filtered shade. Cordylines usually produce panicles of small white flowers, wildly perfumed, heavy with a hint of musk. Propagate from stem cuttings or seed.

Cordyline australis, New Zealand cabbage tree, ti kouka, is one of five cordylines endemic to New Zealand, and is an adaptable small tree, distinctive with its bold fountains of foliage; giant

asterisks against the sky. Most adaptable, cabbage trees can be grown at the coast or far inland. They are cultivated extensively in many countries of the world, and are a feature of coastal Devon and the French Riviera. Ideal as specimen trees, or as a focal point in a garden, these versatile cordylines can also be grown in large containers, and there are most handsome cultivars bred especially to grace jars and pots. Although New Zealand cordylines are grown mainly for their structure, the typical creamy white panicles of flowers are pleasing. Their only fault is their habit of shedding old leaves, which can be untidy, but you can use them for fuelling the barbecue.

C. fruticosa, red ti or ti ngahere, possibly had its first home in New Guinea and Malaysia, but has naturalised in many islands of the South Pacific where it grows lavishly. Red ti develops in an upright fashion, on either a single or several stems, and can grow tall, but is usually around a metre. Fountain-like rosetted clusters of multi-coloured leaves erupt from the stems of these long-lived plants in dazzling shades; crimson, glowing red, plum, coral, emerald green — there is no end to their colour combinations. Shiny, waxy and lasting well in water, ti leaves can be short and fat or long and thin. Popular for floral arrangements in the South Pacific and Hawaii, they are used as food wrappings, plates and ropes, as well as for decoration. Leis are plaited from ti in Hawaii, too. These plants are seen at their best when grown in groups, perhaps mulched with scoria. Colourful cultivars are readily available. Warmth and water are necessary for success, and watch out for mealy bugs.

C. indivisa, mountain cabbage tree, likes misty, moist conditions, and is most ornamental, with broad, bold leaves and a prominent ruddy midrib. Surprisingly, this species does well in the tropics as well as the subtropics, provided it receives regular rain.

C. kaspar, from northern Three Kings Islands, has shorter and fatter leaves than most species, and is a nuggety tree too, with a sturdy appearance, designed to put up with salt-laden winds.

C. stricta, slender palm lily, an Australian, lives up to its common name, and has jungle-green leaves on slim stems. It makes a satisfying feature plant with its elegant form, will thrive in full sun or shade, and can be grown in pots. The slender palm lily bears panicles of soft white to purple flowers, followed by black berries which germinate readily. Other cordylines are sometimes available; *C. rubra* is one to look for.

Delonix
Fabaceae

These magnificent trees originate in Arabia, India, Africa and Madagascar, which gives some indication of their needs. With five species of tropical and subtropical deciduous and evergreen trees, the genus includes what is often described as one of the most beautiful trees of the world. *Delonix* species have bipinnate, ornamental leaves and brilliant flowers on wide-spreading branches. They prefer full sun, rich, moist soil, humid heat and not very strong winds, although they can be grown at the coast. When young, a tree should be mulched, and pruned to keep just one single trunk. You can propagate from seed.

Trees produce very long seed pods.

Delonix regia is also commonly called royal poinciana, flamboyant tree, flame of the forest, and peacock flower — no hyperbole! From Madagascar, this rather special quick-growing tree will attain a medium height, but with a spread much larger than usual — a canopy composed of well-made feathery leaves that will provide a shady outdoor room. Clusters of glowing crimson or deep terracotta-red flowers are borne in brilliant clouds at the top of the tree. To view the royal poinciana at its best, you need to be able to look down upon it. Its only drawback is that it is a slow developer and does not produce flowers for many years, but they are worth the wait.

A relation of the royal poinciana, and also from Madagascar, is Colville's glory (*Colvillea racemosa*), which enjoys similar conditions and is a small tree with ornamental feathery leaflets. It is crowned with terracotta flowers in large trusses, usually in autumn. This spectacular tree does well at the coast, and is rather slow growing.

Dracaena
Dracaenaceae

Dracaenas originate in Africa and Asia. They are evergreen trees and shrubs usually grown for their bold, architectural form, and valued as landscape plants. Much used as potted

Delonix regia

Colvillea racemosa

specimens, dracaenas enjoy a warm climate, and when grown outdoors require a friable, open soil, and a sunny or lightly shaded position. Some species prefer a humid region, away from prevailing winds. Dracaenas do not seem to need fertilising often, and require no pruning, although the usual method of increase is from stem cuttings. You may find mealy bugs and scale to be a problem.

Dracaena draco, dragon tree, is from the Canary Islands, and will grow to a good size but takes a long time to do so. It has a topknot of sage-green leaves on a stalwart trunk, and should be carefully sited to get the attention it deserves. Dragon trees are dramatic plants, and look well when underplanted with groundcovers such as mondo grass, or mulched with rocks and pebbles. This species is drought tolerant.

D. marginata, from Madagascar, has irregular, twisted stems, and is a modest size at maturity;

Dracaena draco and vireya rhododendrons

Erythrina crista-galli   *Eucalyptus ficifolia*

no more than 6 m, which makes it an ideal landscape tree for small gardens. Its handsome, lance-like leaves are embellished with a red margin, while 'Tricolor' is further adorned with a cream stripe.

Watch out for less well-known types, such as *D. fragrans* 'Massangeana', which has a broad, bright yellow stripe right down the centre of the green leaves, and small, fragrant flowers.

Close relations, and the only other member of the family, are the sansevierias, tough perennials. The species cultivated for the garden is *Sansevieria trifasciata*, unfairly nicknamed mother-in-law's tongue, and presently enjoying a renaissance. With prominent, stiff, vertical fleshy leaves of up to a metre, embroidered in grey green, sometimes framed in yellow, sansevierias are often planted in pots for courtyard accents, but can be grown easily outdoors in warm places. Combine them with low-growing succulents in well-drained soil where they will provide height and interesting contrast. 'Laurentii' is an old favourite, and interesting new selections have been developed.

Erythrina
Fabaceae

Thorny deciduous and semi-deciduous trees and shrubs, erythrinas come from tropical and subtropical areas of the world, and are much admired for their showy flowers and ease of growth. Among the hundred or so species there are several that stand out and are cultivated for the striking flowers in shades of red, orange and sometimes pink or white. The large kinds make ueful shade trees, and all are attractive to birds. Erythrinas are at their best after a dry period. Grow in full sun for success, and watch out for borer and red spider mite. Prune to keep in shape. They are child's play to propagate from quite large cuttings — simply heel them in.

Erythrina caffra, South African coral tree, is a large deciduous tree (although only briefly so), and in late winter or early spring in most areas flaunts a cockscomb of vivid scarlet blooms with pronounced stamens on bare banches.

E. crista-galli, coral tree, originates in Brazil, and is a small tree, carrying clusters of vivid flame-red pea-like flowers in late summer and large, fresh green leaves, which fall for a short while. Coral tree is a tough customer, and adaptable, and possibly the most popular of the species. You can train it as a shrub or use it as a specimen and allow to grow to up to 9 m.

E. fusca, a larger tree, flowers profusely in long trusses of scarlet, followed by giant seed pods.

E. variegata, whose habitats range from

eastern Africa to Polynesia, also grows to be a large tree. Its big deep green leaves drop in the dry season, to be superseded by brilliant furnace-red blooms in great profusion. Occasionally a white-flowered kind is to be seen, and there are cultivars with variegated leaves.

Eucalyptus
Myrtaceae

Where would Australia be without its gum trees? Part of its wealthy botanical heritage are the ubiquitous eucalypts, fast-growing, drought-resistant trees in sizes from small to immense. The 700 or more species are all native to Australia except for a mere handful. Known all over the world, eucalypts are exemplary immigrants, and have settled in many areas, from hot climates to cool, depending on species. Many are well shaped and have attractive, often aromatic, foliage and profuse fluffy flowers. Some are further ornamented by their colourful bark — think of the ghost gums. Easy to grow, eucalypts are so numerous it is difficult to identify some, but quite a few stand out for their decorative good looks. They differ in their cultural requirements.

Eucalyptus cinerea, silver dollar gum, is admired for its juvenile foliage and later rounded leaves of a cool, soft grey-green, used extensively in bouquets and floral arrangements. Keep clipping back to maintain the young foliage, and to keep the tree in bounds, as it grows to a size too large for the average garden. This applies also to *E. gunnii*, with young foliage of a delightful silver.

E. deglupta has several common names, rainbow-bark gum being one, and is grown extensively in parks, where its displays of multi-coloured branches and trunk are magnificent. This gum can be seen to advantage in Hawaii, and does very well in warm areas.

E. ficifolia, red-flowering gum, from Western Australia, is the most spectacular of all, and throughout summer is covered with blossom in colours ranging from bright tangerine through to vivid scarlet or crimson. The red-flowering gum does very well at the coast, and develops into a rounded, pleasant, thickly canopied tree of medium size.

As a colourful alternative, try the black penda (*Xanthostemon chrysantha*), a relation from the rainforests of Queensland. Great for warm gardens, where it grows to a medium size, the black penda in wintertime is illuminated by glowing lemon-yellow flowers with prominent anthers.

Ficus
Moraceae

What a large genus this is, with many first-class trees for the subtropics, plus delicious fruit trees and easy-care house plants. *Ficus* species, all popularly known as fig, originate in tropical and subtropical areas all over the world, and are mainly cultivated for their pleasing foliage and landscaping suitability. Much used in parks and for shade, some fig trees are far too large, or even invasive, for the home garden — banyan trees, for instance — but others are small and adaptable enough to grow in containers for home or office. They bear tiny flowers on the inside surface of

Ficus dammaropsis

Hymenosporum flavum

Jacaranda mimosifolia

the fleshy receptacles (rather eccentric, really) and employ a very involved form of reproduction. Birds appreciate the fruit, and bats too. Most figs have strong, invasive roots, and will colonise and take over other plants with ease. Figs are not difficult to grow, but prefer part shade or sun, and well-drained soil.

Ficus benjamina, weeping fig, is from Asia, and forms an impressive big tree, much used in parks in hot countries for its shade. Its spread is greater than its height and provides a shady canopy for alfresco dining. Its leaves are small and shiny, its shape graceful, and this makes the weeping fig a very good choice for a container in a courtyard or in the house. Cultivars are specially bred for this purpose.

F. carica, common fig, is the scrumptious edible species. Its natural habitat ranging from Turkey to western Asia, this fig has the distinction of being the first fruit mentioned in the Bible. It is a deciduous small tree, with the well-known, distinctive, three-lobed leaves and succulent fruit. Adaptable and decorative, fruiting figs will grow in arid Mediterranean areas as well as the subtropics and warm temperate zones.

F. dammaropsis, dinnerplate fig, a small tree, has foliage more impressive than any dinnerplate, comes from New Guinea's mountainous regions, and boasts immense leaves, deep green, shiny as though polished, and prettily pleated. These leaves are heavily veined, and lined with a lighter celadon green. Dinnerplate fig has a slender trunk, can easily be accommodated in a small garden, and is an exceptional foliage plant. It will form rounded, scaled fruit which ripen to a deep purple.

F. lyrata, banjo or fiddleleaf fig, comes from tropical Africa, and grows to mammoth proportions in the tropics, but can be curtailed in genial climates. It is worth growing for its well-made leaves, and they *are* violin-shaped, bold, heavily veined, polished a shiny bright green. The fiddleleaf fig is right at home in a pot, decorative inside or out.

There are *Ficus* species for many other situations — for instance, Moreton Bay fig (*F. macrophylla*), the gigantic ornamental tree that thrives in seaside positions. There is also the bo tree or sacred fig (*F. religiosa*), steeped in history and religion as the tree Buddha meditated under when he received enlightment.

Hymenosporum
Pittosporaceae

From subtropical rainforests of eastern AUnited Statestralia and New Guinea, this genus consists of just the one species, an ornamental flowering small tree with an intoxicating scent. It has deep green lustrous leaves, and can grow in an untidy fashion, long and lanky, so should be kept clipped back. Suitable for gardens grand or small, it grows rapidly. Site your hymenosporum where you can take advantage of the flowers' subtle fragrance, which intensifies at night. These delightful trees will grow readily at the seaside, although very strong winds may break the branches. Fortunately they reshoot very readily.

Hymenosporum flavum, Australian frangipani, is well named for its perfume. It produces profuse clusters of highly fragrant, small cream flowers which turn bright yellow and finally golden. The blossom starts in spring and lasts till summer in most areas, and is much appreciated by nectar-seeking birds. A recent development has been a most useful groundcover kind, called 'Little Elf', with all the fragrance of its parent.

Jacaranda
Bignoniaceae

Deciduous and evergreen trees from subtropical and tropical parts of South America, with about 50 species, jacarandas flaunt pretty tubular white, pink or mauve flowers and fern-like foliage. One species is favoured above all others, and is cultivated in warm areas throughout the world. So many are seen in subtropical areas of Australia, they are often thought to be natives. When in bloom, jacarandas are among the most enchanting of all flowering trees. They can stand quite long periods of dry weather, and are used for street planting, but are admirable for the home garden. Give them full sun and a good soil with ample mulch. They like a place to themselves, and few plants thrive in the area directly around jacarandas, as they are shallow rooting and greedy feeders. Seed will germinate readily, and pests do not worry them, other than borer.

Jacaranda mimosifolia is a medium-sized, spreading tree, its decorative, ferny foliage divided into little leaflets, which fall just before flowering time. The flowers are of a soft lilac, tubular, and come in large clusters, making a froth of misty mauve in a glorious canopy. When the flowers fall, they form a delightful carpet round the tree.

Lagerstroemia
Lythraceae

Although this is a genus of over 50 species, only a few are judged suitable for gardens. They are indigenous to several countries in eastern and Southeast Asia, and one comes from northern Australia. Lagerstroemias are evergreen or deci-

Lagerstroemia indica

duous, generally compact trees, characterised by large trUnited Statesses of crinkly flowers, as though fashioned out of crepe paper. Another disting-uishing feature is their smooth, pale bark that falls away in long strips, giving a two-tone appearance.

Lagerstroemias prefer full sun and shelter from winds as the flower panicles are vulnerable. Fertile, friable, slightly acid soil is needed, with a good proportion of humus. Keep moist when the trees are in leaf, but in higher rainfall areas additional water will only be needed for saplings. Prune back to maintain a good shape, and after flowering. Powdery mildew can attack in humid areas. However, mildew-resistant types have been developed in the United States. Increase from cuttings or from seed.

Lagerstroemia indica, crepe myrtle, is thought to come from China, and is a small, rounded, compact deciduous tree with little oval leaves. It erupts into glorious colour when the weather is very warm, usually in high summer. The crowded heads of flowers are held away from the tree, and arrive in shades from white, baby pink, to rose, crimson, or hues of mauve, and a few are two-toned, one like coconut ice. When they drop, a rosy carpet forms around the tree. There are many cultivars to choose from, and this tree is adaptable, tolerating heat, humidity and even drought.

L. speciosa, queen's flower or queen of flowers, from jungles of Southeast Asia, is a larger tree, perhaps up to 10 m, also deciduous, and develops a dense, spreading crown topped with bold spikes of filmy mauve or rosy pink flowers, and foliage that turns golden or bronze in autumn.

Floriferous new varieties have been developed and if you are on the lookout for a special shrub, choose from a range of lagerstroemias especially designed for smaller gardens, and available in many shades.

Lagunaria
Malvaceae

One of a kind, this species is a staunch tree from Norfolk Island, Lord Howe Island and coastal

Lagunaria patersonii

Magnolia grandiflora

Queensland, places where it puts up with strong, salt-laden winds. It is able to do so as it has felted, small, tight, grey-green leaves resistant to salt, so for the seaside, lagunarias are ideal. They are also compact enough for small gardens, and planting on streets and foreshores. Slow growing, but eventually becoming pyramidal large trees, lagunarias do best in open soil and full sun, but can be left alone for the most part as the trees are almost self-sufficient, and even self-seeding. Great for beach gardens that are only visited at holiday times.

Lagunaria patersonii, Norfolk Island hibiscus, is studded with dull, old-rose-shaded flowers, hibiscus-like, but they are most numerous, contrast well with the greyish leaves, and almost completely cover the tree, usually in summer, though seasons can differ according to area.

Magnolia
Magnoliaceae

The very name 'magnolia' conjures up visions of steamy heat, romance and mystery. There are a hundred or so species, and innumerable hybrids, with new selections appearing yearly, so it is perhaps just as well the genus bears a mellifluous name. Magnolias are superb flowering plants, and come as shrubs or trees,

both deciduous and evergreen, from the Americas and eastern Asia. To get those you desire, you may have to purchase from a specialist mail-order firm.

Magnolias need to be sited carefully, as they do not like being transplanted, and some species grow into very big trees. In general, despite wide differences in their natural habitats, magnolias require fairly rich soil, well drained, and slightly acidic for most, though a few prefer it alkaline. Magnolias are adaptable, but none of them like to be crowded, needing room to themselves because their roots are easily damaged by greedy, neighbouring plants, or disturbed by close cultivation. It is wise to supply a generous mulch, especially for young plants. A few magnolias like it at the beach, but away from the strongest winds. Small-growing deciduous shrubs look well in oriental gardens; larger evergreen types make good specimen trees. Do not prune unless absolutely necessary. Magnolias are blessed with having a good resistance to pests and diseases.

Magnolia delavayi is an evergreen native to southern China, and will grow to a medium-sized tree. The leathery leaves, almost grey-green in colour, are ornamental throughout the year, the fleeting, fragrant flowers ivory and cup-like.

M. grandiflora, southern magnolia or bull bay,

Metrosideros excelsa

is the classic evergreen species from southern USA. The state flower of Louisiana and Mississippi, this is the epitome of the Deep South. One of the showiest magnolias in a spectacular genus, it forms a large, generous tree, a fine specimen for the larger garden, with bold, decorative leaves, long and shiny, of a dark green, lined in a paler shade. The giant flowers are fleshy, with a tantalising scent, hard to describe, but with a hint of citrus, sweet and powerful, never to be forgotten. There are many cultivars, mostly developed in the United States, and some specially promoted for the smaller garden.

Other magnolias shine in the subtropics, including varieties of southern sweet bay (*M. virginiana*), which share parentage with the southern magnolia of many outstanding cultivars.

Metrosideros
Myrtaceae

Containing about 50 species of trees, shrubs and vines, endemic to the South Pacific, with one species from Hawaii, this genus is pretty tough. Most species are coastal dwellers. Their leathery, grey-green leaves repel salt winds, and they are known for their bright pompom flowers, uually red, but sometimes yellow, and very occasionally white. Some small species and hybrids can be contained in pots, and they prefer full sun and a fertile soil. You can propagate them from seed or cuttings.

Metrosideros excelsa, pohutukawa, New Zealand Christmas tree, is splendid for the coast. It will bloom while still very young and small, a bright display of distinctive, fuzzy scarlet to crimson flowers, with the occasional tree sporting yellow blooms. Pohutukawa is a New Zealand icon, and flowers in summer when people are at the seaside. It will take salt-laden prevailing winds in its stride, and is long lived. Pohutukawas have their vulnerability, however, and in New Zealand possums have destroyed thousands of trees, but thanks to conservationists, they are still flourishing.

The pohutukawa will grow eventually into a large tree, but can be trimmed back, and even used as a hedge plant. You can find floriferous shrubby types for the smaller garden, with names such as 'Springfire', 'Scarlet Pimpernel' and 'Tahiti'. The Hawaiian species, *M. polymorpha*, has similar flowers, and grows in great abundance in the uplands of the islands.

M. kermadecensis, Kermadec pohutukawa, has smaller leaves than the New Zealand varieties, with a longer flowering season, and the variegated types, with lighter flowers, are those usually seen in gardens. They are more compact, too.

Michelia
Magnoliaceae

Michelias consist of shrubs and evergreen trees in the main, and are indigenous to tropical and subtropical Asia, with a few from the foothills of the Himalayas. Their flowers are very like those of magnolias, but that is not surprising, as they are close members of the same family. Some species are appreciated for their heavy scent, and, in India, are cultivated for their fragrant oil, used in cosmetics. Give michelias gritty rich earth, well drained, on the acid side, and a position in the sun or with a little shade. They do well at the shore, away from strong winds. You can propagate from seed or cuttings, but the latter

Michelia doltsopa

are very slow to take root.

Michelia champaca, champak or champaca, from the foothills of the Himalayas, develops into a medium-sized tree, and has long, glossy leaves, finely veined, hanging elegantly from horizontal branches. This tree is widely grown in Southeast Asia, where its delightful perfumed flowers are commonly used as temple offerings. The blooms are many-petalled and of a yellow or sometimes orange shade, their scent heavy, rich and sweet, with an intoxicating fruity fragrance. This is the national flower of the Philippines, but is also popular in all warm areas of the world. Champak flowers intermittently throughout the year, but is at its best in summer.

M. doltsopa hails from the Himalayas too, and is variable in form, usually slender and upright when young, but developing widthways as it matures. It has thin, leathery, dark green leaves, and big creamy or white fragrant flowers. They open, usually in late winter, from furry brown buds, and festoon the tree during its short season.

Pandanus
Pandanaceae

An adaptable genus of 700 or so ancient plants from Africa, Malaysia, Pacific islands and northern parts of Australia, it contains some species which line subtropical and tropical beaches, eventually becoming small trees, while others are ideal for garden decoration. Their common name is screwpine, because of the appearance of their long prickly leaves, which open in a whirly arrangement. Several species are ornamental, and valued for their bold structure and survival techniques. Stoic plants, pandanus prefer well-drained, light soil and warm, dry conditions. Cuttings take root effortlessly and quickly, although you can increase from seed.

Pandanus odoratissimus, found all through the Pacific and parts of Asia, is a stalwart coastal small tree able to withstand strong salt winds. It has a rounded stem and supports itself on pole-like buttress roots. Female plants are distinguished by their large knobbly fruit, while the male of the species is decorated with fragrant white flowers.

P. sanderi, a popular species for gardens, usually has green and yellow striped, spiny leaves and will make a fine specimen, eventually becoming tree size, albeit small.

P. tectorius, hala screw pine, is to be seen on seacoasts in the Pacific, and was formerly much used for weaving, medicine and food. Its unusual appearance, with propped roots, spiralled, spiky leaves and knobbly, pineapple-like fruits, makes it instantly recognisable.

Close relations of *Pandanus* species are the climbing freycinetias. With sword- or palm-like leaves, these are handsome plants, prized for their ornamental bright bracts. These climbers will thrive in humid areas, and are easily increased by division. The hardest part may be finding freycinetias in garden centres.

Saraca
Fabaceae

With over 70 species to its credit, this genus comes from Southeast Asia, and consists of small evergreen rainforest trees. Several species boast masses of long-lasting, dazzling flowers among the pinnate, attractive leaves. The new foliage has hues of pink, and hangs like tassels at branch end. Borderline for the subtropics, they need plenty of warmth, humidity, shelter and a little shade. However, these trees are so delightful it is worth a try. Rich, moist soil, well mulched, will help, and you will need to keep saracas amply watered. You can propagate from seed. Watch out for scale.

Saraca indica, asoka, has a dense, pyramidal structure, and glossy leaflets. It carries big tight clusters of bright golden-yellow flowers. This tree excites attention wherever it is seen, and is the subject of innumerable photographs. Site the asoka tree carefully, where you can fully appreciate the flowers from beneath. This is a sacred tree to Buddhists and Hindus.

S. thaipingensis grows to several metres in height, and its massive flower clusters are bright orange to tangerine in colour, changing as they age, often turning red. It is considered to be the showiest of the species.

Schefflera
Araliaceae

An extensive genus of plants from small trees and shrubs to climbers, scheffleras range over the tropics and subtropics for the most part. Only a few are cultivated, mainly for their ornamental leaves, which are divided into leaflets. They require moisture and warmth, prefer semi-shade and appreciate shelter from wind. Some species are used as indoor container plants. You can increase from cuttings or seed.

Schefflera actinophylla, Queensland umbrella tree or octopus tree, gets its common names from its appearance; the spokes of umbrella-like leaves and the bright red flowers form topknots on the tree in a radiating, sinuous, writhing shape, octopus-like and unique. The flowers are full of nectar, and in their natural habitat of Queensland rainforests, umbrella trees are visited by Ulysses butterflies as well as many birds. The flowers last for many months of the

Schefflera actinophylla

Meryta sinclairii

year before being replaced by red seeds. The trees are picturesque all the time, with their shining, large, much divided, vivid green leaves held elegantly aloft on many divided trunks. You can grow your umbrella tree in a container for several years, as it will not mind being confined. In nature these trees often grow as epiphytes.

S. digitata, pate, is from New Zealand's north, where it grows on the edge of bush. It is typical of the genus, sporting fresh green leaves extravagantly divided into leaflets. Not often seen for sale, pate is well worth growing. This small tree bears greenish flowers, but is most admired for its splendid foliage.

Another New Zealand native, belonging to the same family, and with bold, tropical-looking foliage, is puka (*Meryta sinclairii*), a small, rounded tree with immense, thick, glossy leaves. Puka is grown for its architectural form, and is eminently suited to small or large gardens, where it probably does best in half sun. It will thrive at the coast, as long as there is plentiful water. Sometimes seen is the outstanding variegated form 'Moonlight'.

Schizolobium parahybum

Schizolobium
Fabaceae

What intriguing trees they are, the two species of this genus from South America. Schizolobiums soar to a great size in the wild, and have straight, slim trunks topped by a spreading, filmy cover of fern-like leaves. Give them rich, friable soil, ample sunlight, plenty of water, and a sheltered site, and you will be quite quickly rewarded. Plant these fern trees in groups or as specimens. Propagate from fresh seed.

Schizolobium parahybum, Brazilian fern tree or bacurubu, has a straight, slim, cylindrical trunk and shiny fresh green bipinnate leaves, a metre or more long, which form an elegant canopy, and are seen at their best when silhouetted against the sky. These are designer trees, and almost impeccable, except that, being deciduous, they lose their leaves for a short time in winter. However, they make up for this, and surprise with clusters of buttercup-yellow flowers, usually in spring, followed by long pods, each containing a single seed.

Spathodea
Bignoniaceae

From a genus with one species, so spectacular that it is a great shame there are not more, this evergreen tree is native to warm regions of Africa, both tropical and subtropical. Fast growing and best suited to larger gardens, it is a favourite in many countries and frequently used as a street tree. Once established, spathodeas will tolerate long periods of drought, but need a good rich free-draining soil, ample sun and shelter from strong winds. Propagation is from seed.

Spathodea campanulata, African flame or tulip tree, has large leaves divided into oval leaflets, but it is the flowers that are so amazing. Globes of frilly, molten-red, tulip-shaped blooms form from a central cluster of velvety brown crescents and stand above the deep green foliage. They

Spathodea campanulata

appear almost year round, depending on climate, and attract numerous birds to the nectar. The woody seed pods are used in floral arrangements, and the frosted, winged seeds are used in lei-making in Hawaii. This is a tree to treasure.

Syzygium
Myrtaceae

Hundreds of species of these evergreen shrubs and trees exist, and are confusing because not long ago they were placed with *Eugenia* species. Syzygiums call Africa, Southeast Asia and Australia home. Admired for their form, foliage, flowers and fruit, they are a handsome lot, often nicknamed lillypilly. Aromatic cloves are collected from the dried flowerbuds of a species from the Moluccas. In the garden, syzygiums flourish in full sun, moist, friable soil, and a somewhat sheltered position. Some species are far too large for the home garden, but all can be ruthlessly pruned back.

Syzygium jambos, rose apple, is native to Southeast Asia, but has naturalised in many places, Hawaii chiefly. It was introduced there as a garden plant, but liked the surroundings so much it can now be found in damp forests. This medium-sized tree has long, slender leaves and pompom flowers of soft lemon-yellow, followed by its unusual, crunchy, egg-shaped fruit, which have a definite fragrance of roses, and taste just as you imagine roses should. You can make them into a delicate jelly.

S. luehmannii, small-leafed lillypilly, an eastern Australian, is one of the more popular trees of the genus, as it boasts several flushes of shiny, pink-tipped leaves, creamy fluffy flowers, and quantities of small oval berries, usually of a rosy pink. Best kept for shelter hedges, it will ultimately grow large, but can be kept clipped.

Obviously with such a big genus, other species are available. *S. wilsonii*, powderpuff lilly-pilly, fits the bill for neatness and shrub size. It is small and rounded, with bright red new leaves, fluffy deep red flowers and oval cream fruit.

Tabebuia
Bignoniaceae

Outstanding members of a very handsome family, tabebuias are from the West Indies and tropical parts of Central and South America. Several of the 100 or so species are cultivated for their clusters of brightly coloured flowers, ornamental foliage, neatness, and rapid growth. They can be recommended for home gardens, parks and as street plantings. As a rule, tabebuias are evergreen, but can lose their leaves for a short while, especially when they flower. They demand warmth and a humus-rich soil to give of their best, and will thrive at the coast away from the worst winds. It is thought that dry conditions may promote profuse flowers. A general fertiliser applied annually will keep the trees healthy. Propagate from hardwood cuttings, and do not worry about pests and diseases.

Tabebuia chrysantha is one of many tabebuias to have yellow flowers, and is a small deciduous tree from Venezuela. Brilliant when in full bloom, the saffron-yellow tubular flowers appear in bold clusters on leafless stems.

T. chrysotricha, golden trumpet tree, from Brazil, has trumpet-like flowers in shades of deep rich gold, which cover the crown when in full bloom.

T. heterophylla, from Brazil, is breathtaking when in bloom, its glorious blossom, in various shades of pink, from cool to shocking, all sublime, arrayed on almost leafless branches. When you see this tree against an azure sky, it is a sight to remember. This species will bloom at intervals during the year.

Other tabebuias are sometimes available, and delight with their enchanting blossom, in either pink, yellow or shades of gold.

Close relation is *Tecoma stans*, commonly called yellow bells. Featuring serrated leaves in attractive leaflets, this small tree is alive with glowing yellow, trumpet-shaped bells in bold clusters for all the warmer months. Yet another relation with ornamental foliage and yellow flowers is *Radermachera sinica*, boasting several common names such as Canton lace and Asian

Tabebuia chrysantha

bell-flower. It carries shiny, fresh green bi-pinnate leaves, and as it ages bears great trusses of white to yellow tubular blooms.

Terminalia
Combretaceae

Native to subtropical and tropical regions of Australia, Asia and Africa, this is a large genus of evergreen and deciduous trees. Some species are cultivated for their handsome leaves and ability to repel salt-laden winds. Terminalias produce small fruit, and a few are edible. Sun, sea and well-drained soil suits the variety described here.

Terminalia catappa, sea or tropical almond, is evergreen, and abundant in seaside areas of the tropics and subtropics, where it revels in the sea breezes. It lines beaches, rocky foreshores and parks with its spreading, almost horizontal branches carrying rosettes of oval leaves, which turn colour as they age and fall at any time of the year. A surprising yellow, red, orange, auburn and rusty brown bring a permanent look of autumn to the tree and all around it. Small, almond-size fruit follow summer's inconspicuous white flowers, and they are edible.

35

Tipuana tipu

Tipuana
Fabaceae

Just a single species of this genus exists, and it hails from subtropical parts of several South American countries. An evergreen in warm, wet climates, and deciduous and semi-deciduous in drier regions, this quick-growing legume develops into a large and spreading tree, an ideal shady specimen for big gardens. Hardy and dependable, often employed as a street tree, the *Tipuana* species is easily grown from seed. It appears pest free, will adapt to almost any soil, other than a very alkaline type, and requires maximum sunshine.

Tipuana tipu, pride of Bolivia, is a graceful, charming tree, with a flattened crown, and no wonder it is the pride of Bolivia. Anyone whose garden hosts this delight has good reason to feel proud. *T. tipu* boasts a profusion of fresh, bright green leaves, divided into many leaflets. In spring, a dazzling glow of yellow, gold and sometimes apricot pea-like flowers cover the tree, the sprays unfolding at the tips of the branches to give an ephemeral display for a fortnight or so, and then it is all over for another year. No matter, it is worth it, and winged seed pods dangle and decorate the tree for some time.

Vitex
Verbenaceae

A large group of mostly subtropical and tropical evergreen and deciduous trees and shrubs, with showy, divided leaves and pretty flowers, this genus is adaptable and most species do well at the coast. They are able to deal with many soil types as long as drainage is good, and they are usually increased by seed.

Vitex lucens, puriri, is a handsome large evergreen tree originating in New Zealand, where it grows in northern parts. Puriri has a sturdy trunk and provides a dome-shaped canopy of deep green, glossy leaflets of a supple leathery texture, and fuchsia-pink flowers, followed by rounded red fruit in clusters. Both flowers and fruit are food for birds. Often seen as street trees and in parks, puriri need room to grow.

V. negundo is a good choice for the garden. A shrub-like little tree, indigenous to Asia, it is grown for its pleasant aromatic foliage and small, fragrant flowers of a delicate mauve.

V. trifolia is an evergreen shrub or small tree from Australia and Asia, noted for its sprays of lavender-blue flowers, ornamented with white spots on their lips. The small fruit that follow are a blue black. Often used as a hedge, and at the coast (its natural habitat), this useful plant is available in several named selections.

Shrubs

Shrubs are woody plants with numerous stems, none dominant. Some are dense and bushy, others open and willow-like. While it is not easy to gauge their eventual height, as this varies so much with climate, soil, site and care, shrubs are usually up to 3 m tall.

These plants are among the most serviceable and useful of landscaping subjects, providing the intrinsic framework of most gardens. Reliable evergreen shrubs that shine all year with attractive foliage as well as flowers are the ones to grow.

Foliage plants offer fantastic opportunities for real drama in the garden, and for form and texture many subtropical species are unsurpassed. At the same time, warm-climate flowering varieties provide us with some of the most ravishing blossoms imaginable, frequently perfumed, and in every shade and hue.

With so many varieties to choose from, it is tempting to display one each of many, but aesthetically it is more pleasing to group several of the same species together; cocktail planting can be restless. Coordinate the colours in a harmony of tones and contrasts. Check flowering times and plant to ensure ongoing colour and year-round interest.

Shrubs can be persuaded to grow against walls, as hedge plants and in containers, as well as embroidering the general garden. Some shrubs do well in shade, but many appreciate sunlight. Most soils can be modified to suit shrubs, as they are adaptable, but prepare it well and incorporate fertiliser in the form of slow-release pellets, regularly applied, especially in areas of consistently high rainfall. Give plants the benefit of compost and mulch, and extra water for varieties that demand this. Small plants are less expensive than larger specimens, and usually do just as well, with less shock at planting time. Healthy shrubs are generally pest and disease resistant, but all garden plants need checking regularly for predators.

Abutilon
Malvaceae

Although this is a genus of 150 or so species, just a few deserve garden status. Evergreen, woody, erect shrubs, abutilons come mainly from

Abutilon megapotamicum

Abutilon x *hybridum*

South America. Popularly called Chinese lanterns, on account of their papery, hanging flowers and rounded stamens, reliable abutilons have been cultivated for centuries. The colourful blossoms attract nectar-seeking birds.

These shrubs will succeed in full sun or filtered shade, and are adaptable and easygoing, with a long flowering season. They need some shelter from the worst winds. Prune them back rigorously in spring, and tip prune thereafter, otherwise they will get leggy and fail to flower. Abutilons are child's play to propagate, and grow readily from cuttings. They are not susceptible to pests.

Abutilon x *hybridum*, Chinese lantern, develops typically untidily unless trained, or grown against a sunny or partly shaded wall. It makes a useful background plant. The flowers come in many colours: white, pink, lemon, yellow, orange, red and deep burgundy. The papery, tissue-thin petals are conspicuously veined, and in a deeper colour in some varieties.

The deckle-edged leaves are a dull green, and some are variegated.

A. megapotamicum, Brazilian bell-flower, is a small groundcover, or may be allowed to grow into a clambering shrub. The little hanging flowers are gorgeously coloured, in scarlet and gold, and look as though designed as costumes for dancers. The Brazilian bell-flower probably is at its best against a sunny wall or fence, where its charming flowers will adorn the cane-like branches for many months.

Acalypha
Euphorbiaceae

Heat-loving acalyphas are shrubs from tropical parts. There are a lot of them, but only a few are considered ornamental enough for the garden. Acalyphas grow fast and are densely structured, making them highly suitable for road frontages or hedges with their radiant foliage. They can withstand heat, but not hot, dry winds, which can burn their leaves. Rich soil will help

Acalypha wilkesiana

acalyphas to grow quickly, as will moisture in dry periods. Look out for good varieties, as leaf colour can vary. You can grow these useful shrubs in full sun or part shade. Insects enjoy the foliage, and caterpillars can be a curse. Cuttings will take readily.

Acalypha wilkesiana, copper leaf, is a vigorous evergreen shrub from Fiji, now grown all through the South Pacific. You never see two bushes the same. The shapely, serrated, large leaves vary widely in tones and tints, and are captivating; red, gold, orange, yellow, green and cream can all appear on the one leaf. The tassel flowers are only incidental. *A. wilkesiana* has many cultivars. 'Macafeeana' is an old favourite and still popular with its bronzed, coppery leaves, blotched with glowing red. Others have yellow or cream deckle-edged margins. Another species is *A. hispida*, the chenille plant prized for its long tassels of red flowers. This is really a tropical dweller, but can be grown as an annual beyond the tropics.

Alyogyne
Malvaceae

Alyogynes come from Western and South Australia, and are handsome erect shrubs which will grow to 3 m in warm, sunny places. They have divided, usually hairy leaves, and fragile flowers in either pink, lilac, cream or white, hibiscus-like, which is not surprising as they are related. Alyogynes can withstand dry conditions, and prefer a friable soil, but do not require cosseting. You can take cuttings or grow them from seed.

Alyogyne hakeifolia is commonly called the red-centred hibiscus, and flaunts mainly lilac flowers with a crimson centre and stamens of a rusty red. The flowers are not large, but most attractive, and arrive in spring and summer.

A. huegelii, the lilac hibiscus, has open flowers with five overlapping petals, slightly bigger than those of its red-centred relation, and can vary in tone from lilac to pink and occasionally white. The flowers are numerous and come in quick succession for many months, and the semi-deciduous bush needs pruning to keep in shape. If you have a difficult rocky area, you could safely plant these alyogynes there, but remember that the petals are delicate and harmed by wind.

Another Australian member of the same family to consider, growing in a similar area is *Gossypium sturtianum*, Sturt's desert rose, with flowers very similar, in a cool blue to purple, set off by a red centre. The leaves are round and glaucous. This useful shrub deals admirably with hot dry conditions, and has two claims to fame. It belongs to the same genus as cotton, one of the world's important commercial crops, and

Alyogyne huegelii

Aphelandra squarrosa

Aphelandra sinclairiana

Sturt's desert rose itself is the floral emblem of Australia's Northern Territory.

Aphelandra
Acanthaceae

Tropical Americans, aphelandras total almost 200 shrubs and subshrub species. Beyond the tropics many are used as house plants, cultivated for their lavishly designed leaves. In the subtropics, aphelandras develop well-made, vivid, cone-shaped flowers with contrasting bracts, and they flower profusely for the best part of the year.

In drifts and groups these are valuable landscape plants, adaptable and tolerant, though they will not do well where winds are strong. Light shade or sun suits them, and they are not particular about soil, although a granular fertiliser will keep the plants strong and growing. Prune vigorously after flowering to help the new growth and flowers.

Aphelandra aurantiaca var. *roezlii* is a low-growing, very ornamental subshrub with leaves of a deep, metallic navy-blue colour, highlighted by silvery veins. Spikes of furnace-red bracts and tubular orange flowers erupt from the middle of the plant and last for some time, exciting comment wherever they are seen. Grow these aphelandras in groups at the front of a shrubbery, away from wind, and in semi-shade. Moist conditions and humidity are right for these treasures.

A. sinclairiana, coral aphelandra, comes from rainforests in Central America. A tall shrub, it has deep green, softly textured foliage and flowers of a brilliant contrast. They are in clusters of cone-shaped, velvety bracts of bright coral and cerise blossom. You can use several for group plantings or as background shrubs.

A. squarrosa, from Brazil, is the zebra plant, so-called because of its striped foliage. Usually employed as a house plant, it does well in a humid atmosphere and bright light, but not sun, and it will bear a terminal spike of yellow flowers. A bush-house is a good place to grow this plant, which requires regular doses of liquid fertiliser, copious supplies of water, and protection from winds and draughts. Cultivars are available, even bolder than the species.

Other members of the Acanthaceae family are noted for their foliage. One to look out for is *Strobilanthes dyerianus*, Persian shield. This is a small-growing shrub with illuminated leaves of metallic purple, adorned with prominent veins of deep green. Best placed in partial shade, in rich soil with some leaf mould, Persian shield plants will only thrive in a garden that receives high rainfall.

Another relation with conspicuous foliage is *Graptophyllum pictum*, the caricature plant, from New Guinea and thereabouts. A dense, woody shrub, the caricature plant delivers croton-like foliage in splashes and patterns of colour, a glorious mix of green and yellow, or pink and purples to cream and white. Two common forms, seen in the islands of the Pacific, are green-edged with cream-to-white blotches and scarlet veins; and yellow-edged with bright green splashes.

Banksia
Proteaceae

Sir Joseph Banks, the eminent naturalist, is honoured by the naming of this genus, and indeed he discovered a species in Botany Bay in 1770, when on Captain Cook's epic voyage. Banksias contain at least 75 species, found throughout Australia and straying into New Guinea. They are fine representatives of the protea family, staunch in the face of adversity, and well known for their tolerance of dry conditions. The flowers are arranged in cylindrical upright heads, brush-like, and made up of a thousand or so individual blooms, irresistible to nectar-seeking birds. Banksias come in various sizes, from prostrate shrubs to trees, and flower in warm colours at different times of the year. Most shrubby banksias flourish in sunlight and gritty or sandy soil. Judicious tip

pruning helps maintain their shape. The majority of species are easily raised from seed.

Banksia ericifolia, heath banksia, bears heath-like leaves and stiff, golden to henna flowers. It grows readily in a variety of climates, and is a cinch at the coast. The hybrids come in unexpected colours; pink to deep red. And watch out for 'Giant Candles', which lives up to its name and is a sturdy shrub, able to deal with adverse conditions.

B. spinulosa, hairpin banksia, a tolerant, compact shrub, has narrow, serrated leaves lined with silver. The flower cones are yellow with golden-brown tips. Cultivars are available. Many more banksias are being developed for the subtropical garden, some enjoying moist soil.

Brugmansia
Solanaceae

Tree-like shrubs or shrub-like trees? It is difficult to place brugmansias, as they develop trunks and most can grow to tree size. However, there is no question of why brugmansias or, to give them their previous name, daturas, are cultivated. It is for their bold, trumpet-shaped, highly perfumed flowers. Brugmansias bear large, soft, sage-green leaves, are evergreen, and develop their grand trumpets after a year. Their original habitat is in the Andes.

The plants have hallucinogenic properties, and all parts are poisonous. Snails do not seem to know this and treat brugmansia leaves as haute cuisine. A warm climate suits these plants, and some species grow happily at the beach. In fact, several types have naturalised in odd pockets of many countries in seaside areas. Free-draining soil is needed, and moisture. It is best to pinch plants back as they grow, otherwise they develop into ungainly, untidy shrubs. Watch out for whitefly, spider mites and mealy bug, as well as voracious snails. Brugmansias are easily propagated from cuttings and make handsome container plants in marginal climates.

Brugmansia aurea is illuminated with long golden to apricot, open-faced trumpets, trimmed with flares.

Brugmansias make ideal pot subjects

B. x *candida*, angel's trumpet, grows to tree size in rather a raffish way if left to its own devices. The hanging white trumpets end in a delightful flare, like a dancer's skirt. This species has fragrant flowers, intensifying in the late afternoons and at night, heavy and sweet. There are several good cultivars, too. 'Plena' is fancy, with an extra flounce, and others are in shades of apricot. Semi-shade will suffice for the angel's trumpet.

B. x *insignis* is a very good hybrid, in colours from white to cream or apricot, and other brugmansia hybrids and cultivars abound, too, usually in blush pink to darker pink, apricot and gold, while *B. sanguinea*, red angel's trumpet, boasts two-toned flowers in brick red and yellow. It is not as elegantly structured as most, nor as vigorous.

Closely allied are *Datura* species, a genus of about eight annuals and perennials. Among them is the moonflower (*D. innoxia*). This perennial is often treated as an annual, and grows quickly from seed. Its alabaster-white flowers, edged in a soft lilac, emerge in the evening and perfume the air with a spicy aroma. Moonflowers reach a height of around 1 m, and are ideal for containers, or in small groups in the flower garden.

Brunfelsia
Solanaceae

Brunfelsias are delightful evergreen shrubs from tropical America, with an abundance of bloom. The flowers have the ability to change colour as they fade, thus decorating the shrubs for many months in a kaleidoscope of colour. Brunfelsias do not develop rapidly, although they are adaptable, and the species differ in their wants, some preferring partial shade, others full sun. They grow well as container plants or in groups, and need to be pruned quite rigorously after flowering to maintain shape and encourage blooms in the following season. Thrips can trouble brunfelsias. As they seed profusely, new plants are always available from the fresh seed.

Brunfelsia americana originates in the Caribbean, where it is called lady of the night

Brunfelsia australis

for its heavy, overpowering scent all through the dark hours. The tall shrub, with glossy, light green leaves, can be pruned back, and bears open, white-faced flowers that alter to cream and yellow as they age. Lady of the night should be placed in a sunny position and can be used as a hedge plant, or left to develop as a specimen shrub. It will thrive in the heat as long as it has good, friable soil and ample water.

A close relation, and from the same area, is *Cestrum nocturnum*, commonly called queen of the night, and this shrub, too, has an over-powering nocturnal scent. It will naturalise when it likes the conditions, and should be used in the background of the garden, and not allowed to wander. It can become very untidy, but its clusters of white flowers, tinted a pale green, are attractive.

B. australis, charmingly nicknamed yesterday-today-and-tomorrow because of its multi-coloured blooms, is a compact, medium-sized shrub whose flowers change from sapphire blue to violet before fading to white. Yesterday-today-and-tomorrow blooms from late winter onwards, through spring to summer, and likes a semi-shaded position. The flowers are fragrant both by day and night, and it is an amenable shrub for a container or any spot away from harsh winds.

43

Caesalpinia
Fabaceae

Caesalpinias are a genus of evergreen to semi-deciduous shrubs, trees and climbers from warm regions of the world. They have fern-like leaves with abundant leaflets, and the shrubs are elegant and most decorative. However, caesalpinias are cultivated primarily for their glorious flowers, clusters of blooms in bright, hot colours, distinguished by exceptionally long stamens. The shrubs prefer a friable, fertile soil, well watered, and a desirable spot in the garden, perhaps against a wall in the sun. An organic mulch is beneficial. Propagate from seed, which arrives in long pods. (After all, they are legumes.)

Caesalpinia gilliesii, dwarf poinciana or bird of paradise bush, has subtropical parts of South America as its home, and is admired and grown in most warm areas of the world. It is tolerant of dry conditions at the coast, but may be semi-deciduous there. This is a precocious plant and will flower quickly, the bush erupting in spikes of yellow flowers with lovely long crimson stamens. Dwarf poinciana is not that small, sometimes reaching 3 m.

C. pulcherrima has common names that honour its brilliance — peacock flower, red bird of paradise, pride of Barbados. Whatever you call it, this shrub produces upright clusters of vivid scarlet and shiny gold flowers, topped with deep red stamens, for months at a time. Furthermore this species has other uses; the shrubs provide red dyes and laxatives, and the hard wood has been used to fashion violin bows. You can keep *C. pulcherrima* compact by hard pruning. Yellow pride of Barbados is another form, and there are also deep pink and crimson types, all worth growing.

Calliandra
Fabaceae

Not many of the hundreds of species of calliandras are cultivated for their beauty. They mainly come from the Americas, and it is the evergreen shrubs that are favoured for gardens. These have bipinnate, fern-like leaves, sensitive to the weather, and will close at night. The blooms are in clusters, soft and furry, bottlebrush-like, and usually pink or red in colour. Calliandras are fairly adaptable and will thrive in many areas, but they appreciate a position away from wind, good open soil, a reliable water supply and full sun, if possible. Most important is the free-draining soil. You can propagate calliandras from seed.

Calliandra californica, red fairy duster, from Mexico, thrives in dry conditions, as its Baja homeland would indicate. A small, upright shrub, the red fairy duster obliges with fluffy flowers of cerise, set off by grey-green leaves.

C. emarginata, powderpuff plant, from Central America, is an ethereal shrub, but its appearance belies its toughness. Usually cultivated as a specimen, it bears white or pink to red fluffy, pompom-like flowers with an explosion of stamens — most floriferous. Blooms appear throughout the year, and are followed by typical legume seed pods. As the seeds ripen, the pods curve back to eject the seeds, so you may find new plants growing quite a distance from the parent. You can confidently plant this shrub in a container, and it is often seen as a bonsai subject, too. *C. haematocephala*, blood-red tassel-flower, is similar.

Caesalpinia gilliesii

Calliandra californica

Carissa
Apocynaceae

Carissas are dependable plants, numbering about 20 species, mainly from Africa. Evergreen shrubs, usually compact, they have spines, white, fragrant flowers and bold red fruits. They are often planted as hedges, their spines being a deterrent to unwanted wildlife. Gritty soil, heat and a subtropical climate will ensure flowers and fruit nearly all year, once a plant is established. Some species are wind resistant, a decided asset at the coast. You can increase carissas by seeds or layering.

Carissa bispinosa, hedge thorn or num-num, inhabits southern Africa, has shiny, dark green leaves, numerous vicious spines, and small, perfumed white flowers, followed by red, edible fruits which ripen to plum colour. A compact bush which can be clipped back and kept to 1 m, this carissa will tolerate heat and dry weather.

C. macrocarpa, Natal plum, grows on bush edges and along beaches in Natal, and can deal efficiently with salt-laden winds. Natal plums produce white flowers, seductively scented, evocative of gardenias, with a jasmine overtone perhaps, but a fragrance to remember, and intensified at night. They bloom for many months, and the plump, round, crimson fruit come quickly, decorating the shrub at the same time as the snowy white flowers. The fruit, the size of small plums, can be made into pies, scrumptious jams and jellies, or sauces and chutneys. Left on the bush, they are very ornamental.

In Hawaiian coastal gardens carissas are a feature, cascading over lava rocks right by the shore. A Californian cultivar, 'Boxwood Beauty', is a favourite. Its thorns are blunter, its flowers and fruit larger than the species, all on a compact, spreading bush that can be used as a groundcover. Carissas are a feature of Malibu gardens, too.

Clerodendrum
Verbenaceae

Clerodendrums are a diverse lot, including climbers, shrubs, trees and perennials. Some like it hot, shrubs among them, and some species are tropical, rapid growers and need shelter from

Carissa macrocarpa

Clerodendrum paniculatum

shining leaves are a satisfying contrast. This clerodendrum grows into a medium-sized shrub. You may find other red-flowered species to try, such as *C. buchananii*, but you will not find one with such a cavalcade of bloom.

C. ugandense, blue butterfly bush, is aptly named, and grows into a small, slender shrub liberally sprinkled with delightful little blue 'butterflies', in shades of celestial blue and a deeper royal, with conspicuous arching stamens. Typical of the genus, the flowers are followed by round berries, in this case almost black. The blue butterfly bush is an adaptable plant, and will grow readily in either sun or partial shade, preferring a good, moisture-retentive soil. Its leaves are modest, and when the bush is not flowering you would not give it a second glance, but it is irresistible when in bloom.

Codiaeum
Euphorbiaceae

Plants with brilliant foliage are features of the tropics and subtropics, but few can rival codiaeums for razzle dazzle and a kaleidoscope of colours. Evergreen shrubs and small trees, this

Codiaeum variegatum

wind. They have bright, charming flowers, often two-toned, with characteristic long stamens, followed by small, shiny berries. As a rule, their leaves are somewhat coarse, and if you crush them they give off an unmistakeable odour. Clerodendrums should be transplanted when very small, and you can increase them by cuttings or seeds. Some species are short lived, but you can forgive them that, and have more waiting in the wings.

Clerodendrum paniculatum, the pagoda flower, from Asian hot spots, favours the tropics, but is good to grow in the subtropics when provided with shelter and lush, jungle conditions. It is worth it, as its flowerheads are in bold tiers of bright flame red, opening to a salmon pink, the whole resembling an oriental temple, hence its common name. And they are in bloom for most of the time, too. The dark, heavily veined, is a small genus of some 6 species from the Pacific, Malaysia and Asia, and it is from one species, the croton, that all the hundreds of variegations and chromatic colours come. Of Pacific islands origin, codiaeums are seen all over the South Pacific, Hawaii and in warm areas of Australia.

These adaptable shrubs are usually pruned back to a manageable size, and can be planted as hedges, in containers or as a specimen. The cultivars are more compact, and, if possible, come in even more outrageous colour schemes. Full sunlight is necessary for the best displays of foliage. Mulch, a moist soil and regular applications of a general garden fertiliser guarantee vivid leaves. The ever-present mealy bugs, thrips and spider mites find crotons attractive. Propagate from cuttings, and you could try some air layering, too.

Codiaeum variegatum, croton, and all its permutations, are South Pacific shrubs for the humid garden. They do have flowers, but these are small, white, and incidental. Leaves in lemon, yellow, red green, pink, purple, and hues and highlights in between, are the glories of crotons, and the flamboyant foliage comes in differing

Coffea arabica

leaf shapes, too. The leaves are enhanced by rain, when the colours intensify and glisten more than ever, while the shrub revels in the moisture. Look out for the named cultivars.

If you find crotons too vivid and not part of your colour scheme, try a near relation, one that enjoys the same conditions, the snow bush (*Breynia disticha*), also from the South Pacific. The snow bush is a medium-sized shrub with a pleasing weeping habit. Its leaves are its glory, the delicate-looking fresh new ones being softly white and a gentle pink, the older ones turning a light green. Snow bushes can be used in the garden in the same positions as crotons, and enjoy similar conditions; ample rain and humidity and full sun for maximum foliage colour.

Coffea
Rubiaceae

There is only one distinguished species among the 40 in the *Coffea* genus, and that, of course, is coffee, from Ethiopia. Most species have glossy leaves and fragrant white flowers in clusters along the branches, followed by berries. Rich soil is needed to produce strong bushes, also warmth, semi-shade, and a liberal mulch. Coffee bushes are rapid growers, and do not care to be transplanted. Fresh seed germinates readily. Watch out for scale.

Coffea arabica, Arabian coffee, is the favourite species, and coffee is cultivated for commerce by at least 50 countries. Coffee bushes are decorative, with glossy, deckle-edged leaves on slim branches, and the fragrant white flowers (the plant belongs to the same family as gardenias) are held horizontally on slim stems. The compact bushes are agreeable shrubs for the garden, their flowers abundant and exuding a delicious aroma. These are followed by green berries that turn bright tomato red and dark crimson when ripe. Do not expect to make coffee from them; it is a long, involved process. Best just to admire the bushes, taking care to site them well, as they are long lived.

It might be interesting to try a tea bush or two as well. The famous brew is made from the foliage of *Camellia sinensis*, another pretty shrub, whose leaf tips are picked at just the right moment and processed. However, in the home garden *C. sinensis* can be planted for its ornamental, picotee-edged leaves and small sweet white flowers, without a thought to making tea.

Crotalaria
Fabaceae

Although there are many *Crotalaria* species, the genus is complex, containing plants from many countries of the world, but including only a very few worthwhile garden subjects. These are the shrubs with yellow or lime-green pea flowers and leaves divided into three leaflets. Not hard to grow, crotalarias like sun or part shade, are not fussy over soil, and some species will put up with dry conditions. Most crotalarias are untidy in growth and should be pruned back after flowering, which will encourage more flowers, too. They grow rapidly. Propagate from tip cuttings or seed.

Crotalaria agatiflora

Crotalaria agatiflora, canary-bird bush, is a variable species with several subspecies, and roams over many warm parts of Africa. Its flowers are yellow with a lime-green tinge, and bird-shaped, on long, upright stems.

C. capensis, Cape laburnum, found all over South Africa, bears drooping spikes of bright yellow flowers at the tops of branches at most times of the year. It appreciates more rainfall than other species, grows in a loose fashion, and should be curtailed.

C. laburnifolia, bird flower, has its habitat in the northern states of Australia, is similar to the canary-bird bush, and a delightful shrub to have. Its chartreuse flowers are for all the world like tiny, exotic birds attached to the stems by their beaks. The bird flower prefers open, gritty soil and will put up with salt winds and quite cool conditions. It flowers for many months, and the long racemes can be picked for the vase, where they will last for many days.

C. cunninghamii, the green bird flower, is another Australian, and is also bird-like, but with purple stripes on its petals. A few other crotalarias are also well adjusted to garden conditions.

If you have a penchant for lime-green or chartreuse flowers, grow *Salvia mexicana* 'Limelight', Mexican sage. It is a rounded, albeit leggy shrub with appropriate sage-green leaves, and right through summer and autumn explodes in a startling array of terminal flowerheads. The whole bush is illuminated with sharp lime-green bracts at first, and slowly produces deep blue to dark purple flowers. Best as a background shrub, because the plant is fairly nondescript until it delivers its dazzling flowerheads, Mexican sage needs pruning rigorously after flowering to maintain a good shape and strong growth in ensuing seasons.

Cuphea
Lythraceae

Useful and dependable, rather than showy, probably best describes the shrubby cupheas. There are plenty of them — annuals, perennials, subshrubs as well as shrubs — and Central and South America are their natural habitats. Small, ground-hugging plants for the most part, cupheas produce tubular flowers, usually two-toned, all year long. Simple to grow, with few demands, they prefer well-drained soil but moist conditions, and sun. You can use cupheas for groundcovers en masse, and in containers. No diseases or pests appear to worry these shrubs, which are propagated from seed.

Cuphea ignea, cigar flower or cigarette plant, from Mexico, is popularly named for its long, tubular flowers, bright orange or pink in colour, flaring to dark wine with a white tip. The flowers are small, but cover the little bush of tiny, glossy green leaves.

C. micropetala, a fellow Mexican, mimics the cigar flower in looks, but is larger, and the flower tubes are more of a tangerine to golden colour, fading to a soft yellow green at the tips, and with bigger leaves.

Dombeya
Sterculiaceae

Although over 200 species of *Dombeya* exist, and range over parts of Africa, Madagascar and islands in the Indian Ocean, only a few exceptional shrubs and small trees are cultivated. It is their compact habit, ornamental leaves, and profusion of clustered, often fragrant, blooms that please. In shades of white to red, dombeyas can be cut for the vase. Some dombeyas are deciduous, others semi so; many more are evergreen. Extremely easy to grow, these amenable plants are useful and undemanding, and can be propagated from cuttings or seed.

Dombeyas require sun to flower well, and humidity suits them, plus a well-drained soil enriched with some organic matter. A mulch is beneficial as the roots like it moist, although as they mature dombeyas will tolerate dry conditions. It is good to have several species, as

Dombeya 'Pink Cloud'

Euphorbia pulcherrima

not all bloom at the same time, and as the spent flowerheads turn rusty brown and tend to stay on certain shrubs, some grooming may be called for.

Dombeya cacumina, red dombeya, grows rapidly into a large shrub or small tree, and is useful as a screen or specimen. This outstanding species blooms later than most, with generous downfacing clusters of glowing, coral-red, white-centred flowers on terminal branches.

D. x cayeuxii is a rounded shrub with abundant clusters of delightful blush-pink blooms, like fruit blossom, and they cover the bush from summer to autumn. Its origins are uncertain, but it is a superior plant to grow.

D. rotundifolia, called the South African wild pear, a large shrub or a small, deciduous tree, is transformed from head to foot in spring, or earlier, with clusters of creamy-white bloom, although species cultivated in Australia tend to produce pink flowers. The new leaves emerge with the flowers or as the flowers fade. No trouble to grow from seed, as long as the soil is moist, this South African is a good species for a shrubbery.

D. tiliacea is commonly named the Natal wedding flower, on account of its origins, and its large, milky-white fragrant flowers. It blooms from late summer to early spring, a great asset.

Several other species are well worth trying, and are stalwart in gardens ranging from the tropics to warm temperate regions, and by the sea. Look out for the robust hybrids, in vibrant pinks and reds.

Euphorbia
Euphorbiaceae

Although there are about 2000 species of this immense genus, not many are shrubs. Euphorbias are natives of tropical, subtropical and warm temperate areas. Mostly they will thrive in sun or part shade, and all like well-drained soil. Many species tolerate cold conditions, while others bask in the heat. When cut, they will exude a milky sap which can irritate the skin and eyes. You can propagate the shrubby types from cuttings and stems.

Euphorbia leucocephala, with the appropriately common name of snowflake, is a dense, compact, rounded shrub covered with ice-white bracts for many months, imparting a cool look to the warm garden, and a fine contrast to its kin, the poinsettia. Easy to grow and increase, snowflake is a delight to have.

E. pulcherrima, poinsettia, from Mexico, is a favourite all over the world for its brilliant flaming-scarlet bracts. Poinsettias are dependable, easy-going shrubs in warm areas, and will flower for many months. Look out for the dazzling cultivars, too, in colours from rich cream to yellow, apricot and crimson. Those with big shaggy double heads revel in the heat and can be seen all over the tropics and subtropics, and their bracts are darker red, a vivid crimson.

The blooming period of poinsettias is conditioned by the daylight hours, and they are called 'photoperiod' plants. Short days and long nights stimulate the growth and colouring of the leaf pigments. Commercial growers regulate daylight hours, and use chemicals to dwarf plants, so we can have potted poinsettias at Christmas, regardless of where we live. In warm areas, these plants can afterwards be planted out to flourish in the garden.

Gardenia
Rubiaceae

Gardenia — the very name evokes images of hot, tropical nights and seductive scents. Evergreen shrubs, with a couple of hundred species, gardenias hail from warm areas of Asia and parts of Africa. They are cultivated for their overpowering fragrance, and in parts of Asia yellow dye is extracted from the fruit of some species. Gardenias have shiny, bottle-green foliage, and most do better in sheltered, semi-shaded places. Rich, dark acid soil is the preference of most species, in a humid atmosphere with abundant water in the hottest months. Be generous with fertiliser, and the addition of Epsom salts will ensure healthy foliage. Pests are partial to gardenias, and thrips, scale and mealy bug can be a problem. Increase by taking tip cuttings.

Gardenia augusta, common gardenia, is from China and Japan, and has been cultivated there for centuries as an ornamental shrub. Common gardenia grows freely in South Africa, and that has led to its other erroneous common name of Cape jasmine. The flowers can be single or double, lily white, yellowing as they age. The scent is like no other; heavy, sweet and alluring. It is a compact shrub, medium sized, and can be persuaded to grow as a standard. A prostrate form is 'Radicans'. Gardenias are best grown in

Gardenia augusta 'Magnifica'

groups, and ideal near a swimming pool or deck where their scent can be appreciated .

G. taitensis, tiare or Tahitian gardenia, has islands of the South Pacific as its home. Tiare blossoms are pure white, pinwheel shaped, perfumed to delight the senses, and of course the shrubs do well at the seaside. In Samoa and Tahiti, tiare flowers are used to make leis, as crowns for the hair, and to scent coconut oil. This species grows to quite a large shrub, inclined to sprawl, but can be cut back, and likes the sun.

Other gardenias are obtainable, but if your garden is not suitable, you could try growing *Bouvardia longiflora*, scented bouvardia, instead. It comes from the same family and has highly perfumed white flowers, with overtones of gardenia and jasmine. This is a small shrub, widely grown for the florist trade, the flowers being very popular for wedding bouquets.

Grevillea
Proteaceae

The amazing protea family has several representatives in Australia, and the enchanting spider flowers are among the best and most ornamental of these. Grevilleas are distinguished by their spidery clustered flowers and ferny foliage, and range from forest giants to ground-hugging shrubs. The flowers come in a wide colour assortment, too, from white to yellow, through to orange and red. With over 230 known species and countless hybrids and cultivars, grevilleas are without peer as trouble-free trees, shrubs and groundcovers, generous with flowers over a long period.

Grevilleas require a fairly light, well-drained soil, more acid than not, and plenty of sun. Some species are more suited to subtropical climates than others, but there is a wide selection for most regions. You should prune grevilleas right after they flower to keep them within bounds. Pests do not harm these dependable, strong, reliable plants. You can propagate from cuttings, but they do not take readily.

Grevillea banksii, Banks's grevillea or red silky

Hibiscus arnottianus

Mixed hibiscus in a subtropical setting

Hibiscus rosa-sinensis hybrid

oak, named for Sir Joseph Banks, is a handsome large shrub or small tree from subtropical parts of eastern Australia. A stalwart fast-growing shrub for the seaside and exposed positions, and one of the most popular grevilleas, it has deeply divided sage-green leaves which contrast delightfully with the spikes of summer-blooming carmine flowers.

G. longistyla x *johnsonii* enjoys warmth and grows quickly to a medium-sized shrub, with an abundance of bloom. The flowers, bright pink with glowing red styles, have a very long season.

There are so many kinds of grevillea to choose from, it seems churlish not to describe dozens. With names such as 'Coconut Ice', 'Honey Gem', 'Pink Lady' and the ever reliable 'Robyn Gordon', who could resist these charmers?

Then there is the always dependable *G. robusta*, silky oak, which ultimately becomes a massive tree, in late spring bearing a wealth of golden to orange, fringed clusters of nectar-rich blooms, and notable year round for its handsome cut leaves, with a silvery lining. Suitable for large gardens, parks and as a street tree, silky oak is a success in many warm countries.

Another Australian member of the Proteaceae family, renowned for its flowers, is *Alloxylon flammeum*, tree waratah. From warm rainforests, it eventually reaches tree status, but is shrub-like for many years. The flowers of the tree waratah have some resemblance to a waratah, producing blood-red terminal blooms over several weeks in summer.

Hibiscus
Malvaceae

This genus, with about 220 species, ranges from trees to annuals. Those suitable for the subtropics are mainly the sublime hybrids of *Hibiscus rosa-sinensis*, but there are other worthy shrubby species. At least one tree for the beach can be grown on warm shores. Hibiscus flowers come in many shades, but are distinguished by their five petals and conspicuous stamens. These plants all appreciate full sun, a genial climate,

friable soil, and ample water in dry periods, also regular fertilising. However, the hybrid shrubs demand extra care and attention to give of their best, with specialised feeding, regular watering and annual pruning essential for success. These plants are easily propagated from cuttings. In hot climates hibiscus are plagued by a voracious beetle, and elsewhere aphids and scale can be a problem.

H. arnottianus, white hibiscus, from Hawaii, is blessed with several superior qualitites. Not only do the shrubs bloom profusely, but the pure white, elegant single flowers have an irresistible fragrance, and are adorned with prominent crimson stamens. Then there are their stalwart genes, with built-in resistance to root rot and borer. Hawaii's white hibiscus is used for hybridising, and you will find many aromatic hybrids in Hawaii. You can expect this shrub to grow to a respectable size. Another Hawaiian is sometimes seen, although endangered in its own habitat. *H. brackenridgei* is Hawaii's official state flower, and is a bright daffodil yellow.

H. calyphyllus, from Africa, was once thought to be endemic to the island of Kauai, Hawaii, so well does it flourish there. It is distinguished by its deep burgundy throat, surrounded by golden yellow petals.

H. heterophyllus, rosella, an Australian, is cultivated in the main for its edible buds, although it is decorative in flower as well, having blooms of white or soft pink, occasionally yellow. It is a large shrub, adaptable, and easy to grow. The buds are used to make a delectable jam.

H. mutabilis, cotton rose, a Chinese hibiscus, is an interesting shrub to grow. The big fat flowers first open white, and then progress from baby pink to rose, so all colours are to be seen on the sturdy shrub, which has strong, felted, soft green leaves.

H. rosa-sinensis, and its thousands of hybrids and cultivars, is indisputably the crowning glory of the hibiscus family. For beauty, form, size and colour, very few flowers can compete. Its origins are slightly obscure, but today's magnificent blooms have been developed by hybridists in

Iochroma cyaneum

Ixora chinensis

enchanting flowers, coral hibiscus has reflexed, extravagantly cut, ruffled, deep-coral petals with a long, fragile-looking staminal column, the whole hanging on a slender stem. This hibiscus has been used for hybridising with *H. rosa-sinensis*.

H. tiliaceus, cottonwood tree or hau, is a spreading, medium-sized tree of the seashore, one that arouses thoughts of tropical vacations. The cottonwood grows right up to high-tide mark, and delights with its near year-round topaz flowers highlighted by bold crimson centres. As they age, these fade to a warm orange. A variegated-leaf cultivar is widely used by florists and island peoples in the Pacific.

A near relation is *Malvaviscus arboreus*, the sleeping hibiscus or Turk's cap. Easy to grow, it likes the same conditions as hibiscus and forms a dense, rounded shrub with heart-shaped leaves and bright scarlet flowers, like furled hibiscus. The sleeping hibiscus will flower for six months of the year.

Iochroma
Solanaceae

Evergreen shrubs from tropical and subtropical parts of the Americas, iochromas have tubular, hanging flowers in jewel colours of purple, indigo, garnet red or pearl white. Filtered sunlight suits them well, and well-drained soil. Iochromas can be ungainly shrubs, and should be pruned back regularly. Whitefly and aphids attack the young shoots. Propagate from cuttings.

Iochroma cyaneum, with the lacklustre common name of violet tubeflower, can take on a sombre appearance, with its hanging clusters of indigo or deep purple, tubular flowers against a background of grey-green, furry textured leaves. Best grown as a background shrub, with lighter companions. A bigger flowered species is *I. grandiflorum*, from Ecuador.

I. fuchsioides is a brighter proposition altogether, although similar in shape to the violet tubeflower. It carries scarlet flowers with orange throats as a good contrast.

Australia, New Zealand, Hawaii, California and Florida. They have produced floriferous shrubs, with king-sized blooms of intense colour and vigour, resistant to disease and frequently lasting longer than one day when picked. With so many to choose from, it is wise to select your hibiscus by colour.

H. schizopetalus, coral hibiscus, is a native of tropical eastern Africa, where it grows in coastal woods. A popular shrub for its strong, arching framework and the intriguing structure of its

Ixora
Rubiaceae

You see ixoras all over the subtropics and tropics because they are as dependable as they are dazzling. Hundreds of species exist, and their home bases are mainly Africa and Asia. Not many species are cultivated, but those that are have a rounded form in tight clusters of bright flowers in red, coral, orange, yellow, pink or white. You often see ixoras decorating carparks and shopping malls, which gives some idea of their survival abilities. A crumbly soil suits them, filtered sun, and warm, humid conditions. They will thrive when given generous amounts of water in the hotter months. Also, as with so many subtropicals, a thick mulch works wonders. Ixoras should be pruned back lightly to maintain their dense, compact shape. Even when they are not flowering, they are attractive, and you can transplant mature bushes. Propagate from cuttings.

Ixora chinensis, simply called ixora, as its botanical name suggests, is from China, but also from Malaysia. The flowers are typical of ixoras, and come in vivid colours of scarlet, brick red, orange, yellow, white and even pink. These shrubs can be relied on to flower for months at a time. They do well in pots, or used as hedge plants. Several cultivars should be available.

A near relation is *Pentas lanceolata*, which will flower continuously in the subtropics provided it has well-watered, well-drained soil. The star-shaped flowers are arranged in clusters in pleasing colours of white through to pink, lavender, purple and cherry-red. Treat it as you would ixoras.

Justicia
Acanthaceae

Evergreen shrubs and perennials make up the 400 or so species of this genus, and they are found in tropical and subtropical areas, mainly in the Americas. Justicias have gone through several name changes, and botanists have obviously dithered over their correct appellation. You will

Justicia brandegeana

see one or other of the species in gardens from warm temperate zones to the tropics, and they are not only ornamental, but easy to grow. The flowers, with bright bracts, are usually in shades of pink, coral, red or white, and are held high. Full sun or partial shade suits justicias, and a good, crumbly soil. It is best to plant them away from strong winds. Cuttings are child's play to propagate.

Justicia brandegeana, the shrimp plant or beleporone (which was its former botanical name), has been cultivated in gardens for many years. It certainly resembles a shrimp or prawn, with its shape and colouring. The bracts are terracotta or coral shaded, the colour of a cooked crustacean, and the flowers are white, dotted wine, for all the world like eye stalks. Although shrimp plants do not do well in salt-laden winds, they grow satisfactorily at the beach in sheltered sites. They are very easy to grow, keep to a small size, and can be pinched back. Although they are so sturdy, justicias do have enemies; snails relish the leaves, despite their unappetising look. There is a superior lemon-coloured type, not as stalwart, but well worth growing for its appealing looks. It requires more shelter and shade.

J. carnea, jacobinia (its common name was once its botanical name), commemorates a town

Luculia grandifolia

in Brazil and has been in cultivation for almost two centuries. This is an erect shrub, over a metre in height, with leaves large, deep green and soft to the touch, but it is the flowers that attract gardeners. Clusters of shocking pink, or maybe deep pink, blooms cover the shrub in profusion. Again, snails find the leaves irresistible.

A close relation to the justicias is *Pachystachys lutea*, with the common names of golden candles or lollipop plant. It bears a resemblance to the yellow shrimp plant, but grows larger. The white flowers sit bolt upright on lemon-yellow bracts, and the leaves are deep green and decidedly decorative. Often treated as an annual, golden candles make good container plants, and are effective in groups. They will bear bright yellow flowers nearly all year long. Look out for thrips.

Luculia
Rubiaceae

A small genus of five shrubs, luculias come from Himalayan regions. They can be temperamental, shining in one garden, sulking in another. If they are happy in their position, luculias are appealing plants, their pink or white flowers having an irresistible fragrance. They like an equable climate, not too hot, not too cold, and a crumbly, well-drained, acidic soil. You can prune them lightly, and increase from cuttings.

Luculia grandifolia has a strong form, with large, dark leaves heavily veined in carmine, and matching stalks. Even when not in flower, this luculia is most handsome, but comes to life when smothered with its snow-white, tubular clusters of sweetly fragrant blooms, usually in late summer. You can grow *L. grandifolia* in semi-shade.

L. gratissima is the most popular of the genus, and beguiles with its mops of soft rose-pink flowers, wildly fragrant. In most places these arrive on the shrub in winter, when fragrance and flowers are generally not so evident. With soft green leaves, tinged bronze, on an upright, medium-sized bush, this luculia likes room to breathe, and no competition from other plants. Sun suits this beauty, and a place where it can be seen and smelt.

Medinilla
Melastomataceae

Most of these 150 or so shrubs and climbers, some epiphytic, call the tropics home. The species for the garden are generally shrubby, highly ornamental, with magnificent panicles of bloom. Filtered shade suits medinillas, and a steady, warm climate, with high humidity. In the subtropics you need to cosset these plants, but they are worth every attention. Regularity is the key; routine feeding and watering. (It is a different story in tropical rainforests of Hawaii, where they have become far too exuberant and are pests.) Propagate from seed or cuttings.

Medinilla magnifica, rose grape, boasts superb hanging clusters of luminous shocking-pink flowerheads, surrounded by paler pink bracts, with yellow stamens. The panicles can be 45 cm long. Small purple berries follow. This medinilla's fantastic flowers need adjectives in the superlative to do them justice. The shrubs,

an epiphyte in its native Philippines, cannot abide wind, and flourish in partial shade and moist, sultry areas.

Megaskepasma
Acanthaceae

One of a kind — and what a kind — this shrub gives a dazzling display for many months. Bright, strong flowers work well in the tropics and subtropics with the contrast of bold foliage, and this species, originally from Venezuela, is cultivated for the brilliant red flowers.

Megaskepasma erythrochlamys thankfully has a common name, Brazilian red cloak. This large shrub explodes with spikes of radiant red, verging on crimson, bracts enclosing small white flowers. You see the red cloaks in botanical gardens in the tropics and subtropics, where they always excite attention and are the subjects of numerous photos. The bottle-green leaves have a slightly quilted effect. It will oblige in light shade or sun,

Medinilla magnifica

Megaskepasma erythrochlamys

Ruellia macrantha

needs high humidity and an open but well-watered soil, fertiliser and mulch. Regular dead-heading is necessary. In other words, give it lots of attention and it will shine. It is easy to propagate from cuttings. Snails like the large, strong, luxuriant leaves, and watch out for mealy-bugs. A shrub for larger gardens, as it can grow tall and spreading, this is truly a delight to have.

A smaller subshrub, and one from the same acanthus family, from Brazil, is *Ruellia macrantha*, not as showy, but most attractive with its tubular flowers of fuchsia-pink, prominently veined in a deeper shade. You need to give it the same conditions as the Brazilian red cloak. Other ruellias are available, and are diverse in size and appearance.

Melaleuca
Myrtaceae

Splendid Australians, melaleucas are tough and dependable, flourishing where lesser shrubs will fail. Fast-growing, versatile and eminently useful, the shrubs provide pretty flowers and dense, fine leaves. Suitable for screening plants and hedges, melaleucas are much visited by birds. Some like the seashore, others are at home in swamps.

Unfortunately several species have become rampant invaders in some places, so be very careful when making your choice. Do not give melaleucas a general fertiliser. Prune regularly to produce a good show of flowers. Once flowering is over, it is best to rigorously cut back these shrubs to a third. Look for interesting cultivars, and the larger tree types, too.

Melaleuca alternifolia, tea-tree, is a tall shrub with narrow linear leaves and stamen-rich, white, misty flowers produced in abundance. It comes from the swamps of warm areas of eastern Australia and is grown commercially for its valuable oil, which has antiseptic and healing properties. The oil is distilled from the foliage.

M. hypericifolia, red honey myrtle, is a useful medium-sized shrub which develops bright scarlet bottlebrush-type flowers among its thick foliage. A miniature prostrate form is 'Ulladulla Beacon', a beach lover.

M. thymifolia, thyme honey myrtle, is a handsome, spreading small shrub with erect, sweet-smelling leaves, hence its common name, and small mauve to purple flowers. Moist soil suits this shrub.

Murraya
Rutaceae

The family Rutaceae contains many genera, and most are known for their delicious scent. Murrayas are no exception. A small genus from India and Southeast Asia, mainly evergreen shrubs and trees, they exhibit creamy, aromatic flowers on fast-growing, dense plants. Murrayas like a good, friable, rich soil, and plenty of moisture. They make useful background shrubs and hedges, being long lived, as are many subjects in the family. You will see old citrus trees, for instance, in abandoned gardens. Murrayas can be grown in full sun or partial shade, and do not sulk when pruned. Usually propagated from tip cuttings, they are no trouble to grow, and suit container cultivation too.

Murraya paniculata, mock orange, is a rounded shrub, compact, with glossy bottle-green leaves. It produces rich, creamy, fleshy

Murraya paniculata

and butterflies are attracted to the flowers. Humidity and warmth are necessary, and filtered sunlight. Mussaendas can be grown on the coast, where they look breathtaking against a brilliant azure sea and sky. Cut off the dead flowerheads. Propagate from semi-hardwood cuttings. Mealy bugs can be troublesome, and scale.

Mussaenda erythrophylla, has an extravagant common name, Ashanti blood, that befits its looks, for it is a small, woody, large-leafed shrub with sepals of blood-red and tiny, creamy, red-centred flowers. It comes from Africa.

M. frondosa, dhobi tree, from India, is adorned with large white sepals and yellow flowers on a small spreading plant.

M. philippica is the most spectacular of all, and offers a collection of hybrids named after prominent women. 'Queen Sirikit' flaunts soft pink to apricot sepals with a frame of darker pink, and yellow flowers. She has great clusters of flowerheads on multiple stems, and will grow to a sizeable shrub. Other hybrids are in similar colour schemes.

flowers in tight clusters. Heavily fragrant, these perfume their surroundings and arrive at intervals throughout the year. Small red berries often follow the flowers. *M. koenigii*, curry leaf, is not as ornamental, but is useful for its aromatic leaves, used in fish curries and other Asian dishes.

Another member of the family to place in similar positions of the garden, and also renowned for its sweet scent, is *Choisya ternata*, the Mexican orange blossom. Glossy, deep green leaves clothe a rounded, compact shrub which is adorned with white flowers, usually in the spring. Mexican orange blossom is able to handle cooler climates than its relation.

Mussaenda
Rubiaceae

Evergreen shrubs, subshrubs and a few climbers make up the genus of mussaendas, among them some of the most sublime shrubs for the tropics and subtropics. Originating in many warm countries (including Asia, Africa and some islands of the Pacific), mussaendas produce small flowers surrounded by large, papery sepals and bracts in shades of white, pink, and apricot or red. Bushes are covered in colour for months,

Mussaenda erythrophylla

Nerium
Apocynaceae

Neriums are a small genus of two species that grow wild in Mediterranean countries and further afield from the Middle East to India. One species has been cultivated for centuries in parts of Asia, and those in the Mediterranean have been known since ancient times, and probably were the shrubs mentioned in the Bible as the 'rose growing by the brook of the field'.

Neriums are stalwart, tough shrubs, and thrive in warm, dry spots. Their leaves resemble those of olives, hence their name of oleander, and they bear clusters of fragrant flowers in white to red. Their elusive perfume has a faint spicy almond scent. Heat and sun are needed, and they can tolerate drought conditions. All parts of neriums are poisonous, and must be treated with great respect. Prune the shrubs back regularly, as they do get untidy, and watch out for aphids and mealy bugs. Neriums are survivors, and they are great at the beach. You can propagate them from cuttings, and sometimes seed.

Nerium oleander, popularly known as oleander or rosebay, is the favoured species, and you can use it for hedging, and anywhere in the sun where a toughie is needed. The cultivars are especially popular, and you can choose from dozens, with

Ochna serrulata

flowers from snow white, through all the pinks to apricot, scarlet, and deepest crimson to cerise, in either singles or doubles. Some boast variegated foliage.

Of the same family, and commonly known as yellow oleander or lucky nut, is *Thevetia peruviana*. This versatile, fast-growing plant produces narrow, glossy dark green leaves. The showy, small, yellow to apricot flowers are funnel-shaped, faintly fragrant, and prettily placed at branch ends. They bloom at any time of year. You can keep your yellow oleander to shrub size, or plant several as a screen or hedge. They require warmth and a well-drained soil.

Ochna
Ochnaceae

From Africa and Asia, these shrubs and trees number about 80 species, but it is only a couple from South Africa and Zimbabwe that are cultivated for their good looks, especially the shrubby type that grows wild in many areas of South Africa. Ochnas prefer full sun and good drainage, but need ample water to keep them fresh and happy. Be generous with leaf mould and mulch. Ochnas grow at the seaside as well as inland. You need to clip the bush back while it is small, to maintain a good, compact shape.

Nerium oleander

Propagation is not easy. Seed needs to be very fresh to germinate. The plants do seem to seed freely in moist garden soil when the seed has passed through birds, which are very fond of them.

Ochna serrulata, the carnival bush or Mickey Mouse plant, is a delightful, spreading, evergreen shrub. It boasts ornamental flowers, fruit and foliage, and is a precocious plant, starting to flower when only about 25 cm high. It will eventually grow to be a medium-sized shrub. The flowers are buttercup yellow, with a froth of stamens. The calyx is bright green, and as the flowers fall the sepals turn vividly red, and the fruit begins to form; green at first, then a glistening black. They remain on the bush for a long while; brilliant in scarlet, green and black. No wonder it is called the carnival bush. That's not all, as in early spring the foliage is tinted a blush-pink with metallic overtones, and later turns a shiny green.

Plumbago
Plumbaginaceae

A genus of only a few species, plumbagos are native to warm regions, and those cultivated for gardens are shrubs from southern Africa, and one indigenous to India. Plumbagos are evergreen, floriferous, with white, blue or pink blooms. They appreciate warm conditions and good drainage, but are not particular about soil. They will require water in drought conditions. Fast-growing and adaptable, these shrubs will flourish at the beach and make successful hedges. You can increase them from cuttings or suckers. Pests do not trouble plumbagos.

Plumbago auriculata, the blue plumbago, is a rambling shrub, festooned with light, sky-blue flowers for months at a time. It carries small, tapered, shiny leaves on long, slim stems. In nature, the blue plumbago scrambles over and through other bushes, and can be left to do this in the wild garden. Usually, though, it is best to keep it manageable by clipping and restraining its activities. The cultivars are more compact, just as easy to grow, and are better for a small

Plumbago auriculata

garden. 'Royal Cape' produces intense blue flowers, does not wander, and is good to grow in a container as well. 'Alba' lives up to its name, bearing soft white flowers.

P. indica, scarlet leadwort, is a small shrub from India, and has flowers of a deep pink with a hint of apricot. Its modest size makes this a good plant for a pot.

Plumeria
Apocynaceae

Plumeria, frangipani — the words evoke memories of lagoon-girt isles, vacations, intoxicating, seductive scents, and steamy warmth, the very essence of the tropics. Trees and shrubs, the eight *Plumeria* species all come from Central America. The flowers of the species are either white, cream, yellow, pink or red, and the cultivars are a delightful mix. In the islands of the Pacific, leis are made of the waxy blossoms. Plumerias have dark green leaves, and in cool conditions are deciduous. Mature plants flourish in dry conditions and crumbly soil, not too rich. Give them full sun, a sheltered spot, and judicious watering till plants are established. You should prune the bushes regularly to keep in good shape, and propagate by stems and branches. These must be left to heal before planting.

Plumeria rubra var *acutifolia*

Plumeria obtusa, white frangipani or Singapore plumeria, can be used as a hedge plant, is evergreen, and produces shiny, bottle-green leaves and flower clusters of creamy white. It blooms almost continuously when it likes the conditions. In some climates it will grow tree-sized, but can be clipped back.

P. *rubra* consists of pink, apricot or cerise flowers composed of pointed petals, and is fragrant and most decorative, but P. *rubra* var. *acutifolia* is the most favoured and frequently seen of all the plumerias. It is yellow-centred, with rich cream petals and an alluring, unforgettable fragrance. There are several sublime cultivars.

Protea
Proteaceae

Proteas travel well, and are cultivated all over the warm world, far from their South African homelands. Surprisingly adaptable, certain varieties are grown commercially from California to Mexico, Israel, Hawaii, and down as far as New Zealand. Prized for the cut-flower market, proteas amaze with their shape, colour and form. Some display feathery, furry toppings to their bracts and are funnel-shaped, while others are rounded and open. Their colours are sophisticated, the flowers usually two-toned in impeccable contrasting hues.

The first essential is to provide perfect drainage and an open uncrowded position for these shrubs, sited in full sun. Poor, acidic soil suits them. Make sure proteas are planted in

Protea 'Pink Ice'

permanent positions as they resent disturbance. Stabilise the plants by placing rocks or stones around them; staking may be advisable. Prune young plants to keep them in shape; pruning of mature plants is achieved mainly by picking the flowers. Propagate from cuttings.

Many of the proteas grown in gardens are hybrids, but some of the species are outstanding. A very moist climate does not suit them. In Hawaii, for instance, these shrubs are grown in the uplands. Proteas are a diverse group, and only a very few can be described here.

P. cynaroides, king protea, is a magnificent species, with huge flowers displayed in a symmetrical bowl of tight pink bracts slowly opening to reveal the silky, silver-backed central mound of wee flowers. A lax, sprawling shrub with leathery leaves, its plain appearance is forgiven when the regal flowers appear. It is South Africa's national emblem.

P. nerifolia is one of the most popular types, with various selections in several colours. Goblet-shaped, with distinctive bracts, fringed with 'feathers', in shades of pink and black, it is a tough species, and the parent of many named selections.

P. repens, sugar bush or honey protea, is well

named, being so nectar rich. Sugar bush is easy to grow, and produces abundant red, crown-shaped flowerheads, good for floral arrangements.

P. sulphurea is a captivating species, a groundcover type with big, cup-shaped, creamy-yellow flowers whose shapely bracts are delicately edged with red. It is useful for planting on dry banks where its pretty flowers can be seen to advantage against the glaucous foliage.

Leucadendron and *Leucospermum* species, also from South Africa, should not be overlooked. Close relations to proteas, they need similar conditions.

Rhododendron
Ericaceae

Rhododendrons are renowned for their magnificent flowers, and are a large genus of some 800 species, diverse in habitat and requirements. There is a rhododendron for every situation, from cold climates to tropical, and with innumerable hybrids and cultivars. The types for the subtropics include the wondrous vireyas, with species mainly from New Guinea, Malaysia and Borneo, the Indica azaleas, and Indicum hybrids. They differ in their cultural requirements, but all need very open, friable soil and sharp drainage, plus mulch and humus to keep their fine hair-roots from drying out. The subtropical and tropical types do well in containers, as rhododendrons do not have a taproot, and can be transplanted with the greatest of ease. Pests and diseases do not strike to a great extent, but again, it depends on species. Most rhododendrons can be increased by seed, cuttings or layering.

Rhododendron Indica azaleas are so numerous, they are listed in categories: Belgian, Kerrigan, Rutherford and Southern. All are suited for warm situations, and come in colours from white, pink and red to lavender and purple, with subtle nuances and sometimes double blooms. Indica types come in an extensive array of hybrids, and gardeners should choose their azaleas from the nursery when they are in flower to obtain the exact tint they require. Indica azaleas are usually

Protea sulphurea

dense, compact shrubs, only a metre or more in height, and with a smaller spread. They respond very well to clipping, and are used in oriental-style gardens, for bonsai, for low hedging and as container plants, as well as massed under trees, or in borders. They prefer acid soil, and will grow in humus. The Indicum and Mucronatum hybrids are similar.

R. Vireya types come in many species and hybrids, and collectors and botanists have had a great deal of fun introducing and developing these masterpieces with vivid, lavish blooms. Already there are countless hybrids and cultivars in glorious colour, from white, cream, yellow, orange and flame red, through to crimson, not forgetting apricot and pink. Two-toned types abound. Some are almost fluorescent in their intensity.

The home gardener is advised to choose plants from the nursery while they are in flower. Vireyas are probably best kept in containers. Their roots are perfectly adapted for imprison-ment in pots, and the plants can be moved to show off the glorious blooms, which will occur in flushes throughout many months of the year. When vireyas are not in flower, as with all rhododendrons, they are not much to look at, so at these times the pot plants can be taken out of the limelight. Some of the hybrids take kindly to hanging baskets. All containerised plants will need regular repotting; some growers do this every 18 months to two years.

In the garden, it is wise to plant your vireyas on raised ground, in a mix of bark, peat, fine scoria, leaf mould and compost. In their natural habitats, vireyas grow epiphytically, so perfect drainage is their number one need. Because of their compact and orderly growth, vireyas are well suited to smaller gardens, but they won't survive strong winds or all-day blazing sun. Thrips, mealy bugs and mites could attack poor plants, so be prepared to lavish food, ample water and mulch on them; they will repay every attention.

Vireya rhododendrons come in vibrant colours

Russelia
Scrophulariaceae

From Mexico, Cuba and Colombia, russelias are a small group of shrubs and subshrubs, with only one species in general cultivation. All over the tropics and subtropics this russelia can be seen, decorating gardens for most of the year with its dependable, cheerful red tubular flowers. While adaptable, the plant requires full sun to achieve its best, and well-drained, humus-rich soil. It is not unduly worried by insects.

Russelia equisetiformis, coral plant, is constantly ablaze with clusters of tiny trumpets of coral to flame red, which cover the weeping showers of green reed-like branches. The coral plant cascades prettily down banks, and is useful for hanging baskets, or to grow on dry ledges. It sprawls gracefully, grows to about a metre in height, and is programmed to deal with heat and drought. Plant russelias en masse. You can increase plants readily from cuttings.

Russelia equisetiformis

Senna
Fabaceae

Sennas are numerous, a genus composed of over 300 species, mainly evergreen shrubs with bright yellow flowers. They come from different areas of the warm world; Australia, Africa and America. Many were formerly grouped with *Cassia* species, and are still popularly known as cassias. Sennas have been cultivated for centuries, some being used as medicines. Their foliage is typically legume-like, with compound leaves of fresh green. Sun is necessary for bounteous blooms, light soil with a mulch the preference. These adaptable shrubs will grow at the beach. Some have the advantage of being in bloom when not many shrubs are on show, during late autumn and winter time. Sennas need to be pruned back, as they can become leggy. They grow readily from fresh seed or cuttings.

Senna alata, candle bush, is native to Central America, and reputed to be used by the Aztecs for its medicinal properties, the leaves and seeds being beneficial for ringworm treatment. Candle bush is aptly named, for it produces upright,

Senna alata

cylindrical, golden-yellow flowerheads, standing clear of the bush, and lasting for many months during winter and spring. Big glossy green leaves cover the sprawling shrub, which can grow rapidly into a large bush, so needs to be pruned rigorously to maintain a good shape and plenty of flowers. Candle bushes are transplantable if you cut them right back first.

S. corymbosa, autumn cassia, is from Argentina, Uruguay and southern parts of the United

States, thrives in warm temperate to subtropical zones, and is most adaptable. Its fern-like leaves are festooned with shiny, buttercup-yellow flowers from autumn to winter. Autumn cassia can get unattractively long and leggy, and needs to be pruned back after flowering, but it grows easily, with no particular fuss. There are several cultivars.

S. didymobotrya is a decorative, medium-sized, upright shrub from Africa, with flamboyant spikes of golden flowerheads, darkening to tan and enhanced by large leaves. This senna will spread further than its height, and you can expect flowers for most of the year if you give it a warm place.

Several Australian species are well worth growing. Some have silvery leaves, and are small, ground-hugging bushes which prefer dry conditions. Other tropical species are tree-sized.

Streptosolen
Solanaceae

One of a kind, the sole *Streptosolen* species is a rambling small shrub from pockets of the Andes. Covered in sage-green, soft leaves, this evergreen shrub displays clusters of dazzling flowers for

Streptosolen jamesonii

months on end. An easy and speedy grower, without many demands, the plant likes sun and open, friable soil. A spot at the seaside suits a shrub or two. Streptosolen are easily increased from tip cuttings, but dislike interference and transplanting.

Streptosolen jamesonii, the marmalade bush, although brighter than any marmalade, thoroughly deserves to be described as showy, for it lights up its surroundings with small, tubular flowers in a hot colour scheme of yellow, gold and tangerine. Marmalade bushes team up with strelitzias very well, or provide good contrast to more sober shrubs and perennials.

Tetrapanax
Araliaceae

This genus has a single species, and originated in Taiwan and nearby islands. Its main claims to fame are its splendid pleated leaves and coastal hardiness. Child's play to grow, this shrub, or sometimes a small tree, spreads from suckers and appears to have no enemies. It does best when in partial shade, but can become long and lanky, at which time you can cut the branches right back and let the suckers grow. This shrub has had other botanical names, and was once classified with aralias.

Tetrapanax papyrifer, the rice-paper plant, was used to make paper from its pithy stems, and is a handsome shrub, imparting an exotic look to the garden with its luxurious pale green leaves, which open to large fans. It produces a topknot of round, creamy green flowers, usually when the days start to cool. Monarch butterflies are attracted to the flowers, and it is a delightful sight to see them covering the creamy panicles.

If you find rice-paper plants too long and lanky, try a close relation, *Fatsia japonica*, another genus once included with aralias. Indeed, its common name is Japanese aralia. This shrub carries ornate, pinnate leaves, so glossy they look polished, succeeds in shade or filtered sunlight, and does well in pots. It has pompom flowers of creamy green. Another relative, the hybrid x *Fatshedera lizei*, is a house plant often used as a

Fatsia japonica with *Tetrapanax papyrifer* in the background

groundcover in the subtropics. Its leaves are ornamental, lobed and glossy, and you can grow it at the beach.

Tibouchina
Melastomataceae

Tibouchinas, formerly lasiandras, are from South America, part of a large genus of evergreen shrubs which bear striking flowers in shades of pure white, soft pink, lavender to purple, often with contrasting stamens. Most bloom for several months of the year, often in winter. Tibouchinas are distinguished by their square stems, and have attractive, hairy, piled foliage with conspicuous veins. Many are known for their aggressiveness and have become pests in tropical parts. Easy to grow, long-lived tibouchinas enjoy sunlight and friable, open soil. As some types can become untidy, it is wise to prune back regularly, especially after flowering. Tibouchinas are successful when used for screens and hedges. You can propagate them almost too easily from cuttings, and pests are seldom a worry.

Tibouchina urvilleana

Tibouchina granulosa

Tibouchina granulosa, from Brazil, commands attention when it is in full flower — usually in the cooler months — its blooms entirely hiding the foliage. It can grow almost tree-like in warm places, and with its vivid, almost strident purple to violet colouring needs to be placed wisely in the garden, as it is almost overpowering in its intensity.

T. urvilleana, glory bush, flaunts royal purple, almost fluorescent flowers, too garish for some. A dense, medium-sized shrub, the glory bush has dark green leaves with a silvery sheen and prominent veins, and the flowerbuds are encased in bright rosy red calyces. Unfortunately, this handsome bush likes to spread its favours and has highly invasive tendencies in some areas. In Hawaii, for instance, it has wiped out native species in parts of the rainforests. A smaller version, and not as likely to rampage, is *T*. 'Jules'; its leaves and flowers are just as comely but half the size. Other refined cultivars have been developed, especially in Australia, and you can find them in new colours, such as the brighter than bright *T. lepidota* 'Alstonville' and 'Edwardsii', both rich purple. Team the loud purple types with softer hued varieties such as pearly white *T. organensis* 'Moonstruck', and pretty pink 'Kathleen'.

Xanthorrhoea
Xanthorrhoeaceae

Grass trees are endemic to Australia, all 17 species, and are an unique group of plants. They are durable, very long-lived, grow at a most leisurely pace and resent transplanting. These intriguing, evergreen, grass-like plants are not true grasses, and were reclassified several times, before appearing in a family of their own. Grass trees produce a fountainhead of fine green leaves and, after many years develop sturdy black trunks. Eventually a spear-like flower spike arises. These strongly defined plants are a distinctive feature of the Australian landscape, and able to survive many bush fires. Place them in rockeries, or in small groups as a focal point. Give them sun, gritty soil, and be patient.

Xanthorrhoea australis is typical of the species, comes from southern parts of Australia, and adapts very well. Usually only the one trunk is formed but this may branch once or twice. Admirable in containers, *X. australis* eventually yields spears of small creamy flowers, with a sweet aroma, but do not expect it to do so for many years. Other species are similar in habit. Do try any you can find; expect them to last for a hundred years or so.

Yucca
Agavaceae

Spiky floriferous plants, yuccas have their beginnings in the drier regions of the United States and Mexico. There are about 40 species of strongly structured evergreen trees, shrubs and perennials. Yuccas adapt well to life in a garden, like full sun, are very tolerant of salt winds, and can survive in most soils as long as they are not water-retentive. Used as accent plants or contained in pots, yuccas are survivors. Propagate from cuttings or suckers.

Xanthorrhoea australis

Yuccas display superb flowerheads.

variegation; combinations of stripes in cream, green and yellow.

Y. elephantipes, giant or spineless yucca, is a popular pot plant, and originates in Mexico and Central America. It develops a sturdy trunk and becomes a tree in nature, but takes a great deal of time to do so. In cultivation it keeps to shrub size in most places. With dark green, serrated long leaves and big panicles of white flowers, the spineless yucca is great to grow in courtyards and entranceways.

Y. filamentosa, Adam's needle, is an amenable plant from Mexico, and will stand either dry or humid conditions. It has rigid, glaucous leaves, prettily edged with white threads but in fact presenting vicious, razor-like prongs. For this reason plants should not be sited where children play or near pathways. The metre-long flower spike is most ornamental, having pendent, creamy white, fleshy flowers in their hundreds. These are often picked individually and used in wedding bouquets.

Y. whipplei, the candle yucca, is distinctly rounded in shape, as though clipped. Its leaves are numerous and narrow, in a pleasing olive green, and it bears typical cream yucca flowers on a very long spike. You can grow this yucca in very dry situations; after all, it comes from the coastal Californian ranges.

Claiming close kinship with yuccas is *Beschorneria yuccoides*, Mexican lily, with grey-green, long, strap-like leaves. A tough customer, it will grow in many areas, by the sea, for example, and in spring sends up very long, lollipop-pink, arching sprays of curious small green flowers with pink bracts.

Yucca aloifolia, Spanish bayonet, has wickedly sharp, dagger-like leaves. It can develop a tree-like trunk, but generally in gardens maintains a shrubby shape. The flowers are hanging bells of a waxy cream, on an upright spike of about 50 cm. Cultivars are popular, and are noted for the leaf

Palms and Cycads

Palms

Ancient plants, palms have been on earth for at least 85 million years, as fossils record. Today the range of palms is overwhelming, with over 200 genera and numerous species recorded. Most enjoy the humid subtropics and tropics, although some are to be seen in desert conditions but only where they can soak up underground water supplies.

A few palms are of great importance to world commerce; the coconut palm, African oil palm and the date palm, for instance. In the domestic landscape palms convey instant opulence, having become fashionable symbols of luxury and pleasure. Dramatic of form, feathery or fan-like, short or tall, clumping or single-stemmed, there is a palm for most gardens. Palms take up little ground space. Another of their many assets is the way they blend so beautifully with other plants, providing a filter of shade for various understorey shrubs and groundcovers. As well as their graceful fronds, the trunks of palms are often most ornamental.

These aristocrats respond to a life of luxury, needing ample water, good drainage, food supplements and warmth. Applications of fertiliser with a high nitrogen content, especially during spring and summer, are essential, for palms are greedy plants. A mulch to retain moisture in the heat is a good idea.

Before planting, prepare the hole carefully by digging a place twice the size of the root ball, and adding good soil and compost. Do not plant out a palm when it is very small. As it is, they often sulk after transplanting, and need to be cosseted for the first year, but even huge mature specimens are successfully transplanted, on account of their neat, compact root system, which can be lifted quite intact.

Pests can attack palms, but a vigorous healthy plant is usually not troubled. However, mealy bug, aphids and scale insects should be eliminated where possible.

Cycads

Whilst palms are ancient, cycads are positively primeval; tenacious survivors evolving over a long period of time. Their ancestors probably predated dinosaurs, and certainly have postdated them for millions of years. Cycads are the most primitive of plants, and the earliest of all seed-bearing types. Although they bear a superficial resemblance to palms, cycads are not related, and differ from them in many respects. You can grow cycads with confidence, secure in the knowledge that they will survive and endure, for that is what they do best. Blessed with inbuilt stamina, they are capable of outliving most other plants. Cycads are true designer plants, and beloved of landscape architects for their strong structural framework; living sculptures.

Cycads have become endangered in some countries and are now protected in many places. Their natural habitats are the Americas, Southeast Asia to Australia, over to eastern and southern Africa, and islands in the Indian Ocean.

Groups of palms and cycads amidst other foliage plants provide texture, form, and a subtle sophisticated colour scheme.

Their wide distribution is thought to be via the buoyancy of the sponge-coated seeds, which are able to float off and catch handy currents to a favourable shore.

Cycads develop very slowly for the first few years, one of the reasons a large plant is so expensive to buy. They concentrate on storing nutrients and starch in their root systems for a while, before doing much above ground. Their preference is for a fast-draining soil, as a general rule. Cycads develop leaves with a waxy coating to enable them to counteract drought, and some species reappear after forest fires.

Put cycads in containers until they expand, and give them a sharp potting mix, similar to that used for orchids. They can be attacked by scale and mealy bug, which should be sponged off. A slow-release fertiliser is beneficial.

Archontophoenix
Arecaceae

Arresting and slender, strongly defined and symmetrical, these palms, with maybe six species, are native to eastern Australia. Quick growing, their natural habitat is the rainforest, and they flourish in areas of high humidity but adjust readily to garden conditions. Mulch them well, and supply liberal quantities of water in dry seasons. Young plants need shelter from the sun and wind until they become strong and established.

Archontophoenix alexandrae, Alexander or king palm, thrives in tropical and subtropical areas, and is found from sea level into the hills, the length of Queensland right up to Cape York Peninsula. This variable, moderately-sized to large palm grows on a straight slim trunk, enlarged at the base, and topped with arching pinnate leaves, feathery and vivid green, with silvery grey undersides. You can expect lavender to creamy yellow flowers, followed by ripe red fruit. An asset to the landscape, probably looking best when several are planted together, Alexander palms are ideal for large gardens and parks.

A. cunninghamiana, bangalow or piccabeen palm, is as elegantly structured as the Alexander palm. Its natural habitat is the coast and surrounding rainforests, and bangalow palms are generally more tolerant of cooler climates. They have an upright trunk, horizontally striped, slightly swollen at the base, and can grow to a good height, but rarely do so in the garden. The arching fronds are feathery, a glossy green, and in maturity this palm displays pink to lavender or amethyst cascading flowers, followed by bright red fruit. Bangalow palms look well planted in threesomes, or as specimens where their elegant form can be clearly seen. They will grow in sun or shade.

Bismarckia
Arecaceae

A single species exists of this magnificent palm endemic to Madagascar, where it is now seldom seen in the wild. Bismarckias grow to a handsome size eventually, and need full sun and room to show off their appealing colour and dramatic structure. They are easily germinated from seed.

Bismarckia nobilis, Bismarck palm, is noted for its splendid, giant, very stiff fan-shaped leaves of a scintillating silvery grey blue, although leaf colour can vary. This is a popular subject for landscaping. Though drought tolerant, small seedlings need plenty of water to prosper, as well as sun and consistent warmth.

Another Madagascan that does well in a subtropical environment, and fairly new to horticulture, is the fast-growing *Ravenea rivularis*, majestic palm. As its common name

Archontophoenix alexandrae

Bismarckia nobilis

shaped palms, some short and stocky, others tall, braheas don't shed their leaves easily, and can have a raffish look. Tough customers, these palms are slow growing, and dependable in dry inland climates. You can propagate them from seed, although germination is erratic.

Brahea armata, blue hesper palm, is from arid regions of Western Mexico, inhabiting canyons, where it grows slowly to about 12 m. The strong, stiff leaf blades are a delightful cool smoky blue, and arise from a thick, nuggety trunk. The conspicuous cream inflorescences are long, drooping and decorative, followed by small brown fruit, usually round. *B. brandegeei* is somewhat similar, and widely used in landscaping. It grows large in its native environment.

B. edulis, Guadalupe palm, comes from this Mexican island, and the remaining stands are in deep ravines, away from the ravages of goats. Stout and strong, the Guadalupe palm is known for its prolific edible fruit, said to be very sweet; when ripe these are juicy and black. The leaf fans are at least a metre across, and of a mid-green.

Butia
Arecaceae

Butias are tough customers, about eight species in all, and are palms indigenous to dry, cool areas of Brazil, Paraguay, Uruguay and Argentina. Some have tall trunks, others display no trunks at all. Versatile and able to adapt to differing climates, butias seem eager to grow. They can deal with wind, and enjoy full sun for preference, but can be sited in partly shaded places. Being deep rooted, they do not require a lot of watering or much attention, once established. Butias are easily increased from their abundant seed.

Butia capitata has several common names; jelly or pindo palm seem to be those most used. This is a smallish palm well known for its feathery plumage of arching, grey-green leaves, shining silver as the sun catches them. One of the few hardy feather palms, it is ideal for coastal areas. *B. capitata* develops a strong, heavy trunk, grey and smooth but well patterned with the leaf scars. Flowers are fragrant, coloured yellow with

suggests, this is a large, refined palm, sun loving, single trunked, and displaying arching sprays of feathery fronds.

From nearby islands comes a palm coveted for its strong structure, *Hyophorbe lagenicaulis*, the bottle palm. Its solitary trunk is bottle shaped, and its pinnate leaves arch elegantly. This small 'designer' palm needs to be sited in full sun where its intriguing form can be easily seen.

Brahea
Arecaceae

Braheas are all hardy palms, 16 species, from Mexico and Guatemala, where they flourish on open hills and limestone slopes, and in dry gullies — places you would not expect to see palms. Fan-

Butia capitata

tints of purple, and followed by striking clusters of yellow or orange fruits. You can cook these and make jelly, or ferment for wine. This butia is the most popular of the genus to grow.

Caryota
Arecaceae

Caryotas are instantly recognisable by their unique leaf shapes, doubly divided, and are commonly known as fishtail palms. They are generally found in humid rainforests of many warm areas from India down to Australia. As long as the soil is moist and the climate warm, fishtail palms will grow. They prefer sun or semi-shade, but need some protection from wind if the leaves are to remain attractive. Some types make good subjects for a large conservatory or sheltered terrace. You can grow them from seed. Be warned, the fruit of caryotas all contain caustic crystals.

Caryota mitis is probably the most widely cultivated version, and is a clustering type, suckering easily, which comes from rainforests and swamps of many Southeast Asian countries. Slow growing in the subtropics, this is a medium-sized palm, its striking fronds almost erect. Although it is mainly grown for its outstanding looks, this fishtail palm is also used to make sago. Rich soil, plenty of moisture and fertiliser will ensure success.

C. urens, toddy or wine palm, is a hardy species, favoured not only for landscaping, but for its sugary sap, from which an alcoholic drink is made. The wine palm has fishtail fronds of a darker colour than the rest of the species and grows somewhat taller, too.

Chamaedorea
Arecaceae

Chamaedoreas roam through several countries, from Central to South America as far down as Brazil and Bolivia. Consisting of around 100 species, these are generally small, neat understorey palms, but they are a diverse group, with some almost ground hugging, and others reaching moderate heights. Their form also differs, and can be solitary or clustering.

Caryota mitis

Chamaerops humilis

Chamaedoreas inhabit rainforests and cloud forests, too; misty and moist to downright wet. Tolerant palms, they adjust and do well indoors in containers where they can deal with the subdued light and even neglect. Many varieties are produced and sold for house plants. These palms bear brilliant red fruit, and propagation is from the seed, which germinates quickly compared to some palms; in about a month if it is really fresh.

Chamaedorea cataractarum, cascade palm, produces pretty cataracts of fine, drooping, fern-like leaves in dense clumps, no more than 2 m tall. Cascade palm prefers moist soil and creeps along the banks of rivers and streams in its Mexican habitat.

C. elegans, parlour palm, is popular throughout the world as an easy-care house plant. It grows naturally in Mexico and neighbouring Guatemala, where it is now considered endangered. This small, dainty palm has a solitary, cane-like stem and bright green leaves. Plant parlour palms in groups under tree canopies, but where they will receive a steady supply of water.

Chamaedoreas abound, and many more are a pleasure to grow. *C. seifrizii*, for example, is generously clumping, with feathery leaves, and is happy inside or outdoors in the shade, while *C. microspadix* clumps in a bamboo-like fashion, and grows fast as well, but never more than a metre or two.

Chamaerops
Arecaceae

Adaptable and tolerant of differing climates, the *Chamaerops* genus has only one representative, a small palm hailing from coastal areas of the

76

western Mediterranean, Morocco and Portugal. It is equipped to deal with salt-laden winds, hot or cold, and conditions on dry mountain slopes, where it thrives in limestone country.

Chamaerops humilis, European fan or windmill palm, is multi-trunked, squat and sturdy, with a dense fan of leaves that can be green or glaucous. Admirable for patio containers, as an efficient hedge, or under tall trees, the European fan palm is a great survivor, but will not tolerate sour, soggy soil.

Chrysalidocarpus
Arecaceae

Graceful palms, despite their awkward botanical name, 22 in number, these evolved in Madagascar and nearby islands off the coast of Tanzania. Some species are single stemmed, others clustered, but all boast arching, feather-shaped fronds, thin and pointed. Moist soils suit these Madagascans and, being island dwellers, they do well at the coast. Only one species is generally cultivated.

Chrysalidocarpus lutescens, golden cane or butterfly palm, is the favoured type, with multiple trunks, golden green, cylindrical and strikingly banded. The lime-green fronds turn topaz in the sun. This fast-growing, clumping small palm lends elegance to the garden, where it needs lots of water but good drainage. It is equally happy in a container; a dragon pot is a good choice, enhancing the palm's oriental air. In its home territory the golden cane palm grows in sand dunes and waterways.

Cycas
Cycadaceae

Some botanists believe this family of cycads to be the most primitive of plants still alive today. *Cycas* species roam from Japan to India, through to Asia, down to Australia, over to Madagascar and around many places in between. Some come from rainforests and arid places; others flourish on moist hills. Slow growing, the various

Cycas revoluta

handsome species differ in their requirements, although most like sunlight, deep and scrupulously well-drained soil and warmth.

Cycas circinalis, queen sago, is an outstanding type, found in many areas from India down as far as parts of the South Pacific. This is a prized plant for the gardener, with its graceful, slightly arching leaves atop a stout, unbranched trunk. A mature plant resembles a small palm in structure.

C. revoluta, the so-called sago palm, is native to southern Japanese islands, and one of the most widely admired and cultivated cycads. Ultimately growing to about 3 m high, this cycad has strong, gently curved leaves, divided into many glossy, stiff leaflets, radiating from its centre. Ideal as specimen plants or in groups, *C. revoluta* is often planted in pots and highlighted in courtyards, patios and entranceways. You can keep this cycad in a container for quite some time as it grows slowly and is a late developer. It does not produce its eminent cone for many years. Larger specimens can be transplanted to a prominent position in the garden later. Dried cycad leaves are appreciated by florists, and are exported from Japan.

Other *Cycas* species are sometimes seen. One that grows naturally in Western Australia's north, on slopes and cliffs, is *C. prunosa*, which needs warmth.

Encephalartos
Zamiaceae

Endemic to Africa, mostly in the south, where they are protected plants, *Encephalartos* species total around 60. In their natural habitats these cycads generally grow in locations with dry winters and rainy summers. This regime should be reproduced in gardens wherever possible. Most are slow growing, taking many years to reach maturity and produce cones. As with most cycads, these Africans take kindly to pot culture and can be contained for a long time. Indeed, one outstanding example is an ancient plant of *Encephalartos altensteinni* in the Palm House at Kew, where it has been thriving since 1775. This is probably the oldest pot plant in the world. The

Hedyscepe canterburyana

species hybridise without difficulty, and some spectacular plants are the result.

E. ferox is a cycad for warm to hot places, and more precocious than some, as it grows fairly rapidly (in cycad time), developing strong, straight leaves up to a metre long, deep green, with spiked leaflets. Eventually this dweller of coastal scrub and sand dunes from Mozambique and South Africa produces a short stubby trunk and several large scarlet cones.

E. horridus, ferocious blue cycad, despite its appalling name, is a handsome, stemless species, boasting grey-green to ice-blue leaves spiked like daggers, and arranged in an elaborate pattern. Although the ferocious cycad will grow slowly and remains small, it will form attractive clumps. This South African type needs sun and warmth and does well at the coast. Site it carefully away from areas frequented by children, paths and walkways, but somewhere to show off its outstanding colours and structure.

E. natalensis is a relatively fast-growing species from rocky places in Natal. It is a palm-like cycad, and produces a slim tall trunk topped with feathery fronds. It prefers full sun, while *E. villosus*, a small, almost stemless breed, also from South Africa, is better in the shade garden.

Howea
Arecaceae

Tiny, isolated Lord Howe Island in the South Pacific is the origin of these two species of world-renowned palms. Commonly known as kentias, they have been favoured as house plants since Victorian times, and can be grown in many places, inside or out, depending on climate. In their homeland, kentias still thrive, and their seeds are harvested and sold throughout the world, as they have been for over a century. Obviously these single-trunked palms do well in coastal regions, and prefer the good life in rich, well-drained but moist soil, and shade while still young.

Howea belmoreana, curly or sentry palm, grows naturally in its island home from sea level into the uplands. Graceful, tall and slender, with distinctly arched fronds, sentry palms grow slowly.

H. forsteriana, kentia palm, grows naturally on sandy soils in lowland forests, and is a superior palm, developing fountains of fine fronds from its slender, soaring trunk; great vertical accents. Place several together, with an understorey of contrasting plants.

Also endemic to Lord Howe Island, with just the one representative, is *Hedyscepe canterburyana*, umbrella or big mountain palm, which occurs in elevated parts of the island, overlooking the ocean. Its nearest relations are *Rhopalostylis*, and there is a good family resemblance. The big mountain palm grows straight and tall on a single, ringed trunk, with a swollen blue-green crownshaft and fronds that fall gracefully. A species for semi-shade and humid conditions, as it would get in its misty island uplands, the big mountain palm will also be happy in any garden near the sea.

Jubaea chilensis

Jubaea
Arecaceae

Just the one species of this colossal palm exists, and it is a native of Chile, where it has become a rarity in the wild, as jubaeas were cut down for their glucose and sucrose content. Jubaeas are giants for large gardens or parks, as not only are they tall, but their straight trunks expand to more than 1.5 m in diameter. Seasides suit them, and they will tolerate drought, and temperate and subtropical climates. A friable, rich soil is needed, and a sunny spot. This palm begins in slow motion, but speeds away once established, its strong roots going straight down. Germination is by seed, which must be fresh.

Jubaea chilensis, Chilean wine palm, is a superb palm with a straight trunk of elephant grey, as tall and symmetrical as a marble column, topped with a great head of deep green fronds; a dinosaur of the palm world. Small yellow flowers arrive in spring, and are followed by smooth, round, brown, hard-skinned nuts, with creamy edible flesh, tasting of coconut.

Livistona
Arecaceae

Livistona is a genus of about 28 palm species, which originate in many warm areas of the world, from Southeast Asia to Australia. They are single-trunked palms, straight and slender, usually pleasantly marked with leaf-base scars. The palmate leaves are large and often arching or drooping. Easy to grow and maintain, livistonas are suitable for many garden uses. All make good container plants when young. Seeds germinate comparatively fast.

Livistona australis, Australian fan or cabbage tree palm, comes from Queensland, down to NSW and Victoria, and grows in many habitats, from the coast to rainforests. Stately palms, with tall, straight stems topped by large fan-like leaves, they ultimately reach a great height, prefer full sun, and are perhaps the most popular of the species.

L. mariae, cabbage palm from central Australia, grows in the moisture-retentive gorges of the Finke River in the MacDonnell Ranges, and needs full sun to display the distinctive reddish tone in young plants' foliage. Tall and elegant, *L. mariae* carries a dense crown of leaves, blue green in maturity. Many other livistonas come from eastern Australia, and all are worth growing.

This area is rich in other species, including the intriguing small *Linospadix monostachya*, walking-stick palm, found in lower Queensland and northern NSW. This little palm requires shade and moisture. *Laccospadix australasica*, the Atherton palm, is a slow-growing, clump-forming type from the Queensland rainforests. It prefers cool nights.

Macrozamia
Zamiaceae

All the 24 species of *Macrozamia* are endemic to Australia, and are fine cycads for the garden, ornamental and stalwart, with decorative deep

A young cycad shows off its excellent lines.

green leaves that can grow to over a metre long. Macrozamias are found in many diverse regions, usually in quite dry locations. Most species are easily cultivated, but only a few are generally available. Filtered shade is best for them, but they will tolerate some sun. Macrozamias of any sort will not disappoint, and this genus seems to grow more quickly than many others

Macrozamia communis, burrawang, from eastern NSW, is a desirable cycad. It grows in luxuriant groves, often under the high canopy of eucalypts, and can be mistaken for a large fern. The trunks are usually subterranean, but can be above ground. After a bush fire, burrawangs rise renewed, phoenix-like, courtesy of their nutrient-rich, long fleshy roots, insurance against fire and droughts. The female plants bear huge cones of brilliant, shimmering scarlet, an unforgettable sight. As with most cycads, burrawangs can be confined in pots, then promoted to a place in the garden when they start to expand.

M. moorei, a cycad from Queensland, carpets the forest floors of coastal and central parts of that state with its abundant fronds, over 150 of them on a mature plant. Easily mistaken for palms, these cycads will produce trunks several metres tall, and are ideally suited for gardens near the beach, where they will need plenty of room to flaunt their long leaves.

Other Australian cycads to cultivate are the two species of *Lepidozamia*, kith and kin to macrozamias, and denizens of Queensland rainforests. Dramatic plants, with long, well-made fronds, these are considered by many landscapers to be the most spectacular of all cycads. Give them a shady or semi-shaded position, in the shelter of trees, but make sure these palm-like cycads receive ample water during hot summers. They make a splendid sight in the wild, where they grow in abundant groves, some close to the seashore.

Normanbya
Arecaceae

One of a kind, from the rainforests of north-eastern Queensland, where it grows in sultry coastal places, usually close to rivers and other moist spots, this black palm is adaptable, and can be cultivated in subtropical home gardens. To grow fast it needs jungle conditons, but given ample water, a warm, somewhat shady position and humus-rich soil, the black palm will be happy. It is not an easy palm to propagate.

Normanbya normanbyi, Queensland black palm, is so named for its hard, blackish wood, prized by native Australian aborigines in days gone by to make spears, and nowadays used in woodwork. Long and slender, the straight trunk is horizontally striped. The deep green leaves are plumose, that is, with the leaflets radiating at different angles from the stem, bottlebrush-like, and these are extravagantly produced in arching sprays from a soft grey-green crown shaft. Profusely flowering, the black palm produces an abundance of apricot to red fruit. When it is young it can be grown as a house plant.

Another stunning Queenslander is *Licuala ramsayi*, also from coastal areas. One of Australia's most shapely palms, it is the largest palm in the *Licuala* genus of over 100 species. A slow-growing fan palm, it boasts large, circular leaves, over a metre across, and is an ideal specimen palm for warm places.

Phoenix
Arecaceae

With about 17 species, phoenix palms are from many dry areas of the warm world; North Africa, Crete, parts of Asia and the Canary Islands. Fossil remains suggest these palms once grew in Europe and North America. They certainly go back till ancient times, and the most valuable species is the prized date palm, cultivated at least since 6000 BC. Quick growing and accommodating, phoenix palms are easy, and able to fill a role in many gardeners' schemes. Most are large and stately, but a few are small, and excellent for containers. *Phoenix* species have strong roots to penetrate dry spots to find underground water. Site them in bright sunlight. They hybridise without intervention.

Dramatic fronds of *Phoenix canariensis* and *P. reclinata* are silhouetted against the sky, and together with small, feathery *P. roebelinii* and a bold *Cycas revoluta* create a delightful oasis.

Phoenix canariensis, Canary Island date palm, is the classic seaside palm, a feature of the French Riviera as well as many other holiday resorts. It grows to mammoth proportions, flourishes in most soil types, and produces a stalwart trunk with heads of long, deep shiny green, curved fronds. The Canary Island date palm provides instant landscaping, as large specimens can be transplanted successfully. A palm to plant where its extravagant size and structure can be appreciated, this species is not recommended for small gardens. You can grow ferns, bromeliads, even small annuals, in its generous lower leaf bases.

P. dactylifera, the inimitable date palm, has long been the tree of life and saviour to desert Bedouins; it thrives by oases. Date palms can be grown for their ornamental value alone, their long slender trunks festooned with arching, grey-green fronds, but their nutritious fruit could also be available to gardeners in the subtropics, provided selected female and male varities are planted — and birds kept at bay.

P. reclinata, Senegal date palm, is a tough, tolerant, clump-forming type, which forms several slightly outward-leaning graceful trunks topped with gently arching feathery fronds — most appealing.

P. roebelinii, pygmy or dwarf date palm, is indeed small for this genus, but shapely. It grows prettily on riverbanks in northern India, Burma and Laos. It will flourish in home gardens. Try growing this miniature by water, where its graceful fronds (softer than those of all the other phoenix palms) will reflect alluringly.

Rhapis
Arecaceae

With 12 species or thereabouts, *Rhapis* are found through China, Vietnam, Laos, Cambodia, down to Thailand. Small, clustering palms, they share cane-like stems, and produce fan-shaped leaves. *Rhapis* sucker profusely, and flourish and increase readily in dry evergreen forests in the wild. In cultivation they are popular for both garden and indoor use, tolerating low light levels and growing slowly. Give them porous soil, shade and a healthy dose of humus and fertiliser, indoors or out. Increase by their efficient suckers, or by seed.

Rhapis excelsa, lady or bamboo palm, is a dainty little plant which forms reed-like clumps, and many superior varieties have been developed in Japan, especially for house plants. Outside in genial climates the lady palm will grow happily in the shade garden where it can wander, but never grow more than 3 m tall. Some types have variegated leaves.

R. humilis, slender lady palm, is similar in most ways, but has even prettier leaf fans, thinner and gracefully drooping. It enjoys the same conditions as its more robust relative.

Rhopalostylis
Arecaceae

Two species and several varieties of these palms exist. They are distinguished not only by their good looks but their location, for one species grows at the most southerly latitudes of any palm. From New Zealand, Kermadec and Norfolk islands, this small genus displays tall, straight, ringed trunks and strongly defined crown shafts. Late developers, *Rhopalostylis* grow slowly at first, and it may be 30 years before they produce seed. Site these beauties in groups in a sheltered, semi-shaded position, in good humus-rich soil, and surround them with ferns and lush understorey plants. Very young plants need heavy shade to prosper. Seed will germinate in a month or so.

Rhopalostylis baueri var. *baueri*, native to Norfolk Island, grows in glades with tree ferns. The species are similar in appearance, but the Norfolk Island version is faster growing, and ultimately is taller. Its stalwart crown shaft is a soft celadon green.

R. baueri var. *cheesemanii*, Kermadec Islands palm, grows in great groves on Raoul Island in the Kermadec group, north of New Zealand. Handsome palms, they carry impressive arched fronds and are easily cultivated.

R. sapida, nikau palm, flourishes throughout New Zealand, growing at bush edges right down to the sea. Nikau need shelter and shade while young. Their solitary trunks grow straight and strong, with upright stiff fronds, and the swollen crown shaft of glossy green adds to this palm's notable appearance, especially when, in adult specimens, the cream to lilac inflorescences tumble down from the base, and bright red fruit forms.

Sabal
Arecaceae

Usually large and slow growing, collectively called palmetto, these 14 species of fan palms are denizens of Mexico, southeastern areas of the United States, and Central America. Some have trunks, some do not. They are tolerant of salt spray, which makes them an excellent choice for gardens at the beach, and they grow in sun or partial shade.

Sabal palmetto, cabbage palm or cabbage palmetto, is possibly the best of the bunch. It grows wild in marshes and coastal plains from North Carolina to Florida, and across to Cuba and the Bahamas. This palm has a lot of growing to do before it soars, straight and tall, to show off its dense head of strong leaves, often pleasantly blue green, strongly defined against the sky. Cabbage palmettos are a feature of coastal cities of southern United States, and are Florida's state tree. Also from the southeastern

Agave attenuata is a good contrast to a background of washingtonia palms.

states is *S. minor*, trunkless as a rule, with blue green leaves, low growing, and as tough as you could wish for.

Syagrus
Arecaceae

All of this variable genus of palms, 32 species, are distributed from Venezuela to Argentina, apart from one lone species native to the Lesser Antilles. Their cultivation demands differing treatment, for some grow in semi-arid places, others in tropical rainforests. *Syagrus* species are adaptable though, adjusting well to their environment, so they can be grown successfully in a wide range of climates and latitudes.

Syagrus romanzoffiana, cocos or queen palm, is one of the best, and grows quite quickly. This palm has a tall, slender trunk topped with arching stems adorned with feathery plumes of a fresh green. It is often used in street planting, because it grows neatly, can deal with pollution, and takes up little ground room. This is a palm for sunlight, will tolerate some wind, grows well at the coast, and is easily germinated from seed. It also hybridises without fuss with several other species.

Washingtonia
Arecaceae

Fast-growing palms, with just two species, washingtonias hail from California, Arizona and northern Mexico. They are most suitable for parks, wide avenues and grand gardens, quickly becoming too big for the average home's surroundings. A feature throughout Florida, washingtonias are happiest basking in sunny places, drought resistant and generally not fussy. They have rather rigid fans of leaves that tend to remain on the trunk when they die, forming untidy skirts, and are not suitable for container growing.

Washingtonia filifera, Californian fan palm, cotton or desert fan palm, is sturdy, with a thick trunk and rather stiff leaves, well apart, and with thread-like fibres a feature. As the leaves mature they bend down, forming a fringed 'petticoat'.

W. robusta, Mexican fan palm, grows taller than the Californian version, with a slimmer trunk. Its head of grey-green foliage, cotton-threaded, is also denser, and the red-lined leafstalks shorter.

Zamia
Zamiaceae

There are numerous species of this cycad genus, but the majority are seldom seen away from their habitats, which can range from rainforests to mangrove swamps and sand dunes. Zamias are as beguiling as any cycad. Native to Florida, they are found down south as far as Chile. All display stiff, fern-like fronds; some have short trunks, while others may be subterranean, or nearly so. As with most cycads, zamias are slow growing, and expensive to buy. They need cosseting with friable but rich soil, and dappled shade, although some like the sun. The following two species are the favoured types to grow.

Zamia furfuracea, cardboard plant, is a stunning Mexican cycad displaying stiff, strong, impeccable fronds. The slightly curved foliage has many leaflets, coloured a soft sage green. Impervious to salt spray, this cycad is a good choice for beach properties, and is often seen in the gardens at luxury resorts. It grows happily in sun or some shade. Contain one or two in courtyard pots. Eventually *Z. furfuracea* will spread to a metre wide and just as high, and form cylindrical cones.

Z. pumila, coontie or Florida arrowroot, from Florida, and occuring also in Cuba, Central America and the West Indies, forms numerous fronds of dark glossy green, narrow leaflets, and is another cycad for the seaside, as it too, is tolerant of sea spray. Filtered shade suits it best.

Fruit

Prolific crops of succulent fruit are available to the fortunate gardener with a subtropical climate, only constrained by the size of the area available. Of first importance is a suitable site, shelter and warmth, sun and excellent drainage, not to forget an adequate supply of water. Seasonal supplies of fertiliser, compost and a generous mulch will ensure good-quality fruit.

Exotic fruit trees can be part of the overall garden design, as many are highly ornamental and give a tropical ambience to their surroundings — bananas and papaya, for instance — or you can consign them to an orchard, making a subtropical fruit bowl. For shelter, which is so essential, consider using spreading, wind-resistant edible plants as part of a productive shelter belt. Feijoas and loquats are undemanding fruitful choices, and sugarcane can be worthwhile, too.

Tempting, luscious tropical fruit can sometimes be persuaded to prosper, too, and it can be a real challenge to produce mangoes and other gourmet delights in a microclimate. With a short shelf life, all these juicy fruits are expensive to buy, providing you can find them, and it is practical as well as satisfying to grow them at home.

Consider groundcovers in the orchard; nasturtiums, pepinos, squash, naranjillas, cape gooseberries, and other heat-loving edible plants.

Be adventurous, and try growing as many fruit as you can. The following are just a few to whet your appetite. New varieties are regularly being introduced, so keep an eye on local garden centres and the catalogues of nurseries specialising in fruiting plants.

Ananas
Pineapple
Bromeliaceae

Bromeliads are not usually cultivated for their fruit but this genus of South Americans, with eight species, contains the remarkable pineapple. *Ananas* species have long, tough, grey-green leaves, spiky-edged, from which the central flower emerges and slowly develops into fruit. The pineapple needs full sunlight and well-drained soil, slightly acid. The fruit varies, so be sure to obtain a good, succulent fruiting kind. Young plants are grown from suckers or 'pups' taken from the parent plant, or you can use the tufted top of a ripe fruit. Once established, the plants should be watered in hot weather, but be prudent, for they can be overwatered. Fertiliser with a high nitrogen content should be spread round the base of the plants, and a mulch to keep down weeds so that you do not need to work around them and become scratched by the wickedly spiked, metre-long leaves. Look out for scale, and sudden wilt, in which case you will have to get rid of the plant.

Ananas comosus, pineapple, a mundane name for such exotica, was commonly called after its supposed resemblance to a pine cone. Pineapples,

Pineapple

from Brazil, were introduced into Europe in the 1600s and caused quite a stir. The plants quickly became a status symbol among the rich and powerful, with gardeners slaving to produce the perfect pineapple in specially heated stove-houses. Each plant produces its composite fruit of up to 200 tiny yellow bracts, and takes a long while to do so, but it is well worth the wait. Do not cut your pineapple until it is ripe; you can tell this by its intoxicating smell. As a general rule, after picking it will not ripen further. Best to eat these delicious fruit fresh, but you can freeze excess pineapple slices by first covering with a little water and sprinkling with sugar.

Annona
Cherimoya, soursop and custard apple
Annonaceae

Annonas come from the warmer parts of the Americas, and comprise 100 species of evergreen and semi-deciduous trees. Those with luscious fruit are the most desirable, and include the creamy sweet cherimoya and custard apple. The trees are low and spreading and have handsome foliage. The fragrant flowers are followed by the unusual fruit, usually round and curiously marked by odd protuberances, scales or even spikes. Some types will flower and fruit off and on all year. Annonas need a warm, sheltered position and a good, rich soil, with a general fertiliser applied regularly and a mulch to retain moisture. Mealy bug can be a problem. Some varieties need to be hand-pollinated. Seed will germinate readily, but it is wise to buy grafted trees.

Annona cherimola, cherimoya, is from high parts of Peru and Ecuador, and the fruit does not look at all promising, being green and knobbly. However, when ripe the interior is smooth and rich, the texture of a creamy custard, with a tantalising fragrance and a delectable flavour evocative of several tropical delights rolled into one. Individual fruit can weigh as much as a kilo, but half that is more usual.

A. muricata, soursop, is a small tree from northern South America, and bears big oval green fruit, liberally covered in short spines. The flesh is sweet, white, and aromatic, of a lighter texture than the cherimoya but just as full of flavour.

A. squamosa, custard apple, is a small semi-deciduous tree, broader than it is long, from various tropical regions. The tree needs pruning to keep it in shape. It is aptly named, with fruit as tempting and as creamy as the other notable species. Again, custard apples are not pre-possessing to look at, being big, green and scaly, but they are a delight to eat.

Averrhoa
Carambola
Oxalidaceae

With only two species to its name, the genus, from Southeast Asia, is grown for the fruit. The trees are small and evergreen, low branching and with dense foliage made up of pinnate leaves.

Clusters of fragrant tiny pink flowers are followed by the five-angled, tangy fruit. Popular as shade trees, or as specimens, averrhoas require full sun and an open, friable soil, away from dry winds. A generous mulch is beneficial and a citrus fertiliser every few months. The trees mature early, and you can expect fruit when they are barely a metre high. Propagate from seed.

Averrhoa carambola, carambola, five-corner, star fruit, produces fruit off and on for most of the year in benign climates. Carambolas are shapely, five-angled, with a waxy, glossy skin, yellow in colour. The flesh is also yellow, and when the fruit is cut across, the sections resemble a star, and are most ornamental. The flesh can be pleasantly sour-sweet, some more honeyed than others, so it is wise to buy a named variety that you have first tasted. The texture is refreshing and as crisp as an apple. Carambola is useful in salads, both sweet and savoury, and

Carambola

for chutneys. You can freeze the slices and serve them in drinks instead of ice cubes or lemon.

The only other species, *A. bilimbi*, carries much more sour fruit, and is useful for pickles.

Carica
Papaya, pawpaw
Caricaceae

A genus of some 20 species, caricas are from Central and South America, and among them is a very important tropical and subtropical fruit, the papaya. Most plants develop a single stem, topped with a crown of handsome, large, indented leaves around which the golden fruits cluster. They are rapid-growing plants, and most precocious, flowering and fruiting when still young. The blossoms exude a heavy, seductive perfume, and although some are self-pollinating, in most varieties the small creamy green male and female flowers are on separate plants. They are distinctly different, the females being in clusters of short-stalked blooms, while the males are on long dangling stalks. It is best to have several plants, and these should be sited in full sun, about 2 m apart, but to be on the safe side, try and get the variety bred in Hawaii, appropriately called 'Solo'. The young trees need to be protected from strong winds, given a sweet soil, deep and well drained, with a good lime content, and amply fertilised. Some types are plagued by red spider, and powdery mildew can be a worry. Seed germinates most readily and plants are best when sown directly in the ground. Cuttings root obligingly.

Carica papaya, pawpaw or papaya, is the species grown all over the warm countries of the world, and flourishes in the heat. Some sorts yield round fruit, others oval, with flesh from yellow to gold, and some a pretty pink or even red. Size varies, too. Papaya can weigh in at 2 kg, but the norm is half a kilo. Grow your papayas against a wall, in the kitchen garden, or in clumps in the ornamental part of your landscape.

Many other species can be cultivated, and although the fruits may not be as desirable as that of papaya, they are easier to grow in cooler

Pawpaw

White sapote

climes. One such is the babaco (*C. pentagona*), which bears large seedless fruit. Although rather bland, the babaco is most useful and can be eaten raw or cooked.

Mountain pawpaw (*C. pubescens*) is also easy to grow. It bears small, pear-shaped yellow fruit which can be made into chutneys. Some caricas are grown for their ornamental qualities. A stunning type with bright scarlet flowers amid splendid jumbo leaves is sometimes obtainable.

Casimiroa
White sapote
Rutaceae

Casimiroas are a Mexican genus of four or five species, and are notable mainly for the type grown in subtropical places, known as the casimiroa or white sapote. Casimiroas prefer a sunny position and well-drained, rich loam, but are tolerant of dry conditions. Trees should be pruned back to maintain a sturdy and attractive shape. Pests do not seem to be a concern.

Casimiroa edulis, casimiroa, white sapote, is a pleasing evergreen tree and will grow to a medium size, complete with fresh green leaves, almost like those of the walnut. The tiny, greeny white flowers arrive in decorative long panicles and are followed by the fruit, which matures to the size of a tennis ball and has a thin skin in shades of cream and green. The flesh is sweet and creamy, and reminiscent of custard apple, pineapple and other delights, all in one. You can expect hundreds of white sapotes, as the tree is most prolific, so you should start picking them before they fully ripen and store them. Eat the fruit fresh, or in smoothies and milkshakes, fruit salads and ice cream. It is thought the fruit is beneficial in helping to reduce high blood pressure.

Citrus
Rutaceae

Citrus are easy to grow, highly ornamental, and usually one of the first fruiting varieties to be planted in a new garden. Not just the ubiquitous lemon, but a big range of citrus varieties can be cultivated without much trouble. Citrus trees, originally from Southeast Asia, have the delightful ability to bear flowers and fruit at the same time, and can be a decorative addition to the ornamental garden. The flowers scent the air all around with their sharp, but sweet, heady fragrance, while the colourful fruit hangs decoratively among the deep green, glossy foliage.

Citrus enjoy a rich soil, liberally fertilised, well drained and well tended to keep down weeds, but always bear in mind these fruit trees are shallow rooted. A generous mulch is a big help. Regularity is important; regular feeding, a climate that does not go to extremes, and regular watering. Unfortunately, citrus are martyrs to many insect pests and diseases. Pruning is not necessary except to ensure that light gets through the whole tree. There are many kinds to grow, all with named selections.

The popular types of lemon are 'Eureka', 'Lisbon', 'Meyer', and 'Genoa'. Oranges come in many guises, and there will be a variety suitable for any subtropical garden. Mandarins are usually small, neat shrubs, often planted in pots. Grapefruit trees can grow large, and there is a wide selection for the subtropics. Look for limes, so useful in drinks and desserts; the Tahitian lime is deservedly popular. The Kaffir lime is an essential ingredient in Asian cooking, where the zest and leaves are used more than the bitter-tasting, wrinkly-skinned, pear-shaped fruit.

Cyphomandra
Tamarillo, tree tomato
Solanaceae

Although in this genus there are about 30 species of evergreen shrubs, trees and climbers from South America, just one, the tree tomato or tamarillo, is widely cultivated for its palatable

Tamarillo

Persimmon

fruit. These are soft-wooded plants, with typical solanum-type flowers and small fruit in profusion, dotted all over tall shrubs or small trees. Tamarillos need shelter from wind, grow very quickly from seed, and are most precocious, fruiting well from their second year. If you do not prune them back, they become lanky and are prone to wind damage. They need good, rich soil to promote growth and fruit, plus an organic manure and a mulch. You can propagate tamarillos easily from cuttings or seed. Indeed, small plants will germinate all round the tree, from fallen fruit, which is just as well, for the trees are short lived. Good for smaller gardens, they can be accommodated against a wall or by a fence. Downy mildew can be a worry.

Cyphomandra betacea, tamarillo, tree tomato, is from Peru, and is covered in small white to soft pink flowers, which turn readily into pointed, egg-sized fruit, usually bright tomato red, or more occasionally, yellow, giving a festive look. The fruit is rich in vitamin C, has a piquant tang, and is eaten raw or stewed, in salads, pies and other desserts, or made into chutneys.

Diospyros
Black sapote, persimmon
Ebenaceae

Hundreds of species of evergreen trees from the tropics and subtropics, with a few from temperate zones, *Diospyros* species are handsome and useful. The cultivated kinds are those that supply timber and scrumptious fruit. The renowned timber, ebony, comes from a Sri Lankan species. The fruit trees like well-drained, warm, moist soil, sun and shelter. They are easy to maintain; pruning is not necessary in the home garden. A little blood and bone is beneficial. Propagate from cuttings and seed.

Diospyros digyna, black sapote, is a medium-sized evergreen tree originating in Mexico and

91

Loquat

that is the loquat. All members of the genus have leathery leaves and scented flowers, and they originate in eastern Asia and roam from the Himalayas to Japan. Easy to grow, loquats like sun and withstand sea breezes. Although they prefer a good, deep soil, they are amenable plants which germinate readily from seed.

Eriobotrya japonica, loquat, is a comely small tree, handsomely decorated with furry, pointed bold leaves, serrated and deeply veined, with a lighter underside. It carries small, fragrant white flowers, with a scent of almonds. These soon develop into perfectly round, golden yellow fruit, complete with several big, glossy brown seeds. Part of the loquat's attraction is the fruiting time, usually very early in spring. In size, the fruit can vary, and larger loquats are being developed, some as big as golf balls, but mainly they are more modest. Loquats are best eaten directly from the tree, but you can make jam with them, adding lemon juice and peel for extra flavour.

Central America. Black sapote has rounded small fruit, ripening to black. The chocolate-coloured flesh is sweet, pulpy, and rich in vitamin C.

D. kaki, persimmon, is the most favoured of the fruits. It is borne on a deciduous tree, cultivated and fully appreciated for centuries in China, where it originated, and in Japan. In early times persimmon aficionados only had the squashy types of fruit available, and not the improved, non-astringent, crunchy varieties we enjoy today. You can eat these like an apple, or slice them for salads, both savoury and sweet. For flavour, colour and shape, persimmons are paragons. Golden orbs of luscious honeyed fruit decorate the small, spreading tree in autumn and winter. Buy a named variety. You also have the bonus of glorious colour from the autumn leaves, which is a decided asset in the subtropics.

Eriobotrya
Loquat
Rosaceae

Only one of the 30-odd species of evergreen trees and shrubs in this genus is readily grown, and

Litchi
Lychee
Sapindaceae

The genus *Litchi* has just the one representative, a scrumptious fruit originally from warm parts of China and Southeast Asia, now cultivated all over the subtropics. No wonder, as this tree is admired for its dense, evergreen foliage as well as fruit, and is not hard to cultivate. Slow-growing, lychees can live for 400 years, but plants demand extra care until established. Young trees are tender and need shelter for their first two years. A shadecloth canopy during the hottest months and a clear plastic surround for the rest of the year will give them a good start. Rich soil, a sheltered spot, heat and high humidity are essential. Your lychee will bear in five to six years, and as it yields heavy crops, requires generous annual feeding. Little pruning is needed, and propagation is usually by air layering. Named grafted varieties are available, and you need to sort out which one is best for your area.

Litchi chinensis, lychee, is a handsome, medium-sized spreading tree, which bears profuse clusters of small, lime-green flowers, followed by thin, rough, hard-shelled crimson fruit, hanging in ornamental baubles, and usually maturing in spring and summer. Inside, and easy to peel, is the sweet translucent flesh, which has a look of pale, light-coloured grapes. Lychees are a most versatile fruit, used for savoury and sweet dishes. The longan, a Southeast Asian delicacy, is similar, and eaten raw, canned or dried. As a snack food, dried longans are very popular.

Macadamia
Queensland nut, macnut
Proteaceae

A genus of 11 species, macadamias come from Australia, New Caledonia and parts of Indonesia. Two Australian species are prized for their nuts. They are all good-looking, evergreen, small to medium trees, easy to grow, and well worth a

Macadamia flowers

sunny, sheltered spot in the home garden. Although they belong to the protea family, macadamia flowers are not as dazzling as most, but they make up for that lack by producing delicious, nutritious nuts. The tiny, modest flowers hang on long racemes, either white or palest pink, and produce nuts nearly all year round in the tropics, but spasmodically in the subtropics and temperate zones. The nuts are creamy, sweet and full of flavour, their only drawback being that the round brown shells are hard to crack. You can increase your trees by seed, but it is far safer to invest in a named grafted variety to be sure of success. A deep soil, with a good constant supply of water, and regular applications of fertiliser, will mean a heavier crop. Macadamias can be infected by leaf miners and borer, and a nasty caterpillar, too. Spraying will knock them back. Rats adore the nuts; some method of safeguarding the crop may need to be employed.

Macadamia integrifolia, Queensland nut, is sometimes called Hawaiian nut or macnut. The tree was introduced to the islands in 1890 and has become a major commercial crop. Many types have been developed in Hawaii, and clever grafting methods and superior stock has been the result. Queensland nut will grow quite high and wide, has glossy leaves and produces splendid nuts.

M. tetraphylla, macadamia nut, bopple nut, is a more compact, bushy tree, with serrated, wavy leaves. The long, hanging clusters of flowers have a decided pink tinge, and its nuts are as scrumptious as any. This is a handsome tree to grow in the garden as an ornamental as well as in the orchard.

Mangifera
Mango
Anacardiaceae

These Indian and Southeast Asian trees are splendid evergreens, with just the one species cultivated for its outstanding fruit. The mango has been nurtured for thousands of years, and grows large in the tropics, but only half the size in the subtropics. Mangoes can be grown outside their preferred tropical zone in microclimates, too. Fertile, well-drained, slightly acidic soil, with ample supplies of water, full sun and shelter from strong winds, should all ensure success. Mulch the plants while they are young, and give them a general fertiliser, but do not overfeed. Pruning is not necessary, and pests and diseases are few. Although seedling trees crop very well, it is prudent to obtain named varieties suitable for your climate, and for superior fruit, free from fibres, and the alleged turpentine smell of some seedlings.

Mangifera indica, mango, becomes a commanding tree with glossy, dense foliage. The young leaves are often tinged pink, and after the tiny pink flowers appear on the tips of branches luscious, golden-fleshed fruit follows. Mangoes come in many skin colours, from yellow, gold and orange, to pink shades, and in shapes from oval to kidney, or banana-like. The fruit is rich in vitamin A, and is ambrosia when eaten raw, or in fruit salads, juice, jams, purées and ice cream. The incomparable mango chutney is made from unripe fruit.

Musa
Banana
Musaceae

Bananas — what would we do without them? One of the most useful fruits in the world, bananas are part of a wider genus that includes ornamental species as well as the fruiting types. Bananas are easy to grow, and require regular amounts of water, full sun for preference, rich, moist soil, albeit well drained, and generous feeding. Their large, banner-like leaves are easily damaged by wind. Banana plants are giant perennial herbs, and new plants are started from the young shoots growing by the main stem. Leave only a couple of these stems to mature and replace the parent after fruiting. A healthy banana plant will flower and fruit when it has made about 40 of its impressive leaves. Pests and diseases can be prevalent in some areas.

Musa x *paradisiaca* is the botanical name given to the myriad fruiting bananas. Bananas have been cultivated for centuries, and have been hybridised and improved out of recognition. Precocious plants, they grow fast and produce flowers when they are still young, from a year to 18 months on. The large flowers are impressive; deep red bracts cover the hundreds of small flowers which soon turn into bananas. Different types are bred for varying climates, and you can find suitable named varieties. Bananas are satisfying to grow, and your main worry will be trying to deal with the hundreds of sweet, toothsome, potassium-rich bananas you will have. It is usual to pick the bunch when the first few fruit start to ripen; and the whole stem should be discarded at this time.

Banana

Passiflora
Passionfruit
Passifloraceae

Although many of the 400 species of *Passiflora* have edible fruit, the most widely grown of all is the type originally found in the wild from Brazil and Paraguay down to parts of Argentina. This is the purple passionfruit, cultivated all over the tropical and subtropical world for its sweet intense flavour and versatility. Many hybrids are available, and constantly being improved for disease resistance, productivity and size. Purple passionfruit are cultivated in the same way as the ornamentals included in the chapter on climbers (see p. 98). Make sure you give the plants ample attention for optimum fruit. Soil should be enriched with organic matter, and water provided in dry periods. You need to site a vine carefully, against a fence or trellis, or draped over a pergola. And make sure you have a new vine growing to replace the old, as passionfruit are not long-lived. Passionvine hoppers can be a nuisance.

Passiflora edulis, passionfruit or purple passionfruit, produces luxuriant, shiny, divided leaves and striking flowers of purple, blue and white, medallion-like, with radiating filaments. However, it is for their fruit of sublime acid sweetness that this type is so desired and cultivated. Egg-shaped, full of honeyed aromatic seeds wrapped in exquisite flesh, purple passionfruit turns a dull blue purple as it ripens, and starts to wrinkle. This versatile fruit can be eaten raw, served as part of a fruit salad, in ice cream, in icing, made into jelly, or used to decorate and flavour soufflés and pavlovas.

Persea
Avocado
Lauraceae

Perseas, numerous evergreen trees and shrubs, originate in warm areas, but only one is cultivated for its fruit, the splendid avocado from Central America. Leafy, handsome trees, growing to medium size in the main, but depending on the

Avocado

variety, the avocado is popular world wide, and a prize to grow in the garden. A sheltered position is required, and a benign, settled climate. A deep, rich, composted soil, well drained, and the best you can possibly give your tree, is essential for success. Young trees should have ample water until they are well established, and be provided with a thick mulch and nitrogen-rich fertiliser in warmer months. Prune to keep in shape, and trim lower branches. Do not be tempted to sow an avocado seed. A grafted tree is the way to go, and you can obtain named varieties that will fruit in just a few years.

Persea americana, avocado, bears fruit either round, oval or pear-shaped (which accounts for one of its common names of alligator pear). The better varieties are still 'Hass', with wrinkled skin that blackens as the fruit ripens, and 'Fuerte', thin-skinned and glossy green. 'Sharwil' will grow at the coast, and is very vigorous. Avocados are nutritious, their succulent, smooth, lime-green pulp being rich in beneficial oil and several vitamins. You do not have to pick them all at once. As avocados do not ripen well on the tree, harvest when the fruit is fully formed, then ripen indoors in a brown paper bag with a lemon or apple, as needed. Avocados seldom seem to be cheap to buy, so make good gifts for appreciative friends.

Physalis
Tomatillo, Cape gooseberry
Solanaceae

A genus of over 80 annuals and perennials, *Physalis* species come from many places, but mainly the Americas. Not many are cultivated, but several edible types are most useful and easy to grow. All have small flowers, usually creamy yellow, and form berries that are distinguished by their lacy, inflated calyces. Given full sun and moderately fertile soil, they will thrive. They are child's play to propagate from seed. Pests don't seem to worry these bushy plants.

Physalis ixocarpa, tomatillo, is a sprawling bushy annual, about a metre tall, yielding golf ball size fruit that completely fill and break their papery coverings. The berries are usuallly harvested when green, sticky and tangy, as in Mexican cuisine. You can be misled, as this fruit is sometimes called 'husk tomato' or 'green tomato' in Mexican recipes. Indeed, you can grow your tomatillos the same way as tomatoes, one of their many relations.

P. peruviana, Cape gooseberry, golden berry, or ground cherry, is a perennial but usually grown as an annual. Cape gooseberries (so mis-named because so many were seen growing round the Cape region of South Africa) can naturalise and become a nuisance. However, they are useful for covering a bank or waste ground, and they do well right by the seaside. They bear round, small, yellow to gold fruit, fun to pick, useful raw in fruit salads, or lightly poached for a breakfast treat, and most delectable in jam.

Other bushy, fruity members of the solanum family are easy to grow too, and include naranjillas and pepinos. *Solanum quitoense*, naranjilla, is a spreading, shrub-like plant which can be featured in a container, so handsome is the foliage. The young leaves are lined with purple velvety hairs, and soon grow large and conspicuous. Naranjillas have fragrant flowers, followed by small, sweet, juicy golden fruit. You can eat them raw, make into jams and jellies, or process for juice.

S. muricatum, pepino, is a bushy small plant. It grows quickly, soon producing attractive yellow, oval fruit, often streaked with purple. The aromatic flesh can be eaten raw and in salads, both savoury and sweet.

Psidium
Guava
Myrtaceae

From South and Central America, psidiums number over 100 species of evergreen shrubs and trees. A few tasty species roam the warm areas of the world, famous for their fruit and foliage

Cape gooseberry

Strawberry guava

96

and popular on account of their ease of growth, compactness and pleasant appearance. They grow rapidly, have strong, small leaves, and will flower and fruit from an early age. The typical fluffy flowers of the family are small and fragrant. Psidiums naturalise where they like the climate, and prefer an open soil, rich in nutrients. The fruit has a high vitamin C content, more than many citrus, and loses little in cooking. Pruning keeps the bushes shapely and compact, ideal for the small garden. Guavas are propagated from seed or cuttings.

Psidium cattleianum, cherry or strawberry guava, can be kept to a modest shrubby size by judicial pruning. It has neat, shiny dark, green leaves, lightly bronzed when young, is precocious and grows rapidly. It is a stalwart, tolerant plant, not needing a great deal of nurturing, and will thrive at the beach, away from the strongest winds. This guava is a good choice for small gardens, where probably one bush is all you will need. Eat the cherry-sized red fruit raw, or process into jellies and jams, or wine, if you have a surplus. There is a yellow variety, but it is not as popular.

P. guajava, common or yellow guava, thrives in genial hot places, and will spread with reckless abandon if left to its own devices. This guava has leathery leaves and clusters of white flowers that quickly turn into oval fruit the size of duck eggs, with a thin yellow skin and bright pink flesh within. Guavas have a tantalising, exotic aroma that makes you want to try the fruit at once. Eat them raw, very lightly poached, in pies, jams and jellies, in honeyed sweetmeats and pastes, or juiced. This variety gives you crops several times a year in benign climates, being a

Feijoa

prodigous producer.

Feijoa (*Feijoa sellowiana*), another member of the Myrtaceae family, also produces abundant fruit, is easy to grow and well suited to smaller gardens. Treat them as you would cherry guavas. The shrubs are ornamental, bearing bright crimson flowers among their grey-green leaves, and are often grown as hedges. The fruit, green in colour, have a sweet scent and a taste all their own, but must be ripe and blemish free. Pick them carefully as they bruise easily.

Climbers

Climbers, vines and creepers are flexible, versatile plants, a boon to gardeners. Eager to grow, economical of ground space, generous in flower and foliage, climbers are ideal for many positions in the subtropical garden.

A great number of climbers enjoy warm climates, as most started life in jungles and rainforests, where they rapidly rose above the dense tree canopies in whatever way they could, to catch the light. With so much competition, these climbing vines have to be aggressive to survive, often smothering trees as they ruthlessly look for light. They ascend by various methods; aerial roots, suction cups and tendrils. Some twine, others cling, while a few loll about and need to be persuaded to use a support.

With sparkling blooms and handsome foliage, climbing plants are among the most flamboyant and dramatic subjects in the garden, with so many uses; as screens, camouflage, shelter, to give privacy, but mainly to show off their considerable charms. These paragons can be kept under control by guiding them to grow where you want them: trained over a pergola or archway, adorning a wall or trellis, cascading theatrically down a bank, curtaining mundane fences, or forming cool arbours and leafy bowers for alfresco dining. Some species will efficiently carpet the ground, others scale tall forest trees. Whatever direction you wish them to take, tying, shaping and pruning will be needed to keep most

Opposite: *Beaumontia grandiflora*

climbers in bounds. They will also appreciate a cool root run and a humus-rich soil, with maybe the benefit of a mulch in hotter months.

Climbers are intrinsic to the subtropical garden style, and the range of varieties available seems to increase each season, with many hybrids and cultivars vying for attention. Throughout the year, one or more climbers enchant with obliging generosity and reckless prodigality. Most are long lived, full of amazing energy and stamina, but one should also consider the annual vines, such as morning glories and other ipomoeas with their blaring trumpets, tough climbing nasturtiums, and the short-lived black-eyed Susans. You get more for your money with climbers.

Allamanda
Apocynaceae

Twining climbers and shrubs, allamandas are a small genus of 12 or so from tropical parts of America. They shine with trumpet-shaped flowers of the brightest yellow, set off by fresh green leaves. You see them all over the tropics and subtropics, where they bear their glorious flowers nearly all year. A warm, fairly sheltered position is perfect, but climbing allamandas can be contained in pots against a warm wall where the climate is not ideal, or planted at the bottom of a sunny slope and trained upwards. They can become straggly unless pruned to keep in shape and ensure abundant flowers. Allamandas thrive

Allamanda cathartica

at the coast. Propagation is from cuttings. Diseases are not a problem, but these plants are subject to mealy bug, thrips and scale.

Allamanda cathartica, the golden trumpet vine, is fast growing and the most admired of the species. The bold clusters of sunshine-yellow, wide, trumpet-shaped flowers adorn the plant all through spring and summer. The cultivar 'Hendersonii' has similar yellow flowers, and is considered to be even more desirable than its parent.

Antigonon
Polygonaceae

Only a few species of these twiners from Mexico and Central America exist, and there is just one thought worthy of cultivation. It is a very useful fast-growing, semi-deciduous vine. Antigonons prefer semi-shade, and moist, well-drained soil, as so many climbers do. They can be increased by seed or cuttings. The bane of warm gardens, thrips, red spider and scale, may all attack the vine.

Antigonon leptopus, the coral vine, clambers by its tendrils, and lopes away quickly. The dark green, heart-shaped leaves set off the arching sprays of blooms, usually of a lolly pink, although there are variations. This creeper will cascade down a shady bank, or ascend an archway or trellis. Winds and full sun are anathema to it.

Aristolochia
Aristolochiaceae

There are over 500 species of this genus, ranging from perennials to climbers, and coming from many areas. It is the climbers that excite the most attention, although only a very few are suitable for the subtropics. These prefer rich, well-drained soil and need water in dry periods, also shelter and sun to give of their best. The flowers are more of a curiosity than beautiful, and this is precisely why they are prized. They are in unusual colour combinations and often strangely shaped, with an alien, pungent smell that attracts insects. Fresh seed germinates readily.

Aristolochia grandiflora, pelican flower, from Central America, is vigorous and has larger flowers than most. These are purple, blotched green, and faintly threatening in colour, shape and smell, but hang down gracefully. Flies do the pollinating, attracted to the malodorous smell. The flowers are followed by intriguing seed pods that look just like small hanging baskets. The seeds are not fertile for long.

A. littoralis, calico flower, from Brazil, grows fast and appreciates high humidity. It also yields unusual flowers, strikingly coloured a deep burgundy, intricately etched in white, and of a shape that almost defies description. You can grow a specimen on a veranda or pergola, and it will not be as strong smelling as most aristolochias.

Beaumontia
Apocynaceae

Fragrant climbers from India to Vietnam, beaumontias boast nine species of evergreen

Aristolochia littoralis

twining plants. Their leaves are glossy and strong, and for months at a time the vines are embellished with long, tubular, mostly white flowers. They require shelter, semi-shade, a rich moist soil and plenty of room. Rather unruly in growth, beaumontias should be rigorously pruned after flowering. These stalwart climbers can be sited to shade a veranda, scale a tree, clamber over a bank or decorate a sturdy trellis. Where winds and winters are cool, plants will be happier in a sheltered patio. You can propagate them from cuttings.

Beaumontia grandiflora, herald's trumpet, is the finest species for the garden, its superior long tubular flowers produced in abundance. The strong foliage is handsome; conspicuously veined leathery leaves of forest green with tones of bronze. You can pick the magnificent lily-like blooms for the house, where their tropical, alluring perfume will pervade the room.

Bomarea
Alstroemeriaceae

A genus of South Americans, bomareas include small climbing plants with bright, unusual flowers, not unlike alstroemerias, to which they are closely related. Most are tuberous rooted, with strong, wiry stems, and they have a definite dormant season in the winter. For ease of growth, dazzling, long-lasting flowerheads and adaptability, bomareas are valuable plants. They decorate patios attractively and can be persuaded to climb trees without harming them. You can plant this climber in a container, bringing it into prominence at blooming time, and storing it away during dormancy. A humus-rich soil is preferred, and ample water during the growing season. Partial shade is acceptable, and bomareas do well on the coast. You can increase this climber by division, best done in spring or just before regrowth commences.

Bomarea caldasii, climbing alstroemeria, is typical of the genus, with brightly coloured tubular flowers hanging in graceful clusters of crimson and yellow. You can pick these for the vase, as they last well in water.

Bomarea multiflora

Bougainvillea 'Scarlett O'Hara'

B. multiflora, from Venezuela, is a good choice, and bears lavish clusters of bell-shaped, glowing red flowers in summer, charmingly spotted with chestnut. There are others to try, and one, at least, has edible roots.

Bougainvillea
Nyctaginaceae

The favourite climbers for warm gardens have to be bougainvilleas, which hail from tropical and subtropical parts of South America, mostly Brazil. There are probably 14 species, but the cultivars are the varieties grown in gardens. Versatile, in brilliant colours, reliable, able to deal with salt winds, there is no end to the appeal of bougainvilleas, the very essence of the tropics.

These plants need sun and room to grow, and are not particularly fussy over soil, as long as it is well drained. They climb easily, too, and a trellis, pergola or fence will show off their dazzle.

Mostly evergreen, bougainvilleas flower nearly all year in the tropics and subtropics, and can be trained to grow as shrubs in containers, as they do in Southeast Asian countries. Bougainvilleas can be coaxed into topiary forms, grown as standards or used to curtain ugly banks. Their one disadvantage is thorns, but they need these to help climb. All bougainvilleas need pruning back occasionally, and the flowers will form on the new wood. Pests leave them alone, and you can easily propagate from tip cuttings.

Bougainvillea glabra 'Magnifica Traillii' is the variety seen in older gardens. With rather strident tones of magenta, it is not everyone's favourite, but it is tried and true, will flower for months on end, and you can tone down its gaudiness by teaming with softer shades, for example pale blue, and then it can work wonderfully.

B. 'Killie Campbell' has large bracts in glowing orange, fading through several nuances to Titian tints. It is not as vigorous as some. The cultivars have been named differently in most countries and so you should buy your bougainvillea according to colour. 'Scarlett O'Hara' is well known, however, and of course blazes with scarlet to crimson bracts; it is always popular and dependable. Some bougainvilleas have both white and coloured bracts on the same plant, and you can obtain them in shades from white to pink, through to purple, as well as gold and scarlet. Others are notable for variegated foliage.

Campsis
Bignoniaceae

This genus consists of two species, from such diverse areas as China and eastern parts of the United States. Lusty climbers, with woody stems and attractive foliage, they are deciduous, producing fine flowers of trumpet shape in warm apricot to scarlet shades. *Campsis* species are useful for growing along walls and fences, or to tumble down a bank. They need sun to do well, and can be planted at the beach, as they are amenable plants which will survive extremes of

Campsis grandiflora

103

climate as well as low rainfall. The flowers arrive in summer as a rule. Vines are easily propagated from hardwood cuttings or suckers.

Campsis grandiflora, the Chinese trumpet creeper, bears shapely, fleshy flowers varying in colour from warm apricot to dusky red and held in big, bright clusters. These are well set off by the attractive leaves which are divided into several oval leaflets. Campsis vines are long lived, and often to be seen in old gardens.

C. x *tagliabuana* is a hybrid of the two species, and a good choice for subtropical gardens. It also has some agreeable cultivars, the most well known being 'Madame Galen', with eyecatching flowers in a deep coral red, displayed in clusters. 'Madame Galen' can be persuaded to grow either as a shrub or winding round a trellis or arbour.

Clerodendrum
Verbenaceae

A genus of shrubs, climbers, trees and perennials, with many appealing plants among them, clerodendrums come from the warmer areas of the world. There are over 400 species, including a few colourful climbers of note. These need high humidity and a warm, sheltered, sunny or only slightly shaded, spot in the garden. A good rich soil and ample water will make for quick growth. These climbers are easily raised from cuttings.

Clerodendrum splendens, glory bower, from western Africa, is a handsome plant with deep bottle-green leaves, deeply veined, and vivid clusters of tubular flowers in radiant red. These appear mainly in the spring and summer, but the vine can bear at other times of the year as well. Against a wall is a good place for glory bower, or spilling over a bank.

C. thomsoniae, bleeding heart, from the same area as *C. splendens*, can remain shrub sized, but will climb if persuaded. Its flowers are striking, and make a brilliant show with their snowy white, lantern-shaped calyces and crimson corollas. As with many clerodendrums, bleeding heart bears colourful fruit in a contrasting pink. You can grow this climber in a container on a terrace, or against a wall or trellis.

Clitoria
Fabaceae

Evergreen climbers that roam over the tropics, mainly the Americas, these 70 or so twining legumes require warm climates to thrive. However, the flowers are unusually shaped, and

Clerodendrum thomsoniae

Clitoria ternatea

Clytostoma callistegioides

hang upside down, designed so the backs of insects are dusted with pollen. The flowers are shaded from white to lilac and blue. Easily grown in the subtropics, clitorias can be sited in full sun at the coast, but a semi-shaded spot is preferable in hot, dry, inland gardens. Rich, well-drained fertile soil will entail good growth and many flowers. Insects do not trouble them, and they grow readily from seed.

Clitoria ternatea, butterfly pea, boasts flowers of an intense cobalt blue, a colour unusual in most flowers in the subtropics. They can vary in tone, through to lilac, with many nuances. Some have flowers prettily marked with lighter shades, and there are single, semi-double and double forms. This is a most useful climber and can be seen growing happily in gardens from the tropics to warm temperate places. It needs support to keep it twining, and it will happily tumble over a fence, its pinnate leaves completely covering the whole plant. After flowering, the butterfly pea yields long bean-like pods filled with seed. The darkest blue flowers are picked and dried and used as a food colouring in many Southeast Asian countries.

Clytostoma
Bignoniaceae

South Americans, with nine species, this genus is useful for its fast-growing capabilities, and plentiful flowers, which all show the characteristic trumpet shape of bignonias. They climb with ease by their tendrils, and appear to have no enemies. Amenable to climate changes, clytostomas survive drought once established, and cold conditions, too. They do well in either full sun or partial shade.

Clytostoma callistegioides, Argentine or orchid trumpet vine, is the species to grow, with its attractive foliage and prolific clusters of blooms in shades of orchid pink or lavender, streaked purple. The vines flower for months during spring and summer, and while the flowers' colouring is not always easy to place in the subtropical garden, this climber is a reliable background plant that will quickly provide a cover and privacy with its curtain of dark, lustrous leaves.

Lookalikes from warm regions of South Africa are the podraneas with two species. They too are fast growing and have similar flowers in shades of white, lavender or pink, being close relations to clytostomas, although from different continents.

Distictis
Bignoniaceae

Arresting climbers from Mexico and the West Indies, *Distictis* species are lavish and large. It is only a small genus, with nine species which all have typical bignonia-type flower trumpets, coloured from white, soft pink and lilac to scarlet and crimson. As with many climbers, all species enjoy moist but well-drained soil, and sun. In the hot weather a mulch is beneficial, plus regular watering. Distictis are efficient, evergreen climbers, clinging easily to their support, which should be sturdy. They have few enemies, and will flower for months, after which they should be pruned back fairly hard. Propagation is usually by cuttings or layering.

Distictis buccinatoria, Mexican blood flower, is the best of the bunch, and bears flamboyant flowers, hotly red with golden yellow throats. Full of vim and vigour, this bold climber is truly outstanding. Planted to cover a large arch or gateway, or up a wall, in a genial climate the Mexican blood flower will bloom for six months.

Gloriosa superba

It needs pruning at least twice a year. 'Mrs Rivers', a variation, produces flowers of a deep mauve with a yellow throat.

Gloriosa
Colchicaceae

From western Asia and southern Africa, and thought to be of a single variable genus, gloriosas are climbing lilies which produce superior flowers with reflexed, two-toned petals. Generally these are coloured vivid scarlet and yellow, although they can vary, some having softer shades; even a purple form is sometimes seen. These flowers are long lasting both in the garden and when cut. As long as they are given rich soil, warmth, protection and semi-shade, gloriosas will astonish with a wealth of dazzling bloom. Leaf mould is beneficial, too. Gloriosas climb with the aid of their tendrils at the end of the long, slender, numerous leaves. In nature, these climbers rely on support from surrounding

Distictis buccinatoria

bushes; in the garden they can be grown through shrubs or supplied with a trellis. Gloriosas resent disturbance, so the tubers should only be lifted and divided every few years, during the dormant season. They die down soon after flowering, and are dormant for six months, during which time they should not be watered as the tubers rot very easily. In fact, it is a very good idea to grow gloriosas in containers, and store them in a dry place while they are dormant. Propagate by division.

Gloriosa superba is aptly named, as its unique shape and colouring are indeed superb. The flowers arrive at the top of the branches in profusion during the warmest months, elegantly structured, with conspicuous stamens and reflexed petals, usually bright red, set off with wavy yellow edges. 'Rothschildiana' is the favoured variety, and has bigger flowers than the species, usually a ruddy red, contrasted with bright yellow edges.

Hoya
Asclepiadaceae

Only a few of the 200 or so species of these climbers deserve a place in the garden. From Southeast Asia, New Guinea and tropical parts of Australia, most produce deliciously fragrant flowers in clusters, some waxy, others as though made of velvet. Hoyas do very well in pots. They need bright light, but not sun, and it is wise to let them dry out between waterings. The new flowers come from the same spot as the spent heads, so leave the old flowers to drop of their own accord. Hoyas strike fairly easily from cuttings, taken at the warmest time of the year. Some varieties are susceptible to thrips, scale and mealy bug.

Hoya carnosa, known as the wax plant, from parts of India, China and Burma, has star-shaped flowers in shades from white to flesh-pink, with a contrasting deep crimson coralla. Its elusive fragrance, evocative of incense, intensifies at night. This hoya can be grown against a wall, where it will cling by its suckers. It has thick, strong leaves that are not worried by pests.

Hoya carnosa

H. carnosa can be left to its own devices in the main, does not need much pruning, and will flower faithfully year after year. Although it will tolerate some wind, it generally needs shelter. The variety 'Compacta' has curious curved leaves, while the variegated type has leaves striped light green and creamy yellow, but is not as sturdy as the species. There are excellent hybrids and cultivars, many developed in Australia.

H. lanceolata subsp. *bella*, sometimes called beautiful honey plant, is from the Himalayas. A dainty plant with modest, narrow leaves and pendent starry white flowers, pink- or red-centred, this hoya is ideal for a hanging basket. It exudes a strong, spicy scent.

The Australian native hoyas are stunning, too. *H. macgillivrayii* bears loose clusters of ruby-red flowers, while *H. australis* produces blooms of white and foliage with a bronze shine.

Ipomoea
Convolvulaceae

With over 300 species, this genus of plants covers climbers, shrubs, perennials and annuals, and they originate from the tropics to warm temperate zones. Many are twining climbers, complete with abundant but ephemeral flowers. This does not matter as they are blessed with continuous blooms, mainly with fragile-looking, papery petals. Ipomoeas are not too fussy in their requirements, but excel when supplied with well-drained soil and sun. Easily propagated from seed, which can be lightly nicked and soaked overnight, ipomoeas are precocious plants, and will be up and running in three or four days. Coastal areas suit them. Watch out for name changes, and those species that can be invasive.

Ipomoea alba is the enchanting moonflower, from tropical parts of America. A night-blooming species, it has naturalised in some warm regions. The moonflower is best grown as an annual, preferably on a terrace or deck or anywhere else near the house where its pulsating ice-white flowers can be observed. They take about half an hour to open and release their intense perfume. If contained in a pot, the plant can be placed on the dinner table to intrigue guests as the flowers quiver open. Moonflowers are quick to grow, and bloom in the warmest months.

I. cairica, from tropical and subtropical parts of Africa and Asia, has naturalised in many countries in coastal areas. The plant is covered in bright green, lobed leaves and for several months produces plentiful flowers, usually pink with a carmine centre, or occasionally red, purple or white. You can train this perennial climber to tumble down a bank or grow on a fence.

I. horsfalliae is the cardinal creeper from the West Indies; its common name refers to its rich rose-red flowers. It will spread and twine to envelop a pergola or fence, and the starry, dainty flowers cover the handsome leaves for months. As with many of the genus, the cardinal creeper thrives at the beach.

I. tricolor, from Mexico, is usually grown as an annual, and every seed sown will germinate in record time. A twiner with strong tendrils, it needs support, and light bamboo stakes do the job admirably. The plant never gets too large. 'Heavenly Blue' is a breathtaking cultivar, its tissue-thin flowers a glorious celestial blue. If planted in full sun, the flowers will fade by midday, so it is a good idea to place 'Heavenly

Blue' where it receives afternoon sun only, and the blooms will persist all day. The leaves are of a light green, heart shaped. Plant several, in containers away from wind, where they will excel.

I. lobata, still commonly called mina lobata, is another Mexican to grow as an annual, but is completely different to look at. Quick-growing, with lobed leaves, it bears racemes of small, tubular carmine flowers fading to orange at the tips. It is a great twiner for creating a temporary screen, short lived, but giving its all throughout the warmer months.

If you are seeking the unusual, consider *Merremia tuberosa*, the famed woodrose, and closely related to the ipomoeas; in fact, it used to be classed as one. Also coming from Mexico, the woodrose will climb rapidly, is vigorous and has small yellow flowers. After these fade the sepals enlarge and, along with the whole seedhead, take on the appearance of a flower in bud. They are like polished leather of a mahogany hue, and are used in floral work.

Jasminum
Oleaceae

Jasmines, from many parts of the world, and with over 200 species, are decorative, with long-lasting pretty flowers, but it is for their fragrance

Jasminum nitidum

that most are esteemed. Mainly jasmines are vines, though there are shrubs among them. Jasmines are widely used in commerce. The essential ingredient for many French perfumes are the jasmines grown in the south of France, locally known as 'Jasmin de Grasse'. Jasmine flowers flavour and perfume tea in China. In Hawaii, the blooms are used in leis.

One or other of the jasmines will thrive in most climates, and the subtropics are no exception. Easy to grow, jasmines perform well in sun, but also survive in semi-shade. Propagation is not difficult from cuttings. The climbers need to be pruned back as they are vigorous vines.

Jasminum azoricum is from the Azores, and accustomed to salt winds. This is a robust climber, takes no time to become established and, depending on locale, displays its pretty white flowers for months on end. Its virtue is in its citrus-type perfume, perhaps bergamot, and its ability to stand up to gales. Its leaves are a shiny jungle green, and attractively divided into three leaflets. You can site this jasmine on a trellis, fence, archway or on the rails of a deck, and be sure it will prosper, provided it has warmth. Pests do not harm it.

J. nitidum, angel wings jasmine, has star-shaped snow-white flowers, not exactly as ethereal as you might expect, but with a heady scent, and larger than those of many other species. Angel wings jasmine is ideal for the subtropics, and flowers for many months, usually from spring to late summer. Its strong, lustrous leaves are dark and remain decorative all year long. You can grow this beauty in a container, too.

J. rex hails from Thailand, and appreciates humidity and heat. Unfortunately, its pure white flowers are not fragrant, but they are numerous and a good foil for the bottle-green foliage. *J. rex* is often used as an effective groundcover in large tropical gardens.

J. sambac, the Arabian jasmine, which actually comes from India, is a small climber with enchanting, strongly aromatic flowers. This is the variety the Chinese use to scent their jasmine tea, and *J. sambac* is grown commercially in Hawaii to produce flowers for leis. This jasmine can be kept as a shrub, or trained against a wall.

Macfadyena unguis-cati

Macfadyena
Bignoniaceae

From Mexico to Uruguay, these three or four species are quick-growing, rampant climbers, and can become ruthless colonisers in the subtropics and tropics, so be careful where you place them. Clinging by efficient, hooked tendrils, the vines all produce bright flowers, trumpet shaped, in generous quantities. Lots of sun and a well-drained soil, away from wind, suit macfadyenas. Copious supplies of water in the summer will be appreciated, and a mulch will help conserve the moisture. Keep pruning when necessary. In temperate climates macfadyenas are not invasive. Cuttings take readily.

Macfadyena unguis-cati is a prepossessing plant with a clumsy botanical name. It has not been served well by botanists, having had various name changes through the years. Commonly called cat's claw creeper for its tiny claw-like tendrils, this is a highly desirable plant, despite its tendency to rampage. It is renowned for its dense decorative foliage, rapid growth and ability to cover unsightly sheds, block out an unwelcome view, or spill over a dry bank. Cat's claw creeper is adorned for a month or so in spring with a dazzling curtain of shimmering buttercup-yellow flowers with a faint, elusive scent. It thrives at the coast, away from the worst winds. Curb the exuberant growth by pruning as necessary; some stems should probably be cut back to ground level every year or so.

Mandevilla
Apocynaceae

Woody-type twiners, mandevillas, also sometimes called dipladenias, hail from Central and South America. Semi-shade suits them, and fertile, well-drained soil. You should mulch mandevillas in the hottest weather, and apply water as many of them come from Brazilian mountains where they thrive in the higher rainfall. Mandevillas are splendid flowering plants with fleshy, open trumpet flowers in colours ranging from white to deepest pink and even red, often with contrasting centres. You can propagate them by seed or cuttings. Mandevillas are generally modest in size, and easily managed.

Mandevilla x 'Alice du Pont' is possibly the most magnificent of the mandevillas. In summer the strong vine is decorated with deep glowing pink open flowers. A warm position is needed for 'Alice' as the plant is quite tender, albeit vigorous if it likes its site. Shade is needed in the hottest part of the day.

M. laxa, often called Chilean jasmine, despite

Mandevilla x 'Alice du Pont'

Mandevilla laxa

its origins in Argentina, is sweetly scented and grows well in cool areas, where it may be deciduous. Myriad pure white flowers arrive for the summer, and the heady perfume, gardenia-like, is intensified at night, so plant this climber where you can appreciate its aroma. Also, the flowers will last when cut. *M. laxa* will twine up a tree or ornament a fence or trellis, and is best pruned in the spring, before it becomes tangled. It grows readily from plentiful seed.

M. sanderi is known as the Brazilian jasmine, and the species has pink flowers, but several cultivars have been developed and some yield blooms of scarlet to crimson. Not only that, some flower nearly all year long in warm, sheltered places.

M. splendens is indeed a splendid sight, boasting flowers of hot pink with a brilliant egg yolk yellow throat. It is a compact climber, reaching 3 m at most, with leaves more decorative than the rest of the species, being bold and glossy.

Maurandya
Scrophulariaceae

Maurandyas are a genus of two species, small, unassuming climbers from Mexico. They have had various appellations through the years, but botanists have now moved from *Asarina* to *Maurandya*. Whatever their name, maurandyas will twine gracefully through other climbers, shrubs or even trees, and flower for a great many months. They can be treated as annuals, as they are quick growers and seed in a prodigal fashion. You can let them crawl up container subjects, or weep gracefully from hanging baskets. It is easier to procure seeds than plants. Sun or semi-shade suits them.

Maurandya barclayana, climbing snapdragon, from Mexico, has refined habits, and climbs daintily through anything handy, without disturbance. It has small, ivy-shaped leaves in a fresh green, and flowers that arrive off and on all year. The colour of violets, tubular, with a white throat and pale markings, maurandya blossoms appear to advantage when teamed with

Rhodochiton atrosanguineus

white-flowered climbers or, surprisingly, against a brilliant bougainvillea.

Another modest climber, one to treat in exactly the same way, from the same area and the same family, is *Rhodochiton atrosanguineus*, often called purple bells. Its form and colouring is unusual, with calyces of fuchsia pink to crimson, and flowers of deep purple within. The whole is prettily shaped, like a half-furled mini parasol.

Monstera
Araceae

Tropical climbers from the steamy rainforests of America, monstera number 25 species in all, and are noted for their spectacular foliage. Mostly they are epiphytic, and lean on trees for support, in rather a lackadaisical way. Monsteras are cultivated for the structural form of their foliage, although most species do produce

Monstera deliciosa

fragrant flowers followed by edible fruit. It is just the one species that is favoured, and it is to be seen as an indoor pot plant all through the world, admired for its jungle-like appearance, and able to cope with a container owing to its epiphytic ways. Monsteras can be used to clothe a steep bank, or as climbers against a wall or up a tree. Humus-rich, moisture-retentive soil suits them, away from the worst winds and in part shade. Child's play to propagate, you simply cut off a stemmed leaf and plant it.

Monstera deliciosa, fruit salad plant, is the type to grow. The opulent leaves bestow a lush, tropical ambience to the garden. Fast-growing, the leaves start off in a typical aroid shape, and develop into mammoth banners of shiny green, majestically formed, and complete with exaggerated lobes, and as they enlarge and mature intriguing, perfect oval holes appear. Monsteras produce spathes of fleshy cream flowers, highly perfumed, and these turn into long cones of edible fruit, also strongly fragrant, and reminiscent of pineapple. Beware of the fine hooks embedded in the fruit, not discernible to the naked eye.

Pandorea
Bignoniaceae

Native to Australia, parts of Southeast Asia and New Caledonia, pandoreas are twining climbers, with perhaps six species. Eager to grow, they consist of shiny, bright green pinnate leaves, typical of many bignonias, and are ornamented with delightful flowers in shades from white to cream and pink. Several cultivars have blooms more brightly coloured. Pandoreas prefer a sunny spot, or somewhere they can climb to the sun, in any good garden soil. They do well at the coast, and dry summers do not worry them. Use one to hide a shed, clothe a trellis, or to give privacy, as well as for beauty.

Pandorea jasminoides, the bower vine, native to Australia, is garlanded with glorious flowers, funnel shaped, with open petals, in ice cream pink, with a deep strawberry centre. There are several cultivars, the most notable being 'Lady Di', pure white.

P. pandorana, wonga wonga vine, an Australian, is an aggressive climber, and needs room. Quick growing, with dense glossy foliage, the wonga wonga vine can be trained along a fence, or used as a screen. Its creamy flowers are small, spotted inside with a wine colour. There is a cultivar in warm shades of gold and brown.

Passiflora
Passifloraceae

Passiflora, passion flower, passionfruit, is a genus with over 400 species, mostly from South America, but many of these vines have naturalised in countries far and wide. Their usual natural habitat is the rainforest where, with the aid of skilful tendrils, they climb through shade to reach the light and sun. Passion plants are cultivated for their intricate flowers and their scrumptious fruit. What more can you ask of a vine? The flower colours differ greatly, in shades from white and pink, through to red and purple, with some two- or even three-toned. Mostly evergreen, these plants need good soil, well drained, and a warm, sunny or partially shaded place to grow. A support such as a trellis or fence

Passiflora coccinea

is necessary, and a generous mulch, away from the stems, will help to conserve water and aid flower or fruit production. Watch out for scale and whitefly, also nematodes.

Passiflora antioquiensis, from Columbia, has startling, flamboyant flowers of rosy red to carmine, hanging from long stalks, which need to be seen from below for maximum effect, so a pergola makes the ideal support. Although this species is grown mainly for its flowers, it produces golden yellow, sweetly flavoured fruits. This passion flower has highly ornamental, deeply lobed leaves, and is the parent to many fine hybrids.

P. coccinea, red passion flower, grows wild in many parts of South America, and one of its local names is monkey guzzle — how inappropriate for such a beauty. *P. coccinea* is a vigorous vine, and flowers freely. It flaunts flowers of ruby red with filaments of deep purple, and white to yellow at the base, and the dark green ruffled leaves set off the blooms well. Several other red-flowered *Passiflora* species are very similar, and all worth growing. *P. quadriglandulosa*, for

example, is often confused with this red passion flower.

P. laurifolia, yellow granadilla, Jamaica honeysuckle, common to the West Indies, Venezuela and Brazil, is of commercial importance for its delicious fruit, but is also cultivated just for its fragrant flowers. They are equipped with extravagant filaments, for all the world like fringed Victorian lampshades. The filaments are banded red, blue, violet and white, while the petals are plum red to purple. The fruit is oval, and yellow or gold when ripe, with a sweet tropical taste. This passion plant has naturalised in many warm areas of the world.

P. quadrangularis, the giant granadilla, has king-sized blooms, the largest of all the passion flowers, produced on a huge vine. For instance, in Java, it can grow to 45 m. It originated in the West Indies and Central America, but has naturalised in many countries, especially Hawaii and the South Pacific. The dazzling, heavy flowers are pendent and of a deep crimson, with well-defined filaments banded in purple and white. The fruit is very large and used mainly in drinks, while the thick yellow rind can be cooked.

P. racemosa is from Brazil, and thought to be the most magnificent of all the passion flowers. For one thing, it dazzles for most of the year, its flowers of flaming red and white hanging from long racemes. Favoured hybrids have been bred from *P. racemosa*, the comely *P.* x *caeruleoracemosa* being one. Dozens of other superior passion flowers can be found, in many different colours and forms.

Petrea
Verbenaceae

A genus of about 30 species of climbers, shrubs and trees, petreas are from Mexico, Central America and the West Indies. Most of them have white or blue to lavender and purple flowers. It is the semi-evergreen woody vine that is the most useful and spectacular in subtropical and warm temperate gardens. This species can be trimmed as a shrub, or encouraged to climb a wall by means of support, or tumble over a pergola.

Petreas appreciate sun, but will flower in part shade. Free-draining acidic soil with a little fertiliser is ideal. Water the small plants until they are established, and be generous with a mulch. Scale insects and mealy bugs can trouble petreas.

Petrea volubilis, queen's or purple wreath, produces arching clusters of violet-coloured flowers, and although these are short lived, the dark calyces will stay. Once established, the queen's wreath will flower year after year, usually from late winter to summer. The leaves are rough in texture, and from this arises one of its less popular common names, sand-paper vine.

Another member of the Verbenaceae family to like similar conditions is *Congea tomentosa*, orchid shower, also a shrubby vine. Its small lavender, soft pink or white flower bracts are borne on abundant sprays that can cover the whole plant. It too prefers an acid soil, but is most adaptable. It will need a sturdy support, or can be used to curtain a wall or bank. To keep it in control you should prune the orchid shower right after flowering.

Philodendron
Araceae

Philodendrons are a large genus, with maybe up to 500 species, and come from the West Indies and hot parts of the Americas. Many have been developed as house plants, and are much hybridised. Dramatic plants, some squat, others climbing, philodendrons are admired for their luxuriant foliage, which imparts a jungle-like atmosphere to the garden. The architectural leaves are often heart shaped; some are split, others bordered with frills or scallops. Their texture can be glossy or velvety; mostly they are coloured green but sometimes splashed or lined with colour. Philodendrons need shade and shelter. The climbing types can be planted

Petrea volubilis

114

Philodendron scandens

near relation, *Epipremnum pinnatum* 'Aureum', the pothos vine, which will quickly scale a tree 18 m tall in its native habitat but is manageable in the garden or conservatory. It displays light green, heart-shaped leaves, often divided, and splashed with gold or cream, and is an arresting, very popular landscaping subject. Not as strapping, but as decorative, is the arrowhead vine (*Syngonium podophyllum*), also a close relation to philodendrons. It can be contained in a pot, allowed to climb, or employed as an efficient groundcover in shady places. There are several variegated cultivars.

Pyrostegia
Bignoniaceae

With few species, pyrostegias are evergreen climbers from the warmer parts of South America. They are as stalwart as any of the esteemed bignonia family, and as spectacular, too. Splendid vigorous vines for many areas of the garden, they will also thrive on the coast.

against the bases of trees where they will take the opportunity of ascending by their aerial roots. Most can be propagated from cuttings.

Philodendron bipinnatifidum, tree philodendron, is a vigorous species, more upright than needing support, and is embellished with glossy deep green leaves, extravagantly lobed and frilled. Cultivars and hybrids of this valuable plant are even more opulent, and boast immense leaves.

P. erubescens, red-leaf philodendron, blushing philodendron, has taro-like leaves, and is a true climbing species from Columbia. The leaves emerge rusty red, and are lined in wine-dark tones, on stems a deep red. Cultivars are numerous, and include 'Multicolor', favoured by many Hawaiian gardeners.

P. scandens, sweetheart vine, presumably so named for its heart-shaped leaves, is from Mexico, and can be persuaded to climb a support via its aerial roots, or employed to trail down.

Other species to scramble up trees include a

Pyrostegia venusta

Pyrostegias have abundant tubular orange or gold flowers that last for many months. Full sun and a well-drained site is important, and they will grow faster in a rich soil, but do well in a variety of conditions. While young, pyrostegias need to be kept moist, but as they develop no particular care is needed. Excellent cover for fences and archways, pyrostegias need no help to climb as they are equipped with strong tendrils. A vine will cover a wall or pergola quickly. These climbers do not suffer from diseases or pests, and can be propagated from stem cuttings, but not tips.

Pyrostegia venusta, from Brazil, has various common names, firecracker vine, golden showers and flame vine being just a few, and all an indication of its theatrical looks. The clusters of hanging, tubular flowers are fiery golden orange, maybe tangerine, and they festoon the vine for months on end, from the start of winter in warm temperate zones.

Quisqualis
Combretaceae

A genus of 16 or so evergreen shrubs and climbers from Africa and tropical areas of Asia, *Quisqualis* species appreciate shelter, warmth, rich soil and moisture. Full sun or light shade suit them. Propagate from seed or cuttings.

Quisqualis indica, Rangoon creeper, is a popular choice for quick cover. It is a twining plant with ovate leaves, and sweetly scented flowers which change colour as they open and mature, from white to pink to deep rosy red, hence its botanical name meaning 'which? what?'. Each bloom consists of a slender tube opening to a starry flower; these are carried in generous clusters all over the plant, generally throughout the summer. The Rangoon creeper is a rampant climber and will need a strong support. It should be curtailed and trimmed back annually to prevent straggly growth. Red spider can trouble it.

Solanum wendlandii

116

Solandra maxima

Stephanotis floribunda

Solandra
Solanaceae

Solandras are king-sized climbers, woody stemmed and rampant. The eight species all come from hot parts of the Americas, and are cultivated for their giant flowers and strong growth. (They have been known to climb as high as a six-storey building.) Producing large, lustrous, thick oval leaves that stay decorative all year, these are not climbers for a small garden, but in the right place are magnificent. Solandras succeed at the coast, unharmed by salt winds. The flowers are larger than those of any other climber, up to 20 cm across, and are chalice-shaped, ranging from creamy white to deep yellow in hue. You can clothe a bank with a solandra, or cover a sturdy fence. Obviously these lavish climbers need to be pruned, and should be curtailed at least once a year, which will also help to promote flowering. As the blooms fade, they should be cut off.

Solandra maxima, chalice vine or cup of gold, is from Mexico, grows to mammoth size, and truly is the best of the bunch, full of vim and vigour. The flowers are its glory, being the largest of the species, goblet shaped, with petals the colour of topaz. Each of these has a contrasting stripe of deep wine red running down the inside.

The flowers are not prolific, but make up for this by their sheer size, and give off a sweet scent reminiscent of vanilla.

For abundance of bloom, other climbing members of the great solanum family do good service in the garden. *Solanum rantonnetii*, blue potato bush, is a scrambling vine, densely leafed, and covered in dark amethyst flowers all summer. It grows untidily, so needs training on a wall or trellis for maximum impact. *S. wendlandii*, blue potato vine, is a good choice for fences, and charms with its fluffy cornflower to lilac flowers. *S. jasminoides*, the common potato vine, is fast growing, and good for a quick solution, but can become over friendly. Its typical solanum-type flowers come in mauve or white.

Stephanotis
Asclepiadaceae

Africa, Madagascar and parts of Asia are home to these delightful vigorous twining plants. There are only a few species, all distinguished by their white fragrant flowers. Stephanotis have pleasant foliage of a waxy texture, and do best in light shade, so are good subjects for bush or shade houses. You can grow one in a tub on a veranda where its scent can be appreciated. It is at its very best in a subtropical situation, away from strong, drying winds, and in well-drained, humus-enriched soil. This climber can be raised from cuttings. If grown indoors, or in a conservatory, watch out for mealy bug.

Stephanotis floribunda, from Madagascar, is the favoured species, with flowers famed worldwide for their perfection — so immaculate they appear unreal. They arrive in clusters of four, are waxy, snow white, tubular with a starry face, and their scent is sweet and strong, without being cloying. Bridal wreath is one of their common names, and the blooms are much in demand for wedding bouquets. Once picked, stephanotis flowers will last in their pristine state for several days and retain their seductive scent. You can usually sell any extra flowers to florists who realise their worth.

Stigmaphyllon
Malpighiaceae

Although there are over 100 species of this genus, very few are suitable for gardens. Those that are come from tropical America, and share golden yellow shimmering flowers and vivid evergreen foliage. Grow them in full sun or part shade, and fertile soil. You should water stigmaphyllons in dry weather, and mulch them, too. These woody vines need regular pruning. Suitable for growing on fences or to wind round a pillar, the plants have few enemies, but aphids can gather on the new growth.

Stigmaphyllon ciliatum, golden creeper, also commonly named butterfly vine or orchid vine, is the favoured species. This is adorned with clusters of shapely frilled golden flowers, usually in spring. The heart-shaped leaves are highlighted in deep red, turn to bronze and then a jungle green. This creeper does well at the coast. Sometimes it is hard to find at garden outlets, in which case another creeper with yellow flowers to try is the Carolina jasmine (*Gelsemium sempervirens*). This too has ornamental evergreen foliage, and carries its golden flowers for many months. Train it up a trellis, or let it trail down. The Carolina jasmine needs full sun and fertile soil.

Tecomanthe
Bignoniaceae

Evergreen climbers all, with only five species, tecomanthes are handsome and bold. Their homelands are New Zealand, New Guinea, tropical Queensland and Malaysia. They are admired for their trusses of strongly defined, opulent flowers, and vigorous growth. Tecomanthes need strong support, and should be planted in semi-shade, in soil rich in humus. Thrips will damage the leaves. Propagate from seed or cuttings.

Tecomanthe dendrophila, the pink trumpet vine, is a strong woody climber from New Guinea, quick-growing once it becomes established. Its glossy, lush leaves are divided into three leaflets, but it is prized for its brilliant clusters of pendent, tubular blooms of coral pink, lined with warm creamy-apricot — a delightful contrast. You can grow this beauty up a tree or trained over a sturdy support. It does well as a container plant, too.

T. hillii, a native of Queensland, is a lusty liana from the rainforests, with dark green pinnate leaves, prominently veined and toothed, and rosy red bell-shaped flowers. This climber prefers semi-shade and some support from a fence or trellis.

T. speciosa has an intriguing history. All the garden climbers have developed from just one plant, plucked from oblivion off an island in the Three Kings group, in northern New Zealand. *T. speciosa* is a stalwart climber, producing large, shining fresh green leaves, divided into three leaflets, on woody stems. In late summer or autumn, it is festooned with rich cream flowers which have overtones of lime green, but these arrive only after the vine is well established. Coming as it does from a small island, this tecomanthe takes salt winds in its stride.

Thunbergia
Acanthaceae

Thunbergias are mainly climbers and shrubby plants from Africa, Madagascar and Asia. They have handsome flowers in various colour schemes, ranging from white to blue and lilac,

Tecomanthe speciosa

Tecomanthe dendrophila

Thunbergia mysorensis

Thunbergia grandiflora

or in warm combinations of yellow, gold and tan to brown. The shapes of the flowers differ too, some being open while others are tubular.

These evergreen climbers are at their best in tropical and subtropical gardens. In fact, they may do too well here, and some species can be invasive. Suited to most soils, and best in full sun, thunbergias are easy to cultivate, and usually flower for a good length of time. They are toughies, rarely suffering from pests or diseases, eager to grow and needing little attention, except to restrain their exuberance. They can be raised easily from seed or cuttings.

Thunbergia gibsonii, orange clock vine, golden glory vine, not only has various common names, but has gone through several specific names as well. It can become too much of a good thing, but if contained in a pot its root run will be restricted. The vivid orange flowers, like flaring trumpets, arrive off and on throughout the year, but mainly in the warmest months. Plants will cover a trellis or fence, or form a groundcover. The golden glory creeper makes a fine background to blue-flowered plants or those in lighter golds and yellows. *T. alata*, black-eyed Susan, which flowers for all the year, is even more invasive and is prohibited in some areas, but it too can be curbed in a pot. The open orange flowers have a black centre, and other varieties come in colours from white to yellow. This thunbergia is most useful for quick cover.

T. grandiflora, the sky flower from Bengal, flaunts flowers of azure to lavender that resemble gloxinias in shape. Cascades and clusters of glorious bloom cover the vines in summer in most places. Unfortunately, this grand climber is a scourge in many areas of the South Pacific, Hawaii and northern Queensland, and should only be planted where it can be constrained. In the subtropics, plant *T. grandiflora* to cover and shade a deck, or pergola, or a fence by a swimming pool, or to climb and ornament a large

Trachelospermum jasminoides

120

tree. Its evergreen, heart-shaped leaves are decorative and resilient, but can burn in fierce hot winds.

T. mysorensis, as its name suggests, is from India. It appears very different from other thunbergias, and is bedecked with very long racemes of golden and auburn to brown inflorescences with bright yellow centres. To be appreciated fully, the flamboyant *T. mysorensis* should be planted to cover a pergola so that its beauty may be seen from below. Other thunbergias include *T. coccinea*, with scarlet flowers.

Trachelospermum
Apocynaceae

Mainly from Asia, with one, surprisingly, from the United States, trachelospermums are evergreen climbers and shrubs. They are reliable plants, prospering in many areas, and cultivated for their efficient, quick cover and fragrant flowers. For faster growth, you should plant your trachelospermums in soil rich in humus, but these species are not too fussy about conditions, and will endure drought once established. Sun or part sun will suit them, and pests are not a problem.

Trachelospermum jasminoides, the Chinese star jasmine, is not a jasmine, although its botanical name suggests a resemblance. Small delicate pinwheels of white flowers almost completely take over the plant for several weeks of the year, usually in spring and summer. They have a seductive scent, as intoxicating as any French perfume. The smooth, dense, dark green leaves smother the whole climber all year, and you can employ one or several as complete groundcovers, as well as to train on a pergola or arbour. If grown on a roadside fence, the Chinese star jasmine will muffle traffic noise, and help to keep down dust, so tightly packed is its foliage. There is a variegated form, but it is not as robust.

Sometimes, *T. asiaticum* is cultivated. It too bears scented flowers, and makes a fine groundcover, but has not quite the same appeal.

Perennials and Bulbs

Perennials

Perennials are mainly grown for their splendid flowers, and the way they persist year after year, provided growing conditions are favourable. Accommodating, dependable plants, perennials have many virtues. Evergreen types will supply interest all year long from foliage, and there will be one or another in flower in most seasons. They arrive in all shades of the spectrum, can be groundcovering or upright, and herbaceous as well as evergreen. Some prefer sunshine, others shade, and while most enjoy well-drained sites, there are those that thrive in watery homes and bogs. Easily propagated and increased, inexpensive to obtain, perennials can be the mainstay of the garden.

Perennial grasses, especially the contentious bamboos and papyrus, are often invasive but can provide a useful element in the subtropical garden.

Plant breeders are constantly improving perennials, and there are countless hybrids and cultivars. Many nurseries specialise in perennials, and bulbs, too, and interested gardeners should explore them for all the latest releases. Those listed here are not difficult to grow, appreciate warmth, and will give endless pleasure in the warm-climate garden.

Bulbs

Bulbs vary in size from small to significant, and have their own food reserves, self-contained storehouses. Convenient to grow, and precocious,

Opposite: *Canna* x *generalis* and waterlilies

bulbs often flower a few weeks after planting.

Bulbs endure, because they mostly lie dormant during miserable weather, and are ready to perform, year after year. Although a few are evergreen, in particular some South Africans, the majority die back after flowering, and are best left in the ground until the leaves fade, when they can be lifted and stored in a dry place. Among the many attractions of bulbs is their ready multiplication and longevity, and they can be passed down through the generations; heirlooms, no less.

Bulbs are simple to grow for the most part, although the conditions they prefer are varied. They can be contained in planters and pots or placed in generous swathes and small groups in the garden. A sampling of those liking subtropical conditions are included here, and all have faultless flowers in pleasing colours.

Annuals

Annuals, true annuals that is, complete their life cycle in just one season. Eager to germinate and get going, as they have a lot of living to do in a short space of time, annual plants are extremely precocious.

Rapid growth and quick garden colour from flowers in an infinite variety of shades, shapes and sizes assure annuals a place in the subtropical garden. Ephemeral they may be, but these plants give a great deal of pleasure to the gardener, with little cost involved. They offer a way of trying new ideas, and provide useful fillers while permanent plants are being established.

Alocasia macrorrhiza

Alocasia x *amazonica*

Annuals, for the most part, prefer a sunny place and friable, well-drained warm soil. Prodigal and lavish with seed, they are raised with little effort, but are also readily available from nurseries for planting out. Choose from old favourites such as petunias, amaranthus, cleomes, celosias, portulaca and zinnias. These transients can be placed in pots and planters, spreading smaller types are great in hanging baskets, and annuals for picking can be grown in the kitchen garden.

As annuals are so well known and widely grown, they do not feature in the following lists, but this does not mean they should be overlooked when you plan your subtropical garden. For all the attributes mentioned above, it is hard to better these useful plants.

Alocasia, Colocasia
Araceae

From tropical Southeast and southern Asia, alocasias and colocasias are rhizomatous and tuberous perennials, dramatic plants whose opulence brings a jungle-like atmosphere to the subtropical garden. While alocasias can boast over 70 species, colocasias include only six. Popular species from both genera have many named varieties and hybrids.

These aroids are renowned for their magnificent leaves, some mammoth, others intricately decorated on elegant stems. Splendid plants for warm, humid places, away from wind and sun, alocasias and colocasias are easygoing provided they receive ample water, a mulch in dry periods and a regular feed. Alocasias can be propagated by division of the rhizomes, stem cuttings or some by seed. Colocasias are easily increased from their stolons. Closely related, both species have some edible varieties, with taro (*Colocasia esculenta*) the most relished. Problem free for the most part, these lavish foliage plants can be attacked by insects.

Alocasia macrorrhiza, commonly called elephant's ear, is perhaps the best known, both for its mammoth vivid green leaves, silky and quilted, and the sheer exuberance of its growth.

124

'Hilo Beauty' is a variety much grown in Hawaii, and is handsomely marked with splashes of cream. These large, generous aroids can be used as specimen or accent plants, or planted in drifts where space allows.

Others to cultivate include *A.* x *amazonica*, with its arrow-shaped, deep green leaves and startling, prominent white veins, and *A. cuprea*. The latter, whose leaves are small for an alocasia, is popular for its colouring of bronze with a metallic sheen, contrasting green veins and a lining of deep red. These smaller alocasias can be placed in the front of the border or in a shaded courtyard, and contrast perfectly with palms, ferns and bright flowers.

Alocasias come in other colours and sizes. The Lyon Arboretum in Honolulu is responsible for developing many choice varieties, even more dramatic, some almost black and boldly patterned, and all worthwhile growing.

Colocasia esculenta, taro, elephant's ear, is a traditional basic food throughout the Pacific, parts of Asia and South America. Mainly it is grown for the starchy tubers, but the leaves are utilised, too. Ornamental as well as useful, you can grow taro easily enough, but it is those with the most dramatic leaves that are so striking. *C. esculenta* var. *antiquorum* produces smaller stems and leaves than the species, and it is at home in the damp garden, or can be contained in pots in shallow water. 'Fontanesii' is a dramatic form with shimmering, pewter-coloured, heart-shaped leaves, highlighted by deep purple veins and margins, elegantly placed on long, slender, velvety stems. Stylish, well-named 'Illustris' boasts leaves dark and lustrous, almost black. Colocasias travel via their runners, and you may find plants coming up in surprising places in your garden.

C. fallax is an ideal, compact groundcover plant for moist areas, and delights with its milky jade, heart-shaped leaves. It multiplies effortlessly, but is not invasive.

C. gigantea carries magnificent large leaves, as you would expect, of a bright green, lined with a pearly bloom, and thrives in a moist position.

Variegated types of colocasia exist, and named varieties can be obtained from specialist nurseries.

Alpinia
Zingiberaceae

The ginger group consists of tropical and subtropical rhizomatous herbs, esteemed for their exotic flowers and superior foliage. Edible gingers have been commercial crops for

Alpinia purpurata

Alpinia zerumbet

centuries. (See also page 149.) A large family, gingers are native to a wide range of countries, and are spectacular plants. Alpinias are as striking as any, with showy, long-lasting flower spikes in brilliant red, pink or white tones, ideal cutting material for the house. They are adaptable, growing in either shade or sun, but prefer protected environments in well-drained rich soil, with ample water and humidity. Equally successful planted as accents, or in generous swathes, alpinias are easily increased by division or by using the rooted plantlets that form among the flower clusters. They should be cut back after flowering. Foliage may be affected by thrips.

Alpinia purpurata, red ginger, one of the most popular, grows tall, about 3 metres, and spreads too, in generous clumps. It needs plenty of room to show off its lush growth and vivid cerise bracts, which are much sought after for flower arrangements, each bloom lasting for over two weeks. Native to Melanesia and the western Pacific, red ginger comes in pink varieties too, 'Eileen McDonald' being popular, and also the delightful 'Jungle Queen'. There is also the double-flowered form, 'Tahitian Ginger', which explodes in a wealth of cascading red inflorescences.

A. zerumbet, shell ginger, is grown throughout the tropics and subtropics, and even succeeds in temperate climates. Originally from misty, cloudy forests in the uplands of Southeast Asia, this adaptable ginger is most appropriately named. Strands of pearly 'shells' on arching, graceful stems make it a stunning sight. From under these pearly bracts the small flowers emerge; frilly in orange and red, bell-shaped, and great for cutting.

Anthurium
Araceae

Anthuriums have the distinction of being the biggest genus in the aroid family, consisting of more than 700 species. Mainly from sultry jungles in tropical America, anthuriums prefer shade and humidity, and in their natural state many perch in branches of rainforest trees.

While a lot are grown for their outstanding foliage, others are admired for their dazzling flowerheads. Some species, destined for the florist trade, are cultivated under controlled conditions, but many have been developed for outdoors, or to be grown under the shelter of a lath house or shade cloth.

These aroids demand protection from wind, rich, moist but well-drained soil, and lots of warmth. Special potting mix is needed for plants kept in containers: soil, bark, tree-fern fibre, charcoal, sphagnum moss — all have their advocates. Use as pot plants, specimens, or in great drifts in the shade garden. You can expect a clutch of insects to attack your anthuriums, including thrips, mealy bug and scale.

Anthurium andraeanum, often called flamingo flower, and its never-ending hybrids, is perhaps the most popular, and boasts shiny, leathery leaves on slender stems. The striking heart-shaped spathes frame the highly visible yellow spadices. Depending on variety, the spathes vary in shades and permutations, but the species itself is fire engine red, as shiny as though sprayed with lacquer, quite unreal looking. The charming Obake hybrids come in subtle shades and tints of white, green, soft pastels, apricot and orange, and are Hawaiian in origin. They have irresistible names such as 'Moonrise', 'Calypso'

Anthurium hybrid

and 'Butterfly'. Flamingo flowers for export are grown extensively in Hawaii, usually under fine shadecloth or netting, although there are also thousands of these stunning plants cultivated in natural conditions, under the shelter of trees.

A. crystallinum, crystal anthurium, is nurtured for its choice foliage. Native to jungles of Columbia and Peru, its luminescent long leaves are wide and dramatic, with a velvety texture, coloured deep emerald green and embroidered with eminent white veins.

A. scherzerianum, pigtail anthurium, produces long, heart-shaped leaves that unfurl at the top of slender stems. White, pink or red spathes contrast with the curled bright yellow 'pigtails'. Prolific when established, the pigtail anthurium flowers almost constantly, and is a good house plant, as well as being happy in shaded, warm gardens.

Anthuriums are being developed and cleverly hybridised all the time. New species may also be waiting to be discovered in their jungle homelands.

Arthropodium
Anthericaceae

Of the dozen or so species of *Arthropodium*, native to Australia and New Zealand, only one or two are cultivated. Adaptable and most versatile, arthropodiums are easy-care, spreading plants for hard or awkward places. Poor or rich soil suits, and the clumps are easily divided. Snails and slugs relish the fleshy leaves.

Arthropodium cirratum, renga renga lily, from New Zealand, will quickly cover banks and ugly areas with compact clumps of arched, bright, evergreen leaves. Denizens of coastal cliff faces in nature, these plants will grow in sun or shade. In springtime, dainty white flowers emerge from the recurved leaves, and of course they thrive at the seashore. Mass renga renga beneath tall trees (they will not mind if the ground is fairly dry) or group in borders with taller shrubs and ferns.

Close kin to the arthropodium is *Chloro-phytum comosum*, nicknamed hen and chickens. Equally adaptable and easy to grow, hen and

Arthropodium cirratum

chicken plants are cultivated for their grass-like foliage, and come from South African coasts. Tough and dependable, it is the striped forms that are cultivated, with recurved cream and green leaves. Chlorophytums develop small plantlets on slender, arching stems, so increase efficiently. Their small starry flowers are quite incidental. Grow chlorophytums as an edging, or where quick cover is needed, and team them with flowering perennials and bulbs, or place in suspended baskets, where they will hang gracefully and need very little attention.

Begonia
Begoniaceae

Native to tropical, subtropical and warm temperate regions, the genus *Begonia* is large and diverse. Central and South America is home to some of the finest species, cultivated for their dramatic foliage in remarkable forms and colours. The showy, fibrous-rooted begonias are happier in cooler climates. Being such a large genus of over 1500 known species, begonias are usually roughly divided into groups; rhizomatous, tuberous, cane-stemmed and fibrous-rooted. A considerable amount of hybridisation has been accomplished, resulting in many superior plants. The types described

127

Begonia Rex-cultorum Group

here appreciate warm, sheltered conditions, slightly acidic, humus-rich, well-drained soil, organic fertiliser, and some shade. Begonias take kindly to being contained, and most types can be potted, using a good-quality potting mix. Caterpillars like begonias, and powdery mildew can strike. If you want to grow begonias seriously, it is well worth joining a begonia society. Few genera present us with such an infinite variety to choose from. The following is just a tiny selection, and new varieties are launched every year.

Begonia 'Cleopatra', of mixed parentage, is a rhizomatous type with translucent, lime-green leaves bearing a deep wine to chocolate contrast. This begonia grows thickly, does not mind sun and, being an easy type, is often employed as an edging or groundcover.

B. *coccinea*, angel wings, is a tall-growing, cane-stemmed type from Brazil. It flaunts delightful thick leaves of a deep glossy green, sprinkled silver and edged with red, and lavish clusters of apricot to coral-red flowers. If it likes its position, angel wings will flower constantly.

B. *fuchsioides*, fibrous-rooting, is so easy to grow it needs curtailing, and becomes bushy in no time. It has small, shiny leaves on graceful, arching stems, and small pink to red flowers.

B. *luxurians*, from Chile, often called the palm-leaf begonia, gives a tropical air with its lavish, drooping, divided leaves. You can keep this tall-growing type in a large container or in a sheltered area of the garden.

B. *masoniana*, iron-cross begonia, a rhizomatous type from New Guinea, is a striking plant with strong, hairy stems supporting large leaves, slightly ruched, and decorated with a definite iron cross in a deep rich brown.

B. 'Orange Rubra', a cane-stemmed, angel-wing type, is a favourite for its delightful clusters of tangerine flowers, constantly appearing, and handsome spotted foliage, not to mention its ease of growth. For a pot or in a garden border team 'Orange Rubra' with the hybrid dwarf *Impatiens* 'Tango' in the same fluorescent tints.

B. Rex-cultorum Group, stunning rhizomatous begonias, are famed for their foliage, which often features silver or bronzed effects. Rex begonias are somewhat fussy, and will not tolerate sunlight, but neither do they like it dark, and they need sultry conditions. Keep their roots on the dry side, and watch for mildew. Their leaves are pointed, not symmetrical, and usually heavily embroidered and coloured. Countless hybrids of this group are available.

B. *scharffii*, a Brazilian beauty, is small and spreading, fibrous-rooted, and grows indoors or out. This begonia boasts furry, broad, ovate leaves, in an unusual yellow green colour with a backing of ruddy red. The flowers are small and prettily pink.

Caladium
Araceae

Deciduous plants from tropical rainforests of South America and the Caribbean, with 7 species, caladiums are admired for their leaves, often wedged-shaped, always intricately patterned and varied, in colours from white to scarlet, with no two plants appearing the same. Some species are edible, like their cousins, the taro. Caladiums have a reputation for being temperamental plants, but it is certainly worth the effort to cosset these prima donnas. Also, tougher varieties are now available.

You can grow caladiums in the subtropical garden, or confine them to pots in the house. Throughout their growth, these plants need a warm, moist atmosphere, filtered shade, shelter from strong winds, and a humus-rich soil. A compost of leafmould is beneficial, and liquid fertiliser, applied each week, will hasten growth and intensify leaf colouring. In hot weather it is beneficial to spray with water. It is wise to keep caladiums in pots, so you can keep track of them. Include a water polymer in the potting mix, which should contain peat. When the plants die down at the end of summer, reduce watering and put pot and all in a dry place to overwinter. If planted directly in a very warm, humid garden, with any luck your caladiums may spread. In some countries these aroids have naturalised.

Caladium bicolor, angel wings, is a dramatic plant with striking foliage in a collection of colours, infinitely varied and patterned, the tones skilfully blended. Rich scarlets, brilliant ruby red, bright green, cream, pink and white are just some of the colours highlighting the extraordinary leaves, which make a vivid tropical display. Numerous hybrids and cultivars are to be found.

Another member of the aroid family with superior foliage is *Dieffenbachia seguine* and its numerous cultivars. With rich, embroidered oval leaves on canes which can reach more than a metre, dieffenbachias enjoy steamy conditions.

Calathea
Marantaceae

With about 300 species, calatheas are noted for their varying leaf shapes and shades, also for a few with spectacular flowers. Calatheas originate in Central America and the West Indies, and come in sizes from groundcovers to specimens over 2 m tall. Columbus reported seeing an edible crop of tubers grown from one species. Masterpieces of patterned foliage, calatheas need warm, moist, humid conditions to give of their best. They should be grown outside in shady

Caladium bicolor

Stromanthe sanguinea

places, or in containers in courtyards and entranceways. They make splendid house plants. Calatheas demand rich, well-drained soil, regular feeding, and ample water during the hot months. They are easily multiplied by division of the fleshy rhizomes, but are martyrs to many insects, including aphids, spider mites and thrips.

Calathea burle-marxii 'Blue Ice' is one of the more spectacular species and comes from eastern

Canna 'Tropicanna'

Brazil, homeland of the landscape architect after whom it is named. This calathea grows to over a metre tall, has bright green leaves and an astonishing crystalline inflorescence of ice-blue bracts, surrounded by tiny lavender or white flowers. So ethereal is the structure and colouring of 'Blue Ice', it instantly commands attention. This exotic variety needs a very sheltered position, constant cosseting, and may be too tender for most gardens.

C. zebrina, zebra plant, another Brazilian, is sturdy, and develops into a compact clump, each stem festooned with big textured leaves of a deep jungle green, patterned with lime-green stripes, and lined with aubergine. The new leaves rise up folded, rather like ice cream cones, and small flowers come in spring as a rule. This handsome species is easier to grow than most, and will spread to form a good groundcover.

Calatheas vary enormously in leaf shape and markings. The peacock plant (*C. makoyana*) comes from jungle floors, and is a small species with oval, textured leaves of silver and green, while *C. rotundifolia* sports thick, leathery, striped leaves as broad as they are long.

Other members of the Marantaceae family are cultivated for their outstanding foliage are *Maranta*, *Ctenanthe* and *Stromanthe* species. Marantas are similar to calatheas, having fascinating foliage, liberally patterned.

Canna
Cannaceae

Cannas, rhizomatous perennials, come from Central and South America, with about 25 species, much hybridised, and many named varieties. Valued highly for their exotic flowers, cannas are also handsome foliage plants with bold, robust leaves, often dramatically spotted or striped, in green, yellow, bronze or deep red. Indeed, types are now being developed mainly for their colourful foliage, the flowers an added bonus.

Every few years, you should lift the rhizomes and discard old rootstock before you replant, to give the best results. Cannas multiply efficiently and may need thinning out before they take over. To keep them flowering for months, cut off the seedheads. Cannas will do well at the coast. They look great in groups of one colour, or skilfully blended, in borders, by pools, in tubs and large containers, contrasting with low-growing foliage plants. Full sun produces best displays. Decayed animal manure is beneficial to cannas, plus a general fertiliser and a good mulch. Water in dry weather, and watch for snails and slugs; they enjoy leaves and flowers. Grow some from seed.

Canna x *generalis* is the name given to the big group of hybrid cannas with vague parentage, with numerous named cultivars, too. The colour range is dizzying, from softest creamy white, yellow, orange, to scarlet and deepest crimson. Many are two-toned in psychedelic shades, some bejewelled and spotted, others almost iridescent. Cannas come in various sizes, from small through to tall, and are usually named accordingly. Selections of those grown for leaf colour include 'Tropicanna', resplendent in deep crimson, striped a deep green to black, and luminescent when caught by the light. 'Bengal Tiger', in green and yellow stripes, is suitably jungle-like.

C. indica, Indian shot, will naturalise in warm areas, and produces splendid leaves on stems over 2 m tall, and flowers with narrow petals in shades of red to yellow. The hard, round seeds are made into leis in Hawaii.

Water cannas, so-called, but no relation, were mainly bred at Longwood Botanical Gardens in Pennsylvania. They include the most well known, *Thalia dealbata*, a deciduous aquatic plant boasting deep blue to violet flowers. Thalias can be planted in bog gardens, as marginals, or in the main garden, where they will need a great deal of water to flourish.

Clivia
Amaryllidaceae

From South Africa come these shade-loving evergreen perennials, noted for their handsome, dark green, glossy leaves and clusters of flowers in warm shades of cream, gold, yellow and red.

Never aggressive, clivias slowly form formidable clumps and make a perfect groundcover under trees, where they appreciate the shade but do not mind the competition from tree roots. Clivias can live off the nutrients from fallen leaves, but like a compost as well. They do not need watering until the heat of summer, and are perfect in pots.

Clivia miniata, Kaffir or bush lily, is the popular species, with stunning clusters of glorious golden to deep orange flowers that are almost fluorescent among the dark foliage. New hybrids and cultivars are even more spectacular, boasting lavish, larger flowerheads in even richer colours; one in deep red is especially desirable. Yellow and cream forms are also available.

C. nobilis, drooping clivia, carries a dense umbel of smaller tubular flowers in yellow and orange, charmingly tipped with green. These appear in early winter as a rule. A handsome hybrid in shades of soft red is *C.* x *cyrtanthiflora*,

Clivia hybrid

an offspring from *C. miniata* and *C. nobilis*.

Also exclusively South African are *Agapanthus* species, both evergreen and deciduous, tough and dependable, and appreciated for their beautiful blues and snowy whites. Good background subjects, these grand plants thrive on slopes and on roadsides, where they deal well with pollution. They do well at the beach, flower in the warmer parts of the year, and need very little attention. Smaller hybrids are available in several shades on the blue and white theme.

Colocasia
see Alocasia, p.124

Costus
Costaceae

From sultry tropical parts of the world, with 150 species, and related to the true gingers, these perennials have fleshy, sturdy rhizomes bearing handsome leaves which grow in a spiral fashion up the strong stems. Costus plants come from humus-rich forest floors, where they enjoy filtered light and jungle-like conditions. The pretty flowers emerge from clusters of colourful bracts and are fast growing in humid, hot areas, slower in the subtropics. You can transplant them easily, and propagate them by division. Plant costus next to pools, in courtyards and patios, and in big tubs and containers. Spreading plants, these so-called gingers need plenty of room and, once flowering is finished, should be cut right back to ground level.

Costus speciosa, crepe ginger, Malay ginger, native to tropical Asia, is composed of velvety, fleshy leaves on cane-like, tall, red-coloured leaf stalks that spring out from the rhizomes. The leaves spiral round the stem in a characteristic way, with the deep crimson inflorescences borne in the centre of the spiral. White or pink-flushed, silky, delightfully frilled flowers, as fine as tissue, emerge from the vivid bracts. The flowers are edible, but such treatment would seem sacrilege. The rhizome is used medicinally in Asian countries. A variegated type is sometimes seen.

C. spiralis, spiral ginger, from the Caribbean,

Mexico and tropical America, has stockier stems, but is similar to crepe ginger, bearing a cone of brilliant red bracts from which emerges small yellow to red flowers. The bracts make great floral decorations. Indianhead ginger or spiral flag (*C. spicatus*) also resembles the other species, except it is a larger plant altogether.

From the same small Costaceae family, with only two genera, and habitats from Southeast Asia to northern Australia, are some 15 species of the genus *Tapeinochilus*, with *T. ananassae*, wax ginger, being the most popular. This plant produces deep red tall canes. The surreal inflorescences, which spring directly from the base, are made up of big bracts, lacquered red, as shiny as sealing wax, in a pineapple-like cone, with tiny yellow flowers. The wax ginger is a fairly compact plant, and can be cultivated from cuttings.

Crinum
Amaryllidaceae

Denizens of the warmer regions of the world, crinums have about 130 species. These are usually notable for big, bold bulbs that produce large plants and flowers. Fast-growing, adaptable, and much hybridised, crinums prefer a rich soil, well watered and well drained for the most part, but being from so many parts of the globe, their requirements can differ. Plant your crinums with part of the bulb exposed, in sun or part shade. Spider mites like them.

Crinum asiaticum, giant or spider lily, is from tropical Asia. It is a huge plant, salt-tolerant, and adorned with seductively scented, spidery-petalled, cool white flowers which bloom continuously. Grow spider lilies as specimens, or in abundance for their lavishness and dramatic structural form. You can plant them right on the edge of the beach, too. 'Mrs James Hendry' is known for its citrus scent and blush-pink flowers.

C. x moorei, bush lily, from South Africa, is deservedly popular. A tough crinum, it carries pretty pink or white lily-like flowers. *C. pedunculatum*, beach or swamp lily, from eastern Australia, is similar, but even bigger, and will

Crinums with a border of white impatiens.

grow in a damp position in shade or sun, on pool edges and with its feet in water, and at the seashore. Its fresh white flowers usually arrive in spring and summer.

Close kin is the belladonna lily (*Amaryllis belladonna*), long-lived and extremely tough, with fragrant, trumpet-shaped, white, soft-to-lolly-pink and sometimes cerise flowers. They flourish in shade or sun. x *Crinodonna* is a hybrid between crinums and belladonnas, and has inherited attractive qualities from both parents.

Also called spider lily in the vernacular is *Hymenocallis littoralis*, a tender beauty from tropical America. The exotic blooms are unique; snowy white and star shaped, but with soft tissue-like membranes between the petals. Grow these clumping low-growing spider lilies in drifts. A good companion plant could be the Amazon lily (*Eucharis amazonica*), native to Columbia and Peru, where it also grows in shaded, warm, sultry, moist conditions, and produces pure white, fragrant flowers, shaped rather like those of a daffodil.

Curcuma
Zingiberaceae

Curcumas were mainly grown for the commercial crop of turmeric in days gone by, but some species are becoming increasingly valued for their spectacular flowerheads. Curcumas range from Southeast Asia as far as northern Australia. Out of fleshy rhizomes, often shaded saffron yellow, arise bright green leaves in which nestle stunning flowerheads of green, white, golden or pink bracts, all with small yellow flowers. The plants are adaptable, flowering in sun or shade, but do best in sheltered places, in humus-rich soil, and with copious supplies of water. They relish humidity and a general garden fertiliser applied every few months. Being so compact, curcumas make very good house plants. Watch out for thrips.

Curcuma australasica, Cape York lily, produces a pretty pink flower spike, and handsome leaves that unfurl to disclose their prominent veins.

C. roscoeana, jewel of Burma, as can be

deduced by its common name, is a dazzling plant with undulating golden bracts that turn deep apricot. A small plant of about 50 cm high, it has leaves closely arranged, and these die back after flowering.

Other curcumas are becoming available, many having been developed as house plants.

Cyrtanthus
Amaryllidaceae

From South Africa, with at least 50 species, cyrtanthus have bulbs usually equipped with strap-like leaves, and flowers in a warm colour range. Best in rich, free-draining soil, cyrtanthus resent disturbance, do well in pots and multiply rapidly.

Cyrtanthus elatus, Scarborough lily or vallota, is the favoured species, and delights with clusters of scarlet, open trumpet flowers, with golden stamens, ideal fur cutting. Vallota flowers in summer several times during the season, and enjoys beach living.

South Africa has given gardeners a wealth of material to choose from, bulbs being no exception. *Haemanthus coccineus*, for instance, is an astonishing two-leaved blood lily with scarlet flowers enwrapped in fleshy red bracts. Warmth and semi-shade are requisites. Closely allied is *Scadoxus puniceus*, boasting a profusion of orange

and scarlet flowers enclosed in vivid red bracts. *S. multiflorus* is a magnificent plant with a starry wealth of flowers like an explosion of red fireworks, and the subspecies *katherinae* is even more dazzling.

Consider other South African bulbs for your subtropical borders. Adaptable, dependable and good travellers are babianas, freesias, ixias, nerines and sparaxis, and that's just a few. Consider the moraeas, too, iris-like cormous perennials, easy to grow, and happy at the seashore; also *Dietes* species, which likewise prosper wherever they go.

Eucomis
Hyacinthaceae

Strapping deciduous plants, nicknamed pineapple lilies, *Eucomis* species, all 15 of them, are from South Africa. They develop leaves not unlike an agapanthus, but broader and decorated on their undersides with speckled brown midribs and veins. The cylindrical flowerheads arrive in spring, and are made up of many small, starry, softly greenish white to pink and lilac flowers, topped with a leaflet crown, thought to look like a pineapple topknot. These bulbs take up a good deal of room, but need it to show off their long-lasting flowers. Both in the vase and in the garden, they are ornamental for several months,

Haemanthus coccineus

Scadoxus multiflorus subsp. *katherinae*

Eucomis hybrid

as the seed capsules continue to be decorative. Slugs and snails often hide in the lavish clumps. Plant pineapple lilies where they can be seen, in front of shrubs, and give them humus and a good, rich soil. Divide clumps when they get oversized. They look very well in pots.

Eucomis bicolor has a fresh white flower tinged with a green hue, and petals edged with purple, while *E. comosa* is similar, but grows slightly larger and is the star of the species, with flowers that vary in colour. They are sometimes white or tinged with pink or deep wine hues, and bloom atop graceful slender stems which are prettily spotted in purple. Varieties in pink and wine are sometimes seen.

Hedychium
Zingiberaceae

Hedychiums, with 40 species, are tougher customers than most gingers, and tolerate colder temperatures than their cousins. From India and uplands of tropical Asia, they are adaptable and easy, so much so several species are aggressive and highly invasive in susceptible areas. Check them out before planting. Hedychiums for the most part are wildly perfumed, filling the air around them with a heavy, voluptuous scent. As with other gingers, the clumps should be cut back rigorously after flowering. Humus-rich soil, and some shade, suits hedychiums.

Hedychium coronarium, white ginger lily, garland flower, has been cultivated in Asia for centuries. The enchanting, orchid-shaped flowers are delicate, with unforgettable, alluring ginger perfume. White ginger blossom is too brittle for the floral trade, but is used for lei making in Hawaii, along with yellow ginger lily (*H. flavescens*), which is just as endearing. Both can be invasive.

H. flavum, golden butterfly ginger, has long been a favourite in southern states of the United States, with egg yolk-yellow to orange dense flower spikes, exotically fragrant and prettily tipped with decorative orange spots.

Hedychium coronarium

H. gardnerianum, kahili ginger, grows in strong, lavish clumps, as wide as they are long, and carries big cones of bright golden-yellow flowers with conspicuous long brick-red stamens. As gloriously fragrant as the rest of the species, kahili ginger will grow in cool parts, as it evolved on mountain slopes of Nepal. Watch out, for it will colonise ruthlessly in some areas.

H. greenei, sometimes nicknamed red ginger lily, has handsome red-backed leaves and produces strong, tall clumps topped with clusters of clear red flowers; alas, no fragrance. You can increase this ginger from the small bulbils that form in leaf axils.

Heliconia
Heliconiaceae

Bold, extravagant flowers and foliage are the hallmarks of heliconias, the amazing perennials mainly from tropical America, with a few from Asia and the western Pacific. There could be over 400 species, with thousands of hybrids and cultivars, and more being developed as their popularity increases. Heliconias are the ultimate in tropical abundance, superior plants, a godsend to florists and flower arrangers, with their long-lasting appeal and ravishing impact. Give them a warm, half-shady position, and after they flower, remove the whole stem back to ground level (it will not flower again), and trim back damaged foliage, too. New shoots arrive close to the old stem.

Plant heliconias in well-drained, rich soil, and use a mulch or compost to cover the tender rhizomes. Hungry plants, heliconias need fertilising regularly. Despite their robustness, they make good container subjects and some are specially bred for this purpose. Water well in the summer, and propagate by division. They are addictive, and once you have acquired one heliconia, you will hanker for more. Some species do better in the tropics. Heliconias are cousins to bananas and strelitzias.

Heliconia bihai has several common names which makes it confusing, and also many named varieties. It is a lavish plant, carrying robust paddle-shaped leaves, and bracts of flaming red lightly tipped with emerald green, and yellow at the base; a popular species for picking.

H. caribaea, wild plantain, is a strong-growing plant with banana-like stems and leaves, carrying waxy clusters of bright yellow or red bracts with small contrasting flowers, usually green.

H. psittacorum, parrot's beak heliconia, is easy to grow and is more cold tolerant than some species. Small and dainty, parrot's beak is good for groundcovers in warm positions, and the flowerheads glow in delightful spangled shades of yellow and red. There are a great many more permutations and named varieties.

H. rostrata is the dramatic hanging lobster claw, so unreal looking that you feel you must touch it. This plant, taller than a man, comes from Peru and Argentina, and its 50 cm flowerheads dangle down in a startling display of red, yellow and green necklaces. In Hawaii, the hanging lobster claws are often seen grown for hedges, and the hanging garlands are for sale

Heliconia rostrata

Hemerocallis hybrid

in the markets.

Only a few of these masterpieces can be described here; there are hundreds to choose from in the catalogues of specialist growers.

Hemerocallis
Hemerocallidaceae

Although many species exist, it is the comely hybrids that have charmed gardeners with their exotic flowers in a wide colour range. These clumping perennials, commonly called daylilies for obvious reasons, evolved in east Asia. They have arching, sword-shaped leaves, and are either deciduous, semi-evergreen or evergreen. Showy flowers stand above the foliage. Daylilies are dependable, long-flowering and so easy to grow they can almost be left to their own devices. The American Hemerocallis Society boasts more than 20,000 named varieties, thanks to dozens of clever breeders. Simple to place in the garden, daylilies marry well with other perennials in similar colour schemes, and look good arranged round water features, and wherever a trusty groundcover is needed. Trouble-free, they will flourish in any type of soil, and plants are easily divided.

Hemerocallis Hybrids are the way to go. Choose your plants by colour and form. Extensive lists from specialised growers are available. In warm areas the evergreen types are best, and will do well near the coast. Plants come in all sizes from small to those almost 2 m tall, and flower sizes range from miniatures to singles or doubles of 15 cm across. Available in creamy white, lime-green, through to lemon, bright yellow, apricot and then all the hot colours, the often fragrant flowers are lily-shaped and velvety to the touch. Some are bi-coloured, many have frilled edges, and all are worthwhile.

Hemigraphis
Acanthaceae

Tropical Asians, these 60 or so species of annuals and perennials are cultivated for their ornamental foliage, often brightly coloured. Useful easy-care groundcovers, *Hemigraphis* species prefer sun or part sun and well-drained soil, and like ample water in summer. They spread rapidly and are simply propagated from cuttings.

Hemigraphis alternata, red ivy, is the most well known, and has spreading stems bedecked with smoky purple metallic leaves, two-toned with green and lined with a deeper purple. Modest white flowers appear intermittently. You can suspend plants in baskets where they hang prettily and need little attention.

Other members of the acanthus family, easy to grow and with attractive leaves, include the polka-dot plant (*Hypoestes phyllostachya*). Its carmine to deep wine leaves are liberally spotted pink. Sun suits these small bushy plants, which are sometimes treated as annuals.

Also kith and kin are the fittonias, groundcovering plants from jungles in South America. *Fittonia verschaffeltii*, painted net leaf, has foliage intricately veined in red, with variations flaunting cream veins.

Hippeastrum
Amaryllidaceae

Hippeastrums are renowned for their brilliant flowers. With over 80 species, they have been much hybridised, and it is the spectacular hybrids that appeal to gardeners worldwide, but several of the species deserve a place in the garden, too. *Hippeastrum puniceum*, for instance, commonly called Barbados lily, is found in many tropical gardens, where it is planted en masse, and makes a dramatic show.

All of these bulbs originated in subtropical and tropical parts of South America, and were introduced into Europe over 200 years ago. More than 100 hybrids and cultivars are commercially available, and breeders are now developing different colour schemes and double flowers, with small, abundant blooms. Seasonal plants, hippeastrums have a period of dormancy in the winter, to emerge and produce within weeks a brilliant floral display. Easy to grow, these bold bulbs need rich soil, organic fertiliser

and water as they sprout. When planted in pots it is good to place them with at least a third of the bulb above the potting mix, and it is wise to overwinter potted bulbs in a cool, dry place. Those left in the garden to grow prefer a half-shady spot, and will even do well under trees as long as they are well fed. Very little goes wrong with these spectacular plants, but snails and slugs find them irresistible, and they can be attacked by a fungal disease, ominously named red spot.

Hippeastrum hybrids, commonly called amaryllis, differ in shape, size and colour. Breeders have tried for years to develop a clear bright yellow hippeastrum, but have been more successful on improvements to the shapes, shades and intensity of the flowers. Blooms vary; some are flamboyant, trumpet-shaped and king size, while others have narrow, pointed petals; miniatures and doubles are new developments. As for colour, this ranges from pure white, softest pink, through lolly pink, vibrant tangerine, to all the reds. Some are rich and velvety, others boast an iridescent sheen, and many are splashed

Hippeastrum hybrid

with a contrasting hue, or smartly striped. A few are exquisitely marked in a delicate lime green, almost iridescent.

Related is the unusual *Sprekelia formosissima*, Aztec or Jacobean lily, one of a kind from Mexico, with scarlet to crimson flowers, spectacularly shaped in the form of a cross. They prefer full sun and well-drained soil, with a third of the bulb planted above the soil. Precocious bulbs, Aztec lilies will bloom in eight weeks from planting. You can grow them in pots, as you would hippeastrums.

From Brazil comes the rare *Worsleya rayneri*, blue amaryllis, a near relation to hippeastrums. This unique bulb produces sickle-shaped, long, arching leaves, and large frilled flowers, more heliotrope than blue, and fading to white at the base. This treasure flowers reluctantly, and takes many years to shine. In its natural state, the blue amaryllis hangs from steep, misty cliffs in acidic soil, and demands perfect drainage. More a plant for collectors, and those patient — and long-lived.

Impatiens
Balsaminaceae

With species galore, this is a large genus of annuals, evergreen perennials and subshrubs from the tropics and subtropics of Asia and Africa, but not many are grown in gardens. Those we do grow are renowned for their abundance of bloom over a very long period. These are usually the valuable hybrids and cultivars, which come in an overwhelming colour selection, and need very little attention to survive.

Impatiens are barometer plants; when they wilt you know water is needed in the garden. Water regularly, fertilise occasionally, and you will have a colourful display all year long. Pest- and disease-free, impatiens are the answer to a gardener's need for instant colour and truly easy-care plants.

Impatiens New Guinea Hybrids are especially bred for their intensity of glowing colour, flower profusion, compact growth habit and ornamental

Impatiens 'Congo Cockatoo'

Impatiens New Guinea Hybrids

139

leaves. You can grow them in pots, hanging baskets or anywhere outdoors, but be careful where you site these wonders. They can look overpowering, and a block of the one colour is better than a hotchpotch. You can choose from vibrant and luminous tangerine, red, yellow, white and everything in between; alas no blue, but the breeders are working on it.

I. walleriana, tried and true busy lizzies, from tropical Africa, are trouble-free perennials that really shine in the shade. Hundreds of strains exist in many sizes, with flat-faced single flowers or doubles like darling rosebuds. The everyday single types are probably best for bedding. Rapid growth, and myriad tints other than blue or a clear yellow colour are to be found, making busy lizzies ideal for new gardens. They flower all year long. Cut them back if they get leggy.

Other intriguing impatiens species and varieties exist. *I.* 'African Queen' is a true yellow, as is *I. repens*, both ideal for hanging baskets, and look out for *I.* 'Congo Cockatoo', with a flower vaguely bird-like in red, yellow and green.

Iresine
Amarathaceae

Mainly from tropical areas of the Americas, iresines consist of 80 species. Cultivated for their vivid leaves, these warmth-loving perennials glow with hot colours. Easy to grow, they like part sun and a fertile, well-drained soil, with a general fertiliser applied regularly. They are upright plants, and need their tips pinched back to keep them shrubby and compact. Use the tips to produce more plants. They dislike wind but will flourish in sheltered coastal gardens. The splendid leaves are relished by slugs and snails.

Iresine herbstii, bloodleaf, beefsteak plant (who ever named it thus?), is a beauty, and charms with spectacular foliage in a spangle of colours, mainly glowing cherry red to deep ruby, with cream to hot-pink midrib and veins. The leaves are usually rounded, but not always, and the varieties arrive in differing colour combinations, some being fresh green with yellow and gold veins, others a shimmering blackberry and raspberry red. Plant

Iresine herbstii among cycads and day lilies

140

iresines near bromeliads to mix and mingle, and with other perennials less fortunate as to foliage.

Musa
Musaceae

Ornamental bananas are as satisfying to grow as the scrumptious edible types. Some of these decorative varieties can be used as house or patio plants, but will grow bigger and better outside. Treat them as you would fruiting bananas, planted in rich soil laced with fertilisers, and provided with liberal supplies of water.

Musa ornata, flowering banana, displays upright bracts of pink to red, lined with a deeper shade, and yellow flowers. The leaves of this medium-sized banana are green, with a red midrib.

M. sumatrana produces splendid jungle-green leaves, splotched dark red, and lined wine red to maroon. Other varieties can be found with leaves of a similar cast.

M. uranoscopus has stems of a deep rich red when young, with banners of green, waxy leaves and brilliant, long-lasting bracts of vivid red, with small yellow flowers. Pick the flowers, as they should last for up to four weeks when cut. The bracts are rigidly upright, unlike the fruiting types.

M. velutina is a small variety, able to fit into most garden sites. Its fuchsia-pink conical bracts unfurl one at a time to reveal the small yellow flowers. These mature into velvety, deep pink 'self-peeling' inedible little bananas; intriguing, to say the least.

The nearest relation to the banana is *Ensete*, with seven species. Commonly called Abyssinian bananas, these are the giants of the family, growing to a mammoth height. *E. maurelli*, the black banana, boasts enormous, dark plum-coloured leaves, prominently veined, and is truly king-sized. *E. ventricosum* can reach 9 m, growing immense foliage, with deep red midribs and a strange flowerhead of dark reddish brown. Ensetes can withstand salt and spray, and so do well at the beach, although their fabulous foliage suffers if exposed to strong winds.

Nelumbo
Nelumbonaceae

The sacred lotus is one of only two species in this family of deciduous aquatic plants, and comes from Asia and northern Australia. *Nelumbo nucifera* is revered by Buddhists, and Buddha is often portrayed sitting on a lotus leaf. Hindus, too, grow lotus round their temples, and the flower is symbolic of the centre of the universe. The other species, *N. lutea*, is from North America, a yellow-flowering type grown in cooler climates. The favourite sacred lotus grows vigorously and in the garden pool needs to be restrained in containers; single plants can also be cultivated in water jars and large dragon pots. The banana-shaped strong rhizome can be planted straight into barrels and tubs, and treated as you would waterlilies. A soil depth of about 20 cm is sufficient to plant the rhizome, and the height of water above needs to be no more than 60 cm. Lotus plants need to bask in the sun to thrive. Propagation is by division or from the abundant seed.

N. nucifera, sacred lotus, is a tropical treasure; the disc-shaped blue-green leaves hover on the water above long, straight, sturdy stems. Drops of water, quicksilver bright, will ornament the otherwise dry leaves. Lotus blossoms are elegant and fragrant, with silky, delicate petals coloured either white, pink or a milky crimson, with golden stamens. Each perfect flower lasts for up to three days. Conical seedpods follow, almost as ornamental as the beautiful flowers, and coveted by florists for their bold pepperpot appearance. If left, the seedheads bend and spread their seeds into the water, so that soon you will have too many plants.

Nymphaea
Nymphaeceae

Waterlilies are the stars of the ornamental pool. There are 50 species from many areas of the world. All have spreading rootstocks, decorative rounded leaves that float on the surface of the water, and delightful flowers in a rainbow of

Nelumbo nucifera

Nymphaea hybrid

142

different colours, including a heavenly blue. These aquatic plants need sunlight to prosper and flower; half a day's sun at least. A minimum water depth of about 30 cm is also needed, and at least a square metre of water surface per plant, but do not supply them with a fountain as waterlilies like calm surroundings. You can choose from tropical types as well as hardier plants, too. Most of the waterlilies seen in subtropical and tropical gardens are hybrids, and are brightly coloured. Buy your waterlilies from a specialist grower, who will issue planting information. You can propagate from seed or division.

Nymphaea capensis, Cape blue waterlily, from eastern and southern Africa, carries fragrant flowers of a vivid, celestial blue, with bright golden-yellow stamens, tipped blue. A large, elegant waterlily, it opens during the day, and stands well above the water on long, sturdy stems. This plant is often confused with the blue or Egyptian lotus (*N. caerulea*), which has flowers of a much paler hue.

Most of the tropical waterlilies are hybrids of *N. capensis*, *N. lotus*, or *N. mexicana*, and not only do they come in enchanting colours, with double or single flowers, and often serrated leaf edges, but you can choose from night- or day-blooming types. You can pick these beauties for indoors, and they are long lasting. Submerge the blooms up to their necks in water for a few hours before arranging in a container.

N. gigantea is a vigorous waterlily with bold, floating, toothed leaves and bears bright blue flowers held high above the water's surface. Its home waters are in New South Wales, northern Australia and Papua New Guinea.

Ophiopogon
Convallariaceae

With 50 or so species to choose from, these evergreen perennials are valued for their carpeting capabilities. All come from eastern parts of Asia and are collectively called mondo grass. The plants spread via efficient rhizomes, and cover ground quickly. Long-lived, mondo

Ophiopogon japonicus

grass is very useful for many areas of the garden. The modest flowers are small, usually white or lilac, and followed by blue to black berries. Shade suits them, and they are admirable plants for under trees, often thriving where other plants fail. Mondo grass is favoured for city landscaping, and deals with the surrounding pollution very well.

Ophiopogon japonicus, mondo grass, is native to Japan and Korea, and creates a jungle-green shaggy carpet, compact and thick. Much used in Japanese landscaping, and in the west as well, this evergreen perennial masquerading as a grass is dependable and versatile. Plants can be set between paving slabs to introduce textural contrast and soften stark edges. The arching dense leaves give instant cover.

O. planiscapus 'Nigrescens', commonly called black mondo grass, is a handsome cultivar with deep wine to ebony foliage, and grows similarly to its green relation. It makes a stunning contrast to plants with silver or white foliage and flowers.

Kin to the above plants are the liriopes, which

143

Xeronema callistemon

do not creep but soon increase. *Liriope muscari* is low growing, with dense, very dark foliage, near black in some cultivars. The arching, strap-like leaves are spiked with white or lilac to violet flowers in late summer. Liriope does well in moist, shady places, as a border edging or planted in drifts. And how about a few aspidistras to plant in the shade? With shining, large deep green leaves, these are further family members which will enliven dark, damp areas in the garden. Aspidistras make admirable pot plants, too.

Phormuim
Phormiaceae

For versatility and ease of culture, phormiums, New Zealand flaxes, take the prize in gardens from high elevations to the sea. They are dramatic, clumping plants with great structural form and presence, cultivated for their splendid leaves, long and graceful or strongly upright. Much hybridised, flax plants now come in various vivid colours, some striped, in many permutations. They will thrive in containers as well as adding impact to garden borders, and their long flowerheads are magnets to nectar-eating birds. Site New Zealand flaxes in solo positions, or in groups among other perennials or shrubs. Regular trimming of the old leaves and removal

of spent flowerheads is all the care they need. To increase, divide and replant, ensuring the foliage is cut back into a fan shape.

Phormium hybrids are the way to go. You can find them in rich deep reds, dazzling hot pinks and bright citrus yellow, many of them two-toned, and in sizes from dwarf to up to 2 m high.

The small Phormiaceae family has just three genera, and *Xeronema callistemon*, the Poor Knights lily, is another outstanding member. Endemic to the group of northern New Zealand islands from whence it gets its common name, and where it grows in uncomfortable conditions, clinging to rocks, this perennial carries ornamental, shiny, sword-like leaves, and produces unusual, brilliant red racemes, usually in spring. The long stamens of the extraordinay flowers create 15 cm brushes which are held horizontally, and although the plant takes a few years to produce these dramatic flowers, it is worth the wait. The plant's major need in garden conditions is perfectly drained soil, aligned to a sunny spot.

Polianthes tuberosa

For allied plants with spiky leaves and unique flowers, try the two *Doryanthes* species, from Australia's east coast. *D. excelsa*, gymea lily, is spectacular to say the least, with bold, sword-like leaves surrounding the enormous, soaring flower spike, up to 4 m high. Atop this huge stem appears a big cluster of dark red flowers, which arrive in spring and summer. You will have to wait up to 10 years before the gymea lily flowers. *D. palmeri* has similar long leaves, from which emerge a spectacular spangle of bright red flowers clustered at the end of almost horizontal stems which can reach 5 m. Slightly hardier than the gymea lily, this species also flowers earlier in its life.

Polianthes
Agavaceae

Renowned for one member, these perennials hail from Mexico, where they relish the hot, sunny conditions. They have succulent leaves, as do all members of the family, and display flowers in a funnel shape, either white or nearly so, on an upright stem. Fertile, friable soil is essential for their wellbeing, with ample water during flowering. The clumps should be lifted each year, the spent bulbs removed, then replanted in spring.

Polianthes tuberosa, tuberose, is the aristocrat of the family. It has been prized and cultivated for hundreds of years for the intoxicating, heavy perfume of its white blooms, much valued as cut flowers. The oil is extracted from the flowers and forms the basis of some of the finest French perfumes, giving them voluptuous overtones.

Ruellia
Acanthaceae

Ruellias are a genus of some 150 species of evergreen shrubs, subshrubs, and perennials, most coming from the tropics and subtropics. Comely plants, diverse in size, shape and flower, they have funnel-shaped blossoms in colours of blue, pink and red. These are lavishly displayed among dark green leaves. Versatile plants,

Solenostemon scutellarioides

145

ruellias can be planted in sun or part shade, and do not mind dry conditions, once established, so consider some to place under trees. Fertilise generously. Prune back after flowering to encourage new growth, and increase from tip cuttings or seeds. Pests are not a problem.

Ruellia brittoniana, Mexican petunia, does have petunia-like flowers, and is a bushy perennial with small, comely blue flowers. It has naturalised in parts of the United States, so watch its progress in your patch.

Solenostemon
Lamiaceae

From tropical Africa and Asia, the 60 species of *Solenostemon* are shrubby perennials, with just a few suitable for gardens. Formerly they were called coleus and this is still the name most of the genus is known by. The commercial variety is allspice (*Solenostemon amboinicus*), famed for its pungent, piquant flavour. You can grow it in a pot, and cut the leaves for flavouring. They bear a slight tang of thyme.

Coleus appreciate rainfall, rich soil, and plenty of food as they are greedy plants. To keep them bushy and compact, nip out the centres every now and again. They grow quickly, and it is fun to raise the ornamental kind from seed, which should produce a kaleidoscope of colours. Pick out your favourites, and grow them in filtered shade. Caterpillars relish the vibrant leaves, as do other leaf-eating insects. Propagate easily from cuttings or seed.

S. scutellarioides, coleus for short, are great plants for brilliant, almost instant colour, and their vivid foliage will delight for months on end. Leaf colour ranges from green, lime, through to yellow, orange and red and brown, often two- and three-toned. These variegated kinds are so dazzling in colour they can be a challenge to incorporate in the garden scheme. Place them among more sober plants, or in pots to brighten patios and courtyards. The dark, single, ruby red shades make a magnificent splash of colour when placed in generous quantities under palms and foliage trees, a perfect contrast to jungle green.

Spathiphyllum
Araceae

About 40 species of these aroids exist, most from tropical America. Glossy, jungle-green leaves, and generally white spathes among the dense leaf clusters ensure their appeal. Spathiphyllums evolved under the canopy of rainforests and so they do not care for strong sunlight, and need shade and humidity to thrive. Plants appreciate a daily shower in the hot weather. They will spread quite rapidly, becoming decorative groundcovers. Spathiphyllums are favoured house plants, often known as peace lilies. Start off with one, and soon you will need to divide it and divide again. They are very easily transplanted. Moist but free-draining soil is needed.

Spathiphyllum hybrids and cultivars are the way to go. Horticulturists have extended the range and hybrids now come in a large array of flower and leaf sizes. Large, lush tropical foliage and snow-white spathes with prominent spadices are popular types; 'Mauna Loa' is one such introduction. Spathiphyllums are most efficient in removing harmful toxins from the air, and have had the privilege of being included on spacecraft to make life more pleasant.

S. wallisii, white sails, is a small version. This

Zantedeschia hybrid — calla lilies

146

Strelitzia reginae

boasts fragrant flowers, is easygoing and makes an efficient groundcover for the shady garden.

The tough aroid, *Zantedeschia aethiopica*, arum lily, from east and southern Africa, is an alternative for gardens in more exposed situations, also boggy areas, but beware, for if it likes the climate, it will have colonising ambitions. *Z. aethiopica* 'Green Goddess' has large leaves and splashes of green on its large spathes, and its foliage stays attractive year round.

Z. elliottiana, golden arum lily, boasts a sunny yellow spathe surrounding a deeper yellow spadix, and striking spotted, heart-shaped leaves. The hybrids, known as calla lilies, come in a multitude of colours and are commercially grown for the flower trade. Not only lovely to look at, these are long lasting too.

Strelitzia
Strelitziaceae

Strelitzias are from South Africa, a small genus of some five species, which are renowned for their dramatic flowers, likened to some exotic bird. South Africa has some remarkable flowering species, but none more dazzling than strelitzias. Five species have interesting structures in various unlikely colour schemes, and every strelitzia is worth a place in the garden, although it is the amazing bird of paradise that is favoured. Easy to grow, these large perennials prefer a sunny position, free-draining fertile soil and an annual fertiliser treat. They are not easy to divide, as they form thick roots and bold clumps. Pests are no problem.

Strelitzia nicolai, giant bird of paradise, or blue and white strelitzia, is the tallest of the family, and needs a large garden to do it justice. This species grows tree-like, its great leaf fans giving it a resemblance to *Ravenala madagascariensis*, the traveller's palm. It develops light blue, navy and white flowerheads, emerging from a dull red bract. This palm-like strelitzia can become raffish and needs grooming as it grows. *S. alba* is similar in form but obviously has white flowers. Both ultimately make exceptionally large thickets.

S. reginae, bird of paradise or crane flower, is the star of the family, known worldwide for its ravishing blooms. The flower emerges from the

Strelitzia nicolai

succeed. It appreciates moist, humid, semi-shady places, and the traveller's part of its common name is apt, as water is stored in its leaf bases, useful to quench the thirst of the needy passerby. This plant grows in a very distinctive shape. From the amazing symmetrical arrangement of the leaf bases, the banana-like fronds rise and fan out theatrically. A warm wall makes a fine background to this masterpiece, although in the tropics it's usually given stand-alone status. It is not without fault, for unless trimmed frequently the traveller's palm becomes very untidy, and it is vulnerable to strong winds.

Tradescantia
Commelinaceae

These perennials, totalling at least 50, from North and South America, are used mainly as groundcovers or container subjects. Be careful; some creeping tradescantias are ruthless invaders and almost impossible to eradicate. Two only are described here. Tough, quick growing and spreading, ideal as a groundcover and edging, these species will not take over. Grow in sun or half shade, and wherever an easy-care plant is needed.

Tradescantia pallida, purple heart, is characteristic of the genus, its clumps quickly forming a carpet of purple lance-shaped leaves which makes a fine cover in full sun.

T. spathacea, moses-in-the-cradle, boat lily or oyster plant, familiarly called rhoeo, its former botanical name, is a strong plant with boat-shaped upright leaves, a dull dark green above, purple below, with small, typical, tradescantia-type white flowers nestled in the 'cradle'. Growing usually to about 40 cm, with a dwarf form half that height also available, rhoeo is always pleasing to look at, and needs very little attention.

Xanthosoma
Araceae

Natives of steamy parts of tropical South America, xanthosomas for the most part bear edible tubers. Early Spanish and Portuguese

hard, beak-like red sheath placed at right angles to the strong straight stem, and consists of vivid orange petals (the bird's crest), and iridescent peacock-blue petals, quite unique. These flowers will keep coming for six months of the year and need cutting back as they fade. The clumps will grow to a good metre and the banana-like leaves are sage green, veined in red. 'Mandela's Gold' carries blooms with a yellow hue. Strelitzias need space around them to be appreciated, perhaps among rocks or surrounded by an appropriate groundcover.

S. juncea has flowers identical to the bird of paradise, but produces very much taller, reed-like, straight leaves, and is not as widely grown as other species.

There is only one other genus in this decorative family, the riveting traveller's palm, *Ravenala madagascariensis*. A Madagascan, obviously, and not a palm of course, despite its mimicry of one, this plant is not as flexible as its relatives, and needs very warm conditions to voyagers introduced the starchy food to many other hot regions of the world, and the plants are closely related to taro. Many among the 45 species of these aroids are valued for their strikingly ornamental leaves. They prefer moist, sheltered conditions and rich soil. Filtered shade is ideal, away from wind and too much sun. You can use xanthosomas in a variety of ways; as specimens, or for planting in great swathes, or highlighted in containers. Propagate by division of the roots.

Xanthosoma lindenii carries long, arrow-shaped leaves with dazzling, extravagant markings of vivid green and white, on fleshy stems about a metre high. Fast growing, and easy to please, this beauty deserves a site where its foliage stands out.

X. violaceum, blue taro, from the West Indies, is a most handsome plant with its prominently veined, arrow-shaped leaves of a bright green, perfectly balanced on long, deep navy-blue to purple stems. You can eat the tubers if you like.

With bold, sculptural foliage plants becoming so popular, many other xanthosomas are being introduced to subtropical gardens, some with really mammoth leaves.

Zingiber
Zingiberaceae

These gingers are treasured for their edible types, as well as for some fabulous flowerheads. Zingibers number over 100 species, and hail from many tropical areas. They consist of succulent, aromatic, knobbly rhizomes and cane-like stems clothed in long, slender leaves. Humidity, heat and a moist, well-drained soil are requisites for these gingers, which are easily propagated from the rhizomes.

Zingiber spectabile, golden beehive ginger, a most apt common name, is a Malaysian species. The shape of the abundantly produced conical flowerhead is similar to that of an old-fashioned beehive, with its waxy, overlapping, intricate layers of scalloped yellow bracts that turn scarlet. Not only that, bees pollinate the strange wee flowers. Grow this ginger in sultry shade, and if it becomes invasive, as it does in genial climates, you can dig up the rhizomes and cook them.

Edible ginger (*Z. officinale*) should be placed in the kitchen garden, as should the other tasty gingers such as myoga (*Z. mioga*), grown for its flowerbuds. These gingers need cosseting to do well.

The fabulous torch ginger (*Etlingera elatior*) is truly tropical, a magical ginger that does not like to roam out of its milieu. However, the waratahs (*Telopea* species) rival it in dazzling colour and form, so grow one instead if you are in cooler climes.

It is easy to get confused by common names. Despite its nickname of blue ginger, the delightful *Dichorisandra thyrsiflora* is no relation, in fact belonging to the Commelinaceae family, but it is as comely as any ginger. Its cane-like stems can grow to over a metre, and are embellished with deep green leaves, deeply etched, which grow in a spiral fashion. The distinctive flower clusters are dark blue to aubergine, very unusual and most decorative in the house.

Dichorisandra thyrsiflora

149

Cacti and Other Succulents

There are about 2500 species of cacti, and the enormous amount of 10,000 or so species of other succulents. Cacti originate in the Americas, while succulents are found right around the world. Many grow in harsh environments, to which they have adapted admirably; desert plains, rainforests and mountainous regions are all home to these survivors.

Cacti and succulents are uniquely shaped, embellished with fleshy ornamental leaves and stems of all shapes and sizes, unlike other plants. Elegant patterns and precise, strongly defined, symmetrical designs, make them endlessly interesting plants to have. Columnar cacti are living sculptures, and all succulents supply year-round interest in subtle shades and form. Some you simply must touch to feel their texture, appearing as though clad in plush or velvet, while others are sleek. A number surprise with exquisite flowers, a decided bonus.

Plants to suit today's homes and lifestyles, where the emphasis is on clean lines and easy-care gardens, cacti and succulents require minimum maintenance. They thrive in pots and rockeries, do well in warm, well-drained gardens, and add interest to patios and decks. Most do not care for subdued light and prefer sunny positions, but not the jungle cacti, of course. These types are cultivated for their opulent, breathtaking flowers, and need different growing conditions from most cacti.

Left: Cacti in a contrast of form with *Echinocactus grusonii* in the foreground.

Generally cacti and succulents are the least demanding of plants to cultivate. Potted specimens should be raised in specially formulated cacti and succulent mixes, as drainage is so important, but these plants are malleable, and choice is determined by location. Water during summer and apply a slow-release fertiliser. Most are pest free, but occasionally slugs and snails like to dine on the succulent leaves of these well-named plants.

Some cacti are colonisers; the prickly pear (*Opuntia stricta*) has an evil reputation for transgressing. Not all opuntias are so ruthless, and the delightful *O. microdasys*, and the variety *albispina*, fondly callled bunny ears, are well-behaved — but in vulnerable areas, cacti are generally not welcomed.

Superb gardens in which to see a multitude of cacti and succulents include the Jardin Exotique de Monaco, set in a stunning location on the side of a rocky incline overlooking the Mediterranean, and the public garden at the nearby medieval hill town of Èze on the French Riviera. The fantasy gardens of Lotusland in Santa Barbara, the Huntington Gardens of San Marino, and South Africa's Kirstenbosch Gardens likewise display striking collections in dramatic surroundings.

Adenium
Apocynaceae

Adeniums are a small genus of about four species of succulent shrubs from southern Arabia and eastern Africa. They are esteemed for their

151

exotic, trumpet-shaped flowers, in colours from pink to red, are slow growing, and popular for container culture. They do not mind their roots imprisoned, indeed, appear to flower more profusely. Sun-loving plants, adeniums appreciate dry heat, and can rot if they are damaged. They demand perfect drainage but need supplies of water as they develop. The foliage is glossy deep green, prominently veined, and the plants are deciduous in droughts. Pests are sometimes a problem, especially scale insects. You can increase from seed.

Adenium obesum, desert rose, mock azalea, impala lily, grows easily, and carries fleshy flowers in white, varying shades of pink and red, usually with a deeper crimson margin. The bright, opened-faced flowers are long lasting, and show up well against the modest foliage which grows on the top of the sturdy round stems. Named cultivars are sometimes available.

Agave
Agavaceae

Agaves originate in the warm areas of the Americas, the majority from Mexico and Central America. Mammoth succulents on the whole, with arresting, fleshy leaves, agaves are designer plants. They do not bloom for many years, and after the flower cluster dies, the whole foliage clump dies, too, and must be removed. Usually there are dozens of offshoots to take their place.

Agaves prefer the drier subtropics, but are remarkably tolerant and resilient plants, invaluable as garden focal points. They do well at the beach, and in Mediterranean-style gardens, and contrast well with rocks and groundcovers or when teamed with smaller succulents. Usually, agaves have sword-shaped leaves equipped with lethal spikes. It is wise to clip their tips. Very good drainage is important

Agave attenuata

152

These desirable aloes have impressive foliage and are embellished with flamboyant flowers.

for their wellbeing, but they do not relish drought conditions. Pests and diseases do not appear to be a concern. Propagate from the numerous offsets.

Agave americana, century plant, from Mexico, grows into a large specimen and needs space to do so. It produces big rosettes of giant, stiff, olive-green leaves, complete with harmful hooked spikes. Place your mature century plants away from pathways. When small they will decorate terracotta pots effectively, especially the popular variegated varieties such as 'Marginata', with leaves piped in bright yellow. Do not expect flowers for at least ten years, but the wait is worthwhile; eventually the century plant sends up a 9-metres spike covered with fluffy flowers in chartreuse to topaz.

A. attenuata is a favourite, having fleshy, milky-jade leaves without spines. It is the clean, sophisticated structure that is so admired, and the fabulous colouring of its rosettes. *A. attenuata*

will produce a mammoth flower spike in lime green, but takes many years to do so. It is an ideal succulent to surround with stones, or display in groups, and needs space to show off its sculptured form.

With their strong silhouettes, agaves are outstanding architectural plants. There are hundreds to choose from and as their qualities continue to be appreciated, new varieties in fascinating shapes and colour schemes are constantly being released.

So closely related to agaves that it is not easy to tell them apart are furcraeas, which come from the same regions as agaves, and like the same conditions.

Aloe
Asphodelaceae

Over 300 species of aloes exist, coming from Madagascar, Africa and the Middle East, in sizes from midgets to giants. These plants are

Aloe polyphylla

renowned for their brilliant flowers as well as their fascinating shapes and textures. Aloes produce flowers in stemmed clusters in warm shades, full of nectar, which birds appreciate, especially in winter when most aloes flower. Sun-lovers, this agreeable genus of succulents are tolerant, easy to grow, and happy at the beach. They are rather shallow rooted, even the large tree-sized types, and are great for containers. Aloes need space around them to grow and show off their strongly defined form. You can put stones against the roots to anchor the plants in position. Well-drained soil is essential, but aloes are easygoing, and child's play to increase from their abundant offsets. Snails and slugs like to dine on their fleshy leaves. Just a few are described here, but the choice is overwhelming.

Aloe candelabrum, candelabra aloe, is one of the larger aloes, well regarded and a handsome plant from the hot valleys of Natal. It produces thick, bright red, upright flower spikes, candelabra-like, from the centre of a big rosette of arched, broad, pointed leaves, which are outlined with small teeth. Candelabra aloe is at its best while still young, as it grows rather raffish as it matures, the older leaves hanging untidily.

A. ferox, bitter aloe, from southern Africa, is also one of the larger types, and develops bright golden orange to red flowerheads on an upright stem from its thick rosette of steel-blue leaves which are deckle-edged in red.

A. plicatilis, fan aloe, is a medium-sized bushy species, with an interesting shape. The leaves fold like a fan, and are bluish green, long and rounded. The abundant fans grow on the ends of the strong branches. It will grow untidily unless checked.

A. polyphylla, spiral aloe, is an endangered species in its original home of Lesotho, and is famed for its intricate spiralled rosette, so precise it might have been measured on a computer. Give the spiral aloe prominence in the garden or display in a container where its amazing architectural qualities can be fully appreciated. The fleshy leaves are bright green. This is one of the smaller species and will take many years to reach flowering size, but it is not grown for its blooms. Try a trio.

A. thraskii, coast aloe, so named for obvious reasons, bears striking, upright, dense, strong flowers, golden and candle-like, most impressive when silhouetted against the sky.

So many aloes are available. Take your pick. *A. vera* is good to grow in a pot, handy to the house, to use for burns and bites, and is soothing on the skin, while *A. stricta*, coral aloe, bears bright, showy coral flowers and pretty foliage, minus prickles, and *A. bainesii*, tree aloe, is indeed tree-size.

Cereus
Cactaceae

With 40 or so species, these columnar cacti are mostly large and impressive, with slate-blue to grey-green stems, clothed in ribbed spines. The night-blooming flowers, white or cream in colour, appear at random all along the fleshy stems. Quick to grow and vigorous, cereus are often used for grafting on to more delicate relations. Their thorns dictate their position in the garden. Place them against walls, or in a place where their definite columns cast interesting shadows, and make focal points. Surround cereus

Aeonium arboreum 'Zwartkop'

Crassula
Crassulaceae

Most crassulas come from South Africa. About 300 species make up this variable genus, with myriad hybrids and cultivars. Many are small, and usually grown in pots; collectors' items. Some are cultivated for their brilliant flowers, and a few of the most popular are described here. Crassulas need well-drained soil as you would expect, and a supplement of leaf mould is beneficial. Easy-care plants, they are simply increased from cuttings.

Crassula coccinea is cultivated for its brilliant, vivid scarlet flowers, massed together in a dense, flat head atop sturdy stalks. It's a small, nuggety plant, so you will need several for maximum impact. Accompanied by spiky succulents and those with grey or green leaves, these crassulas are at their finest.

C. ovata, jade plant, is perfect for pots, and appears to be a miniature tree. Jungle-green, glossy, rounded leaves, framed in red, grow on a strong stem, which soon branches out. In bright sun the leaves change colour and become entirely red. The variety 'Tricolor' is a favourite for its bright leaves of yellow, green and red, colours that turn more intense in full sun.

Crassulas belong to a large family, and are near relations of aeoniums, echeverias, sedums and sempervivums. *Aeonium arboreum* 'Zwartkop' is a spectacular cultivar. Its rich, deep wine to black, glossy rosettes add drama to the garden, and look even more eyecatching when juxtaposed with other dark-leaved plants, such as black mondo grass.

Echeveria
Crassulaceae

Succulents of renown, with over 150 species, mainly from Mexico, echeverias are delightful plants. Easy-care, always attractive, they consist of tightly packed rosettes in cool colours but often flushed pink to red. Perfect in pots or in the open, dry part of the garden, they multiply with great efficiency, and regularly produce

with contrasting shapes, round, smooth stones perhaps, or team with aesthetically pleasing succulent associates. Barrel cactus (*Echinocactus grusonii*), its rounded green globes equipped with golden daggers, is particularly complementary. Cereus increase from cuttings or fresh seed.

Cereus 'Monstrosus' is a notable cultivar, a curious living sculpture, with jade-green contorted stems, ribbed and gently spined. Place it where its unusual structure can be seen to advantage.

C. uruguayanus, Peruvian torch, is native to several South American countries, and a popular species. It produces branching columns, prominently ribbed and spined, which grow to a respectable size, and is a dramatic but stalwart cactus. The attractive white or cream flowers, backed with a deep brick red, arrive from dusk to dawn.

Many more species of cereus will be available for interested collectors. Other cacti were previously placed with cereus, and the botanical name has continued with these genera: *Cephalocereus, Hylocereus, Pachycereus, Pilosocereus, Selinicereus*, and more.

Echeveria pulvinata

nodding, bell-shaped flowers, often two-toned, on sturdy stems. They are almost self-sufficient, but require an open, gritty soil, with some water in dry weather, and need to be groomed every now and then to remove old, dead leaves. Slugs and snails can be a nuisance.

Echeveria elegans, hen and chicks, shares its common name with *E.* x *imbricata*. Both have rounded, symmetrical, ground-hugging rosettes in pleasing, cool slate blue to pearly grey green shades, and the ability to reproduce constantly. In rockeries, containers or in a dry area of the garden, these echeverias will provide a living mosaic.

Echeverias are much hybridised and available in their hundreds, and generally develop big rosettes, some extravagantly frilled, others deckle-edged or even waved. Their colours change with the seasons; pink, lavender, grey, and steel-blue rosettes are usual. You may need to acquire them from specialist nurseries.

Also from Mexico is *Sedum morganianum*, indulgently called donkey or burro's tail, a succulent to grow in hanging baskets to show off its cascades of soft milky-jade fleshy stems. These grow to about a metre long, and are most decorative. Small pink flowers arrive at stem tips, but are quite incidental.

x *Epicactus*
Cactaceae

Epiphyllum species number around 20 and come from the jungles of Mexico and northern South America, but it is their dazzling hybrids that are mainly cultivated today. Thousands of these have been created, and given the general name of x *Epicactus*, orchid cactus. These hybrids share parentage with other beauties from the rainforests. They have unconventional, flattened stems with scalloped edges, without prickles but not particularly attractive. Some are upright, but others flop downwards and are best in hanging baskets where they can appear almost graceful, but should only be brought into prominence when they bear their magnificent flowers.

Orchid cacti can be grown in orchid mix with added humus. Jungle dwellers, in nature these semi-epiphytic species grow in filtered light under the canopy of trees, and good drainage is most important. They appreciate feeding and water in dry periods, especially before flowering, which usually takes place in early summer.

Echeveria elegans

156

Although tough plants, these hybrids are vulnerable to slugs, snails, aphids, scale insects and mealy bug. You can grow them in lath or shade houses, under a veranda, or in trees. Cuttings take readily.

x *Epicactus*, orchid cacti, produce dazzling, opulent flowers in glorious technicolour. Some are as exotic as an Indian sari, in a rainbow of iridescent shades which range from white, cream, through to yellow, all the pinks, red, crimson and many nuances in between. Some flower at night, others are scented, but they all share bold, often luminous blooms, funnel-shaped, spilling out of the spineless stems. Flowers vary in shape and size, too. There are so many species involved in the hybrids that the choice is enormous.

One of the species used in hybridising is the amazing *Nopalxochia phyllanthoides*, sometimes called waterlily cactus, with pendulous flattened stems from which spill exquisite flowers in a cascade of watermelon pink. A cultivar, 'Deutsche Kaiserin', is now placed with all the x *Epicactus*.

Another epiphytic cactus, native to South America, is chain cactus (*Rhipsalis paradoxa*) from Brazil, which prefers shade or part shade, and has slender, trailing, cylindrical stems. This can be grown in hanging baskets or in the forks of trees. It is very different from the flamboyant orchid cactus, and carries insignificant flowers, but is admired for its foliage form. There are other species to try, and they all appreciate humid conditions.

Euphorbia
Euphorbiaceae

The succulent euphorbias are part of this diverse genus, and are numerous. Many hail from South Africa, and appreciate a dry spell, but are amenable plants in the garden, where they do best in a warm, sunny, sheltered position. Some mimic cacti and grow in weird and wonderful shapes, wickedly spiked, as though carved by an imaginative but nasty sculptor. Many of these are more for the collector. All can be propagated from cuttings.

Euphorbia ingens, tree euphorbia, naboom, is a notable tree-sized succulent with a straight, sturdy trunk topped by many upright stems formed of four-winged segments. Tree euphorbias do well at the coast.

E. milii is known commonly as crown of thorns. It's an apt name for this ominous-looking, sprawling succulent shrub, which is cultivated for its very bright red bracts, carried all year round. The plant is armed with bayonet-sharp thorns on twisted stems, and can look effective in a container, sited away from walkways. Crown of thorns is a good coastal plant, and comes from Madagascar. The hybrids come in softer colour schemes that include yellow, orange and pink; they vary in size, but are all equipped with weapons. You can train a plant into a sphere, or latticed, and it is more ornamental this way.

Try other succulent euphorbias, such as the unusual *E. horrida*, which lives up to its name. It consists of thick, undulating stems liberally coated with spikes, and looks like some sea creature from the depths.

Another curious plant to try is *Pedilanthus tithymaloides*, rick rack plant, from the West Indies. From another genus, but belonging to the same euphorbia family, this species is a bushy succulent notable for its zigzag stems. The variegated forms are very popular, and sport white to pink tints on the bright green leaves.

Kalanchoe
Crassulaceae

A variable genus of succulents, climbers, perennials, shrubs and giant tree-like plants, kalanchoes come from Africa and Madagascar for the most part, with a few from Asia. There are about 150 species, mainly grown for their interestingly shaped and textured leaves, and a few for their vivid, long-lasting blooms. Kalanchoes are usually fast growing and will succeed in sun or some shade, and make good house plants. Well-drained soil is essential. They are easily propagated from either leaf or stem cuttings, and many produce tiny plantlets.

K. beharensis, elephant ear, from Madagascar,

Kalanchoe beharensis with *Echeveria elegans*

is noted for its foliage; waved, big leaves of a steely grey green are borne on a shrub-like plant. This needs a sheltered spot, and fertile soil.

K. blossfeldiana, flaming Katy, is a small, neat, shrubby plant, ideal for pots or for planting en masse in the garden. It produces deep green, glossy, deckle-edged leaves in profusion, and big clusters of bright scarlet flowers held above the leaves. It is the hybrids that are most admired. These arrive in bold colours of yellow, orange and red, and shades in between.

K. tomentosa, panda plant, from Madagascar, has striking leaves, silvery grey, furry and fat, edged with woolly brown dots, but not at all like a panda, although it is a pet of a plant. It thrives in pots, on a deck or outdoors, and grows well in the dry garden.

Pereskia
Cactaceae

Pereskias are cacti native to Mexico and Brazil, with 16 species. Primitive plants, these spiny shrubs, trees and climbers do not appear to be cacti at first glance, as they develop leaves and are deciduous. It is their spines that give them away, and you must be careful where you site them. Sun-loving, although they will grow in semi-shade, pereskias bear pretty flowers in many colours. Light soil suits them, and dry conditions in winter. They are easily propagated from cuttings.

Pereskia grandiflora, rose cactus, from Brazil, is a shrubby type, with dense leaves and spiny stems. It makes a good barrier hedge. The shrubs will lose their leaves for a few weeks in winter, but in spring are alight with large flower clusters in glowing rose pink to fuchsia shades.

The climbing kind, *P. aculeata*, flowers briefly, and is equipped with large thorns. Some selections produce golden leaves.

Schlumbergera
Cactaceae

From southern Brazil, schlumbergeras are a small genus of jungle cacti. Long-lived, they can outlast their owners, and are grown worldwide as house plants. These small, bushy cacti, happily growing in trees in nature, are well suited to cultivation in containers, especially hanging baskets. They do best in well-drained, humus-rich soil, or a commercial orchid mix, and need copious amounts of water when they bud and bloom, and a supply of fertiliser such as blood and bone. Place the plants in a dry, shady place in the garden or greenhouse when they are not in bloom and do not water, because they must have a rest period after flowering. Cuttings root readily when placed in damp gritty soil or river sand, or even in water.

Schlumbergera cultivars and hybrids are bred for large flowers and shapely plants, with flat, jointed and arching stems. They carry flowers of many shades and hues: shimmery pink, red, gold and magenta predominate, often with two-toned effects. You will find named varieties.

S. truncata, crab or lobster cactus, is so named for its flattened stems, crab-like and hooked. Its flowers are flame red, with selections in white, pink, orange and apricot, and they have spreading, pointed petals.

Bromeliads

The Bromeliaceae family consists of approximately 46 genera, several thousand species and a bewildering number of hybrids and cultivars. They probably evolved in the Andes region, and now extend up through South America, Panama and Central America, right to some southern states of the United States. There is one exception to this, for a rogue genus comes surprisingly from Africa. Some bromeliads are terrestrial, others epiphytic, flourishing in trees, on rocks, or clinging to cliffs. All are well able to adapt to their surroundings, which can range from steamy jungles to deserts. They are assisted in survival techniques by their rosetted cups, which efficiently catch water and nutrients.

Bromeliads differ greatly in appearance. Some amaze with their brilliant inflorescences in glowing colour, while others are esteemed for the luminous light of their distinctive foliage, strong outlines and structural form. Their diversity makes bromeliads endlessly fascinating. The luscious pineapple (*Ananas comosus*) was the first bromeliad to be enjoyed by westerners, and very much later came the ornamentals. Many are collectors' plants. Tillandsias come from miniature to large (Spanish moss being the most well known), and could be described as the most curious, while billbergias are the most hybridised, and dyckias, puyas and pitcairneas are just a few of the more demanding to grow.

Most bromeliads enjoy high humidity, and some shelter. Ideal plants to grow in or under palms, tree ferns, or perched on branches, bromeliads are exemplary designer plants and excellent container subjects. Whether flaunted in courtyards and entranceways as specimens, or nestled amongst groundcovers to hide the pots, they provide moveable feasts for the eyes, easily shifted to prominence as they colour and flower. Alternatively they can be grown in exuberant drifts, as seen in tropical resorts and parks around the world.

Adaptable plants, bromeliads do need very efficient drainage with an open, porous growing medium, and most require filtered light, although brighter light levels will ensure optimum leaf colouration in certain species. Fertilise sparingly if at all; growers have differing opinions on manure additives. Make sure bromeliads have well-filled 'cups' or 'vases' of water, and efficient air circulation.

Beware; bromeliads are addictive — and they are seldom cheap to buy. Fortunately, most are generous in the production of their offsets or 'pups', and multiply quickly. To find out more about them, join your local bromeliad society, where enthusiasts share their knowledge and new varieties are often traded.

Aechmea
Bromeliaceae

A versatile genus of 170 species, from Central and South America, with numerous hybrids, aechmeas are among the most widely grown bromeliads. Mainly epiphytic, they thrive in pots, and some will grow on rocks. While most appreciate filtered light, a few species need full sun to shine. All like shelter, and humid conditions. Aechmeas have shapely leaves which are frequently decorated with contrasting bands and spots, often in silver or dark wine, almost black. Some have prominent spines, others none at all, and they produce long-lasting, colourful flower spikes, many with bright berries. It is important to make sure their efficient leafy 'cups' are kept full of water, especially in hot weather when they may need a shower every few days. Aechmeas are a pleasure to grow, adaptable and easy-care. The following is just a tiny sample of all the amazing aechmeas you can grow without bother.

Diversity of form and colour from a collection of healthy bromeliads is satisfying to the eye.

Palms and bromeliads are ideal companions, the bromeliads appreciating the dappled shade.

Aechmea caudata, from southern Brazil, is an easy-care species to grow, and has many variegated types too, with leaves striped and banded. Upright flower clusters of bright golden bracts and yellow petals adorn the plants for many months. They like some sun.

A. fasciata, from Brazil, is cultivated for its strong, grey-green leaves, crossbanded with frosty silver swirls, and for its amazing inflorescences; baby-pink, tight clusters of bracts from which peep the bright sky-blue buds and flowers. These pyramidical inflorescences last for many months. Indirect light ensures successful blooming. Many varieties of this species are available.

A. 'Foster's Favourite', has shiny dark leaves as though lacquered with wine-red paint. The drooping flowerheads are prettily coloured in salmon and blue, followed by orange berries. You can grow this beautiful aechmea indoors if you wish.

A. gamosepala, from southern Brazil and Argentina, grows readily in semi-shaded spots, and in no time you will have swathes of these strong plants. Smooth, shiny, bright green leaves surround tall, cylindrical flowerheads of bright pink and blue flowers.

A. recurvata comes from several South American countries. All varieties in this group require strong sunlight to convert their foliage into dazzling, sunny terracotta and orange shades, just before flowering. Vivid coned inflorescences sit in the middle of the recurved leaves.

Above: Ground-covering bromeliads, mainly *Neoregelia* hybrids, make brilliant accents.
Top left: *Guzmania* 'Ostara' in flower with a spotted neoregelia. Top right: *Alcantarea imperialis* 'Rubra'.

Billbergia
Bromeliaceae

Billbergias, epiphytic bromeliads, are numerous, a large genus from eastern Brazil in the main, with some native to Argentina, Mexico and Central America as well. Versatile, tolerant plants, they take kindly to living in pots, but many will grow well in the open ground in the general garden. In their natural habitats, billbergias flourish in bulky clumps in humid places with ample light. They are admired mainly for their flowers, which contrast unusual colours in dramatic combinatons, often in three and four distinct opposite hues. With a bewildering variety of species and hybrids to choose from, you cannot go wrong by starting with any of the following tried and true.

Billbergia amoena produces especially handsome leaves, usually with a red flush, although some stay glossy light green. Bright red bracts open to reveal the small, green, blue-tipped flowers. There are many varieties and named selections.

B. nutans, queen's tears, native to Brazil and Argentina, is the most widely grown species. True survivors, often seen in old gardens along with other plants, queen's tears are not generally recognised as bromeliads. Their narrow leaves are not showy, but the graceful flowers on arching slender stems are dainty and multi-coloured. Shell-pink bracts, brightening more to coral, open to show soft apple-green flowers, bejewelled with violet and red sepals. Pick them for the vase while still in bud — they are long lasting. Other species have similar inflorescences.

B. pyramidalis is as amenable as any brome-liad, and has been a popular plant with gardeners for a great many years. This species from Brazil is robust, forming dense, vase-shaped clumps with bold upright, lolly-pink bracts, and flowers that open to sky blue with hints of mauve. *B. pyramidalis* var. *concolor* is a much admired, medium-sized plant which produces vivid, clear red bracts and rosy red flowers that grow on sturdy stalks.

Guzmania
Bromeliaceae

As lush and exotic as any bromeliad, guzmanias shine with flowerheads as brilliant and unexpected as fireworks. These shoot up, star-like, from central funnel-shaped rosettes of glossy green foliage. Compact and mostly small growing, in general guzmanias are epiphytic. They are native to rainforests of tropical America, and so appreciate high humidity, consistently warm temperatures and filtered shade, but will tolerate some early-morning or late-afternoon sun. Good as house plants, guzmanias are seen gracing hotel foyers, enlivening shopping malls and decorating waterfalls in splendid tropical landscapes, as well as lighting up home gardens. Guzmanias create a luxuriant groundcover, as they multiply most efficiently. Be generous with their water supplies, making sure these treasures have their cups full at all times, and use a porous potting mix, as you do with all bromeliads.

Guzmania lingulata is one of the most familiar of the species. It boasts sealing-wax scarlet bracts and little white flowers, and appreciates shaded areas. A nuggety plant, it reproduces without fuss. You may find several variations of the species.

Much hybridised, guzmanias can be obtained with tantalising names such as 'Cherry', 'Orangeade', 'Grapeade' and 'Fantasia', some as jungle-like and improbable as a Rousseau painting.

Neoregelia
Bromeliaceae

About 70 species of these epiphytes exist, many from Brazil. Neoregelias are probably the most familiar and popular of all bromeliads, widely known widely for their flamboyant foliage and versatility. These plants are competent survivors, being provided with generous rosetted cups, water reservoirs really. They need little attention so long as they have warmth and humidity, and are given generous supplies of water in hot weather to fill their cups. These can become full of debris, or even mosquito larvae, so need to be flushed out every now and then. Neoregelias are much decorated with stripes or blotched with contrasting colour, and many have hearts of vivid red. They need bright or filtered light to bring out the radiance of their leaves, and can be grown in pots, in the ground, where their roots will spread, or as house plants. It is necessary to look down upon neoregelias to appreciate their beauty. Plant them in pots and surround them with carpeting plants for best effect. Pests are not a great problem.

The following are just a handful from the many neoregelias available. Consult specialist catalogues for more; the hardest part will be trying to choose from the dozens on offer.

Neoregelia carolinae, blushing bromeliad, heart of flame, is a superior species, highlighted for at least half the year in a dazzle of flame to cherry-red foliage prior to developing the tiny, inconspicuous, soft violet flowers. These are absolute aristocrats of plants, and if you have room for only a few bromeliads, *N. carolinae* and its numerous hybrids will never disappoint. Look for 'Tricolor', 'Red Nest', and 'Sheer Joy', just for a start.

N. concentrica has strong leaves in a compact rosette, gloriously splashed in deep wine or purple, with red tips and bands of silver on the undersides. The hearts turn purple at flowering time, and just to make things interesting, the small flowers are blue.

Vriesea fosteriana 'Rubra' with its unusual markings is set off by the smaller contrasting bromeliads.

Nidularium
Bromeliaceae

A small genus of about 45 species, all native to eastern Brazil, nidulariums grow in shady, humid rainforests. They are compact but variable plants, either terrestial or epiphytic. Those in cultivation are usually small or medium-sized, and noted for their distinctive nest of bright, long-lasting contrasting collarettes of inner leaves, complete with tiny flowers. Nidulariums are easy to grow provided they receive ample water, and you can pop them in the ground without a qualm, although they are quite at home in containers, too. Site them in semi-shaded areas under trees, palms or tree ferns.

Nidularium fulgens makes a good accent plant. Site it to show off its distinct form and bold brilliance of shiny chartreuse, picotee-edged rosettes, with the contrast of glowing cerise bracts.

N. innocentii, tried and true, is a medium-sized bromeliad with spreading, broad, dark green leaves, darker decided midrib, and purple undersides. The prominent inner rosette is a garnet red. There are many varieties of this species which do well in the garden, especially when sheltered by filtered shade from surrounding trees.

Vriesea
Bromeliaceae

Vrieseas extend from Mexico down as far as Argentina, but most species are native to Brazil. Their way of life differs greatly, with some calling the coasts home, while others cling to misty mountains. Most are epiphytes, and those commonly cultivated are the smaller types from warm, sultry forests. They are a delight to grow.

Vrieseas appreciate moderate, filtered light, and good air circulation. Frequent mist watering is the ideal in the hotter months. Grow them in pots, on tree branches, or in the ground; as long as they have humidity and shelter, they will thrive. Some flaunt highly ornamental leaves, others are cherished for their erect, colourful flower spikes. With so many available, including many new high-voltage hybrids, it is difficult to make a choice, but any of the splendid species described below would be worthwhile garden additions.

Vriesea carinata, nicknamed lobster claw, from rainforests of eastern Brazil, is a small species with soft, fresh green leaves in small rosettes, bearing flowerheads on short, upright stems in fiery, shiny bracts of sealing-wax red at the base, turning to yellow and slightly curved, hence the common name. Easily placed in the garden in pots, or grown in tree ferns, *V. carinata* makes an ideal house plant when it is in colour, as it is for many months. 'Mariae' is a popular hybrid.

V. hieroglyphica, commonly called the king of bromeliads, is aptly named, as it has a regal look and always attracts attention. It bears big, bold, glossy, vivid green leaves, richly marked with jungle-green waves and bands. Eventually it forms a tall flowerhead, not particularly handsome but no matter; this plant is prized for its opulent foliage. Do keep the generous rosettes full of water. This very fine accent plant can grow to a metre high and wide, but is reluctant to produce offsets, and takes many years to do so.

V. splendens, flaming sword, from Trinidad, Guiana and Venezuela, grows naturally on the floors of damp shady forests and on rocks and trees too. This medium-sized species proved an instant success when introduced to western gardens, and was already being hybridised by the 1880s. No wonder, for it carries splendid rosettes of arched, deep jungle-green leaves, crossbanded with deep wine, from which emerges an impressive lance-shaped inflorescence of vivid scarlet and orange.

Orchids

To say orchids are numerous is an understatement, as there are probably in excess of 25,000 species and countless registered hybrids. The great majority of these fascinating plants are native to warm, humid, primarily tropical and subtropical areas, but are certainly found in cooler zones, too. New Guinea has the honour of being home to more orchid species than anywhere else.

Orchids are still waiting to be discovered, and plant collectors venture into the wild to find rare and unnamed species. There is a worldwide ban on importing endangered and very scarce orchids.

Ephiphytic genera are mainly from humid tropical rainforests, while terrestrial types are usually understorey plants, and more likely to be from the subtropics and temperate zones. Plants of infinite variety, orchids are addictive, and it is easy to start with one and end up with hundreds. Some species display flowers tiny and intricate, others can be big and brazen. Part of their allure is their voluptuous looks, and intriguing structure; blatant sexuality on show, not to mention their outstanding tints and tones and vivid colour contrasts.

Some species are fragrant, and many Oriental cymbidiums are bred especially for their bewitching aroma. The Japanese cultivate scented orchids to perfume their houses, competitions being held for the sole purpose of finding the best fragrances.

Not many orchids are used as food products, other than the pods of the vanilla orchid, and the dried tubers of a certain wild terrestrial orchid, made into salep, an edible starch from which is concocted a Turkish ice cream, a renowned national delicacy.

Orchids were once expensive to buy, as they took so long to grow, but now, with meristem culture, clusters of tiny plants are produced very quickly in flasks; test-tube babies, superior hybrids.

The culture of orchid species varies greatly, from light requirements to heat, food and soil and potting mix. In general, it is fair to say that perfect drainage is necessary, regular watering, and application of a nitrogen-rich, slow-release fertiliser, although most orchids have a rest period when watering and feeding is not needed.

Adaptable plants, orchids will thrive in containers or grown outdoors in the comfortable climate of the subtropics. With experience, and help from other growers, you will find orchids are not difficult to grow. Their seductive, fleshy flowers have a mystique all their own, and epitomise the perfume, colour and exotic plant forms that make gardens in warmer climates so alluring.

Cattleya
Orchidaceae

Epiphytes from humid jungles, cattleyas originate in Central and South America. They are a huge tribe, and contain intergeneric hybrids

Cattleya hybrids

Cymbidium hybrids

167

galore, with a bewildering parentage. (More cattleyas and their multitude of hybrids are registered than for any other orchid genus.) Truly dramatic orchids, voluptuous, with romantic allure, cattleyas are famed for their 'look at me' colours, and come in varying sizes. In the subtropics, these orchids will grow in forks of trees, or happily in containers in a loose potting mix; coarse bark, charcoal and spaghnum moss are often used. Consult an expert or acquire a good orchid book before you embark on the cultivation of these prima donnas.

Cattleya Bifoliate Hybrids, cluster cattleya, are quite at home nestling in tree branches, as long as they get a good bright light, and are often seen in the trunks of frangipani and tree ferns in warm areas. These hybrids, from parents almost as colourful, have clusters of dainty flowers in an amazing range of tones.

C. Unifoliate Hybrids are the darlings of the breed, and beloved of florists for their bold ruffled blooms in two-toned extravagant shades.

Other hybrid orchids in the cattleya group include the magnificent x *Brassocattleya* and x *Laeliacattleya*, with an enormous range. A good species to grow is *Laelia anceps*, an uncomplicated orchid needing full sun and miminal attention.

From Central and South America come the oncidiums, a large genus of orchids; those cultivated are the epiphytic types. Flowers are generally in warm colours of brown and yellow, carried on large, arching sprays. Dainty orchids, oncidiums require excellent drainage and filtered shade. They are related to miltonias and odontoglossums.

Cymbidium
Orchidaceae

Cymbidiums are terrestial orchids, and number over 40 species. In the wild they claim southern and eastern Asia and easten Australia as their homes, the species thriving in high regions with good rainfall, but it is the large-flowered hybrids and miniatures that home gardeners grow. Only suitable where the climate is cool at night during

the summer months, cymbidiums can be grown outside, either in pots, or in the ground under the shelter of trees, but they must receive some sun to bloom. You can tell whether plants are receiving enought light by leaf colour; plants with almost lime-green leaves flower more. They are an impressive lot, producing long, arching sprays of numerous flowers in delightful colour combinations. Of all the huge orchid family, cymbidiums are the most widely grown. Orchid mix and perfect drainage are keys to success, and these orchids need feeding regularly. Many gardeners have their favourite liquid fertilisers. After flowering, you can divide your cymbidiums and repot. Snails and slugs enjoy the flower buds, also ants and mites.

Cymbidium Large-flowered Hybrids, are available in countless numbers of named cultivars, and are usually selected by colour. They come in shades of white, cream, lime green to leaf green, and pink, tomato red, through to bronze, full-bodied mahogany and dark choc- olate. Cymbidiums have prominent, brightly coloured 'lips' which contrast with the petals, and some are decidedly brazen in appearance.

C. lowianum is an elegant species from the mountains of many parts of Asia. One of the earliest species brought to Europe, it is still well worth growing in the garden. It develops fine leaves with numerous long, arching flower stems and delicate blooms, finely petalled, in a winning colour combination of light green to chartreuse flowers with a cream and crimson lip. Tough and easy to grow, these orchids are most floriferous.

C. Miniature Hybrids have become increasingly popular because of their neat habit and compact size; their flowers are small editions of their larger relations and just as attractive. They are easy to place in the garden, and make good companions for tree ferns and palms. Many of the oriental cymbidiums are cultivated especially for their delicate fragrance.

If you are seeking wildly fragrant orchids, look no further than the zygopetalums, an epiphytic genus from the Americas. Not only are the flowers stained and spotted in rich, unusual colours, but they exude an alluring perfume, with citrus overtones.

Dendrobium
Orchidaceae

Dendrobiums have the distinction of being one of the largest genera in the orchid family, with about 1200 species, and countless hybrids. Their range is wide, from New Guinea and Australia, to New Zealand, Fiji, India and Japan. So large and variable is the genus that it is divided into sections for convenience. Some like it hot, others prefer a benign climate, and there are those for cool areas. Those mentioned here do best in warm conditions, but are adaptable. Hybrids abound, and many are grown commercially for the cut-flower trade, especially in Southeast Asia and Hawaii. Growing conditions vary, but all dendrobiums require a well-drained potting or planting mix, and coarse bark is often used. Most dendrobiums require a rest period. As with all orchids, it is wise to refer to specialists for cultivation advice.

Dendrobium bigibbum, Cooktown orchid, the floral emblem of Queensland, will flower for many months, and is a doddle to grow in warm gardens. The Cooktown orchid, an epiphyte, can be accommodated in the branch of a tree (but not one that sheds its bark) and does not need any fussing over. It grows from pseudobulbs, and produces strong leaves and sprays of deep rose to fuchsia-pink blooms not unlike phalaenopsis flowers. White, mauve and magenta flowers are not uncommon. Much hybridising has been done with this entrancing species in Australia. Never use soil for the growing medium.

D. kingianum, pink rock orchid, from eastern Australia, forms clumps from the numerous small pseudobulbs. Dull green leaves are

Dendrobium nobile

169

Dendrobium speciosum

lightened by dainty flowers in shades of pink to mauve and white, on arching stems. They usually bloom in winter, and can be grown in pots. This species will put up with cool conditions.

D. nobile comes from Burma, India, Thailand and surrounds, and is mainly cultivated for the stunning hybrids. In nature they are used to wet, hot summers and cool, almost dry winter climates, and this is a guide to their care. These hybrids come in a wealth of colour combinations, and are delicately fragrant.

D. speciosum, king orchid, rock orchid, ranges across the eastern seaboard of Australia, and is a large, robust plant with big pseudobulbs and tough leaves. The amazingly floriferous, arching racemes of white, cream or yellow flowers, with a contrasting lip, hang in profusion, and have an elusive fragrance. You can grow this tree orchid in the forks of two sturdy branches, where the magnificent flower trusses will be displayed to great advantage. Australia has about 50 species of dendrobiums, and all are in cultivation.

Epidendrum
Orchidaceae

Epidendrums number over 1000 species and theirs is one of the largest of the orchid family. Some are reed-like and others have pseudobulbs. As they come from a great variety of latitudes, climates, and altitudes, from seacoasts to mountains, epidendrums require differing conditions, but many do well outdoors in benign climates. Those described here are simple to grow in the home garden. They are child's play to increase, possible by division or from offsets.

Epidendrum ibaguense, crucifix orchid, is the most well known of the tribe, originating in Mexico down to Columbia. Tolerant and adaptable, crucifix orchids will grow from temperate zones to the tropics. They thrive happily in the ground, growing on cane-like stems to over a metre in height. These orchids are inclined to be lax and untidy, but their sprawling stems of strong, leathery dark green leaves are decorated with dense clusters of vivid tangerine flowers. White, pink, lavender or red hybrid varieties are obtainable, but these may not be as vigorous. The 'crucifix' is in the shape of a small golden cross in the centre of each flower. Full sun is needed for the best results. Crucifix orchids can be sited in garden beds, around swimming pools, in raised courtyard gardens, or at the seaside. They are not at all demanding, though will do best if their roots are shaded with some bark or stones.

Other epidendrums to try include those with pseudobulbs such as *E. pseudendrum*, which has flowers of a jewel green with a contrasting lip of vivid orange.

Paphiopedilum
Orchidaceae

Orchids known collectively as slipper orchid, or lady's slipper, the paphiopedilums display flowers with prominent, pouched, pouting lips, in delightful colour combinations. They evolved in tropical rainforests in subdued light on the forest floor among leaf mould. There are at least 60 species, but some are very rare, growing in difficult, almost inaccessible terrain. There are world authorities who have written detailed books on this genus. Mostly, slipper orchids need a steady climate year round, preferring steamy conditions and a well-drained potting mix. Countless hybrids are available, in tantalising hues and shapes, all displaying the typical fleshy, decadent pouches.

Phalaenopsis
Orchidaceae

Commonly called moth orchids, *Phalaenopsis* species total around 50 and there are countless hybrids; firm favourites, and no wonder. Moth orchids boast impeccable flowers on long, arching stems and are widely admired for their ethereal grace and perfection. Epiphytic, these orchids are shade-loving plants from Asia, New

Epidendrum ibaguense

Paphiopedilum hybrid

Phalaenopsis hybrid

Guinea and northern rainforests of Australia. They need consistent warmth and relish humidity; you can grow your orchid in a bathroom where it receives muted light, or outdoors nestling in the lower branches of a tree. Moth orchids must have efficient drainage, and an open, airy compost, but not be allowed to dry out completely. They produce thick, leathery leaves and as many as 20 flowers along their slender stems.

Phalaenopsis Hybrids have been bred to produce cascades of immaculate flowers, large and luxuriant, in enchanting colour combinations. Those with white flowers are in demand for wedding bouquets; many varieties are flushed or striped in pink.

In the same orchid tribe are the endearing vandas, hybrids of which are grown as commercial crops in many countries, Hawaii and Singapore in particular. A renowned natural cross is 'Miss Agnes Joachim', found in 1893 in the Singapore garden of a lady so named, and now the country's national flower. Vandas are epiphytic, climbing orchids which require support and almost full sun. They are amazingly floriferous in various forms, and come in delicate shades of pink, white, mauve and violet. What's more, some are almost ever-blooming.

Index

Page numbers in **bold** refer to illustrations

Abutilon 37
  x *hybridum* 38, **38**
  megapotamicum **37**, 38
Abyssinian banana 141
Acacia 11
  baileyana 12
  fimbriata 12
  pendula 12
  podalyriifolia 12
Acalypha 38
  hispida 39
  wilkesiana 39, **39**
  wilkesiana 'Macafeeana' 39
Adam's needle 70
Adenium obesum 152
Aechmea 159
  caudata 161
  fasciata 161
  'Foster's Favourite' 161
  gamosepala 161
  recurvata 161
Aeonium arboreum 'Zwartkop' 155, **155**
African flame tree 33
African tulip tree 33
Agapanthus species 132
Agave 152
  americana 153
  americana 'Marginata' 153
  attenuata **152**, 153
Alberta magna 12, **12**, 13
Albizia **12**, 13
  julibrissin 13
  julibrissin var. *rosea* 13
Alcantarea imperialis 'Rubra' **162**
Alectryon excelsus 13, **13**
Alexander palm 73
Allamanda 99
  cathartica 100, **100**
  cathartica 'Hendersonii' 100
Allspice 146
Alloxylon flammeum 53
Alocasia 124
  x *amazonica* **124**, 125
  cuprea 125
  macrorrhiza 124, **124**
Aloe 153, **153**
  candelabrum 154
  ferox 154
  plicatilis 154
  polyphylla 154, **154**
  stricta 154
  thraskii 154
  vera 154
Alpinia 125
  purpurata **125**, 126
  zerumbet **125**, 126
Alyogyne 39
  hakeifolia 39
  huegelii 39, **39**
Amaryllis 138
Amaryllis belladonna 133
Amazon lily 133
Ananas comosus 86, 159
Angel wings 128, 129
Angel wings jasmine 109
Angel's trumpet 43
Annona 87
  cherimola 87
  muricata 87
  squamosa 87
Anthurium 126
  andraeanum 126
  crystallinum 127
  hybrid **126**

Obake hybrids 126
  scherzerianum 127
Antigonon leptopus 100
Aphelandra 40
  aurantiaca var. *roezlii* 40
  sinclairiana 40, **40**
  squarrosa 40, **40**
Arabian coffee 47
Arabian jasmine 109
Araucaria 13
  cunninghamii 14
  heterophylla 13, **14**
Archontophoenix 72
  alexandrae 73, **73**
  cunninghamiana 73
Argentine trumpet vine 105
Aristolochia 100
  grandiflora 100
  littoralis 101, **101**
Arrowhead vine 115
Arthropodium cirratum 127, **127**
Arum lily 147
Artocarpus altilis **14**, 15
Ashanti blood 59
Asian bell-flower 35
Asoka 32
Aspidistra 144
Atherton palm 80
Australian fan palm 80
Australian frangipani 27
Autumn cassia 65
Averrhoea 87
  bilimbi 88
  carambola 88, **88**
Avocado 95
Aztec lily 139

Babaco 89
Bamboo palm 83
Banana 87
Bangalow palm 73
Banjo fig 27
Banksia 41
  ericifolia 41
  'Giant Candles' 41
  spinulosa 41
Banks's grevillea 51
Barbados lily 138
Barklya syringifolia 12
Barrel cactus 155
Bauhinia 15
  x *blakeana* 15
  galpinii 15
  purpurea **15**
  variegata 15
  variegata 'Candida' 15
Beach lily 132
Beaucarnea recurvata 16, **16**
Beaumontia grandiflora **98**, 101
Beautiful honey plant 107
Beefsteak plant 140
Begonia 127
  'Cleopatra' 128
  coccinea 128
  fuchsioides 128
  luxurians 128
  masoniana 128
  'Orange Rubra' 128
  Rex-cultorum Group 128, **128**
  scharffii 128
Beloperone 55
Belladonna lily 133
Beschorneria yuccoides 70
Big mountain palm 79
Billbergia 163
  amoena 163

  nutans 163
  pyramidalis 163
  pyramidalis var. *concolor* 163
Bird flower 48
Bird of paradise 147
Bird of paradise bush 44
Bismarck palm 73
Bismarckia nobilis 73, **74**
Bitter aloe 154
Bixa orellana 16
Black banana 141
Black-eyed Susan 120
Black mondo grass 143
Black penda 25
Black sapote 91
Bleeding heart 104
Bloodleaf 140
Blood-red tassel flower 42
Blue amaryllis 139
Blue butterfly bush 46
Blue ginger 149
Blue hesper palm 74
Blue lotus 143
Blue plumbago 61
Blue potato bush 117
Blue potato vine 117
Blue taro 149
Blushing bromeliad 164
Blushing philodendron 115
Bo tree 27
Boat lily 148
Bomarea 101
  caldasii 101
  multiflora **102**, 103
Bombax ceiba 20
Bopple nut 93
Bottle palm 74
Bottle tree 18
Bougainvillea 103
  glabra magnifica 'Traillii' 103
  'Killie Campbell' 103
  'Scarlett O'Hara' **102**, 103
Bouvardia longiflora 51
Bower vine 112
Brachychiton 16
  acerifolius 16, **17**
  discolor 18
  rupestris 18
Brahea 74
  armata 74
  brandegeei 74
  edulis 74
x *Brassocattleya* 168
Brazilian bell-flower 38
Brazilian fern tree 33
Brazilian jasmine 111
Brazilian red cloak l57
Breadfruit 15
Breynia disticha 47
Bridal wreath 118
Brisbane golden wattle 12
Brugmansia 41, **42**
  aurea 41
  x *candida* 43
  x *candida* 'Plena' 43
  x *insignis* 43
  sanguinea 43
Brunfelsia 43
  americana 43
  australis 43, **43**
Bull bay 29
Bunny ears 151
Burrawang 81
Burro's tail 82
Bush lily 131, 132
Bush protea 63

Busy lizzie 140
Butia capitata 74, **75**
Butterfly palm 77
Butterfly pea 105
Butterfly vine 118

Cabbage palm 80, 83
Cabbage palmetto 83
Cabbage tree palm 80
Caesalpinia 44
  gilliesii 44, **44**
  pulcherrima 44
Caladium bicolor 129, **129**
Calathea 129
  burle-marxii 'Blue Ice' 129
  makoyana 130
  rotundifolia 130
  zebrina 130
Calico flower 101
Californian fan palm 85
Calla lily **146**, 147
Calliandra 44
  californica 44, **45**
  emarginata 44
  haematocephala 44
Callistemon 18
  citrinus 18
  viminalis 18
Camellia sinensis 48
Campsis 103
  grandiflora **103**, 104
  x *tagliabuana* 104
  x *tagliabuana* 'Madame Galen' 104
Canary-bird bush 47
Canary Island date palm 82
Candelabra aloe 154
Candle bush 65
Candle yucca 70
Canna 130
  'Bengal Tiger' 130
  x *generalis* 130
  indica 131
  'Tropicanna' 130, **130**
Canton lace 35
Cape blue waterlily 143
Cape gooseberry 96
Cape laburnum 48
Cape York lily 133
Carambola 87, **88**
Cardboard plant 85
Cardinal creeper 108
Carica 88
  papaya 88, **89**
  papaya 'Solo' 88
  pentagona 89
  pubescens 89
Caricature plant 41
Carissa 45
  bispinosa 45
  'Boxwood Beauty' 45
  macrocarpa 45, **45**
Carnival bush 118
Caryota 75
  mitis 75, **75**
  urens 75
Cascade palm 76
Casimiroa edulis 89, **89**
Cassia 18
  fistula 19, **19**
  grandis 19
  javanica 19
  'Rainbow Shower' 19
Cat's claw creeper 110
Cattleya 166
  Bifoliate Hybrids 168
  Unifoliate Hybrids **167**, 168

Century plant 153
Cephalocereus 155
Cereus 154
   'Monstrosus' 155
   uruguayanus 155
Cestrum nocturnum 43
Chalice vine 117
Chamaedorea 75
   cataractarum 76
   elegans 76
   microspadix 76
   seifrizii 76
Chamaerops humilis **76**, 77
Chain cactus 157
Champak 31
Chenille plant 39
Cherimoya 87
Cherry guava 97
Chilean jasmine 110
Chilean wine palm 79
Chinese lantern 38
Chinese star jasmine 121
Chinese trumpet creeper 104
Chiranthodendron pentadactylon 18, **18**
Chlorophytum comosum 127
Choisya ternata 59
Chorisia 20
   insignis 20
   speciosa 20, **20**
Chrysalidocarpus lutescens 77
Cigar flower 49
Cigarette plant 49
Citrus 89
Clerodendrum 45
   buchananii 46
   paniculatum 46, **46**
   splendens 104
   thomsoniae 104, **104**
   ugandense 46
Climbing alstroemeria 101
Climbing snapdragon 111
Clitoria ternatea **104**, 105
Clivia 131
   x *cyrtanthiflora* 131
   hybrid **131**
   miniata 131
   nobilis 131
Cluster cattleya 168
Clytostoma callistegioides 105
Coast aloe 154
Cocos palm 84
Codiaeum variegatum **46**, 47
Coffea arabica 47, **47**
Coleus 146
Colocasia 124
   esculenta 124, 125
   esculenta var. *antiquorum* 125
   fallax 125
   gigantea 125
Colvillea racemosa 22, **23**
Colville's glory 22
Congea tomentosa 114
Cooktown orchid 169
Coontie 85
Cootamundra wattle 12
Copper leaf 39
Coral aloe 154
Coral aphelandra 40
Coral hibiscus 54
Coral plant 65
Coral tree 24
Coral vine 100
Cordia 20
   sebestena 20, **21**
   subcordata 21
Cordyline 21
   australis 21
   fruticosa 21, **21**
   indivisa 22
   kaspar 22
   rubra 22
   stricta 22
Costus 132
   speciosa 132

spicatus 132
spiralis 132
Cotton palm 85
Cotton rose 53
Cottonwood tree 54
Crab cactus 158
Crane flower 147
Crassula 155
   coccinea 155
   ovata 155
Crepe ginger 132
Crepe myrtle 28
x *Crinodonna* 133
Crinum 132, **133**
   asiaticum 132
   x *moorei* 132
   'Mrs. James Hendry' 132
   pedunculatum 132
Crotalaria 48
   agatiflora 48, **48**
   capensis 48
   cunninghamii 48
   laburnifolia 48
Croton 47
Crown of thorns 157
Crucifix orchid 170
Crystal anthurium 127
Ctenanthe species 130
Cuphea 48
   ignea 49
   micropetala 49
Cup of gold 117
Curcuma 133
   australasica 133
   roscoeana 133
Curly palm 79
Curry leaf 59
Custard apple 87
Cycas 77
   circinalis 78
   prunosa 78
   revoluta **77**, 78, **82**
Cymbidium 168
   Large-flowered Hybrids **167**, 168
   lowianum 168
   Miniature Hybrids 168
Cyphomandra betacea 91
Cyrtanthus elatus 134

Date palm 82
Datura innoxia 43
Delonix regia 22, **22**
Dendrobium 169
   bigibbum 169
   kingianum 169
   nobile **169**, 170
   speciosum 170, **170**
Desert fan palm 85
Desert rose 152
Dhobi tree 159
Dichorisandra thyrsiflora 149, **149**
Dieffenbachia seguine 129
Dietes species 134
Dinnerplate fig 27
Diospyros 91
   digyma 91
   kaki 92
Distictis buccinatoria 106, **106**
Dombeya 49
   cacumina 50
   x *cayeuxii* 50
   'Pink Cloud' **49**
   rotundifolia 50
   tiliacea 50
Donkey tail 156
Doryanthes 145
   excelsa 145
   palmeri 145
Dracaena 22
   draco 23, **23**
   fragrans 'Massangeana' 24
   marginata 23
Dragon tree 23
Drooping clivia 131

Dwarf date palm 82
Dwarf poinciana 44
Dyckia 159

Echeveria 155
   elegans 156, **158**
   x *imbricata* 156
   pulvinata 156, **156**
Echinocactus grusonii **150**, 155
Edible fig 27
Edible ginger 149
Egyptian lotus 143
Elephant ear 157
Elephant-foot tree 16
Elephant's ear 124, 125
Encephalartos 78
   altensteinni 78
   ferox 78
   horridus 78
   natalensis 79
   villosus 79
Ensete 141
   maurelli 141
   ventricosum 141
x *Epicactus* 'Deutsche Kaiserin' 157
Epidendrum 170
   ibaguense 170, **171**
   pseudendrum 171
Epiphyllum species 156
Epipremnum pinnatum 'Aureum' 115
Eriobotrya japonica 92
Erythrina 24
   caffra 24
   crista-galli 24, **24**
   fusca 24
   variegata 24
Etlingera elatior 149
Eucalyptus 25
   cinerea 25
   deglupta 25
   ficifolia **24**, 25
   gunnii 25
Eucharis amazonica 133
Eucomis 134
   bicolor 135
   comosa 135
   hybrid **135**
Euphorbia 50, 157
   horrida 157
   ingens 157
   leucocephala 50
   milii 157
   pulcherrima 50, **50**
European fan palm 77

Fan aloe 154
x *Fatshedera lizei* 66
Fatsia japonica 66, **67**
Feijoa sellowiana 97, **97**
Ferocious blue cycad 78
Ficus 25
   benjamina 27
   carica 27
   dammaropsis 25, **25**
   lyrata 27
   macrophylla 27
   religiosa 27
Fiddleleaf fig 27
Firecracker vine 116
Fishtail palm 75
Fittonia verschaffeltii 138
Five-corner 88
Flamboyant tree 22
Flame of the forest 22
Flame vine 116
Flaming Katy 158
Flaming sword 165
Flamingo flower 126
Florida arrowroot 85
Floss-silk tree 20
Flowering banana 141
Freycinetia species 31
Fruit salad plant 112
Furcraea species 153

Gardenia 51
   augusta 51
   augusta 'Magnifica' **51**
   augusta 'Radicans' 51
   taitensis 51
Garland flower 135
Geiger tree 20
Gelsemium sempervirens 118
Giant bird of paradise 148
Giant granadilla 113
Giant lily 132
Giant yucca 70
Gloriosa 106
   superba **106**, 107
   superba 'Rothschildiana' 107
Glory bower 104
Glory bush 69
Gold blossom tree 12
Golden arum lily 147
Golden beehive ginger 149
Golden berry 96
Golden butterfly ginger 135
Golden candles 56
Golden cane palm 77
Golden creeper 118
Golden glory vine 120
Golden shower tree 19
Golden showers 116
Golden trumpet tree 35
Golden trumpet vine 100
Gossypium sturtianum 39
Grapefruit 90
Graptophyllum pictum 41
Grass tree 69
Green bird flower 48
Grevillea 51
   banksii 51
   'Coconut Ice' 53
   'Honey Gem' 53
   longistyla x *johnsonii* 53
   'Pink Lady' 53
   robusta 53
   'Robyn Gordon' 53
Ground cherry 96
Guadalupe palm 74
Guzmania 163
   lingulata 163
   'Ostara' **162**
Gymea lily 145

Haemanthus coccineus 134, **134**
Hairpin banksia 41
Hala screw pine 31
Hau 54
Hawaiian nut 93
Heath banksia 41
Hedge thorn 45
Hedychium 135
   coronarium 135, **135**
   flavescens 135
   flavum 135
   gardnerianum 136
   greenei 136
Hedyscepe canterburyana **78**, 79
Heliconia 136
   bihai 136
   caribaea 136
   psittacorum 136
   rostrata 136, **136**
Hemigraphis alternata 138
Hemerocallis Hybrids 137, **137**
Hen and chickens 127
Hen and chicks 156
Herald's trumpet 101
Hibiscus 53
   arnottianus **52**, 53
   brackenridgei 53
   calyphyllus 53
   heterophyllus 53
   mutabilis 53
   rosa-sinensis **52**, 53
   schizopetalus 54
   tilaceus 54
Hippeastrum 138

hybrids 138, **138**
puniceum 138
Honey protea 63
Hong Kong orchid tree 15
Hoop pine 14
Howea 79
   belmoreana 79
   forsteriana 79
Hoya 107
   australis 107
   carnosa 107, **107**
   carnosa 'Compacta' 107
   lanceolata subsp. *bella* 107
   macgillivrayii 107
Hylocereus 155
Hymenocallis littoralis 133
Hymenosporum 27
   flavum **26**, 27
   'Little Elf' 27
Hypoestes phyllostachya 138
Hyophorbe lagenicaulis 74

Illawarra flame tree 16
Impala lily 152
Impatiens 139
   'African Queen' 140
   'Congo Cockatoo' **139**, 140
   New Guinea Hybrids 139, **139**
   repens 140
   walleriana 140
Indian laburnum 19
Indian shot 131
Ipomoea 107
   alba 108
   cairica 108
   horsfalliae 108
   lobata 108
   tricolor 108
   tricolor 'Heavenly Blue' 108
Iochroma 54
   cyaneum 54, **54**
   fuchsioides 54
   grandiflorum 54
Iresine herbstii 140, **140**
Iron-cross begonia 128
Ixora chinensis 54, 55

Jacaranda 27
   mimosifolia **26**, 28
Jackfruit 14
Jacobean lily 139
Jacobinia 55
Jade plant 155
Jamaica honeysuckle 113
Japanese aralia 64
Jasminum 108
   azoricum 109
   nitidum **108**, 109
   rex 109
   sambac 109
Jelly palm 74
Jewel of Burma 133
Jubaea chilensis 79, **79**
Justicia 55
   brandegeana 55, **55**
   carnea 55

Kaffir lily 131
Kaffir lime 90
Kahili ginger 136
Kalanchoe 157
   beharensis 157, **158**
   blossfeldiana 158
   tomentosa 158
Kentia palm 79
Kermadec Islands palm 83
Kermadec pohutukawa 30
King of bromeliads 165
King orchid 170
King palm 73
King protea 63
Koelreuteria species 19
Kou 21
Kurrajong 18

Laccospadix australasica 80
Lady of the night 43
Lady palm 83
Lady's slipper 171
Laelia anceps 168
x *Laeliacattleya* 168
Lagerstroemia 28
   indica 28, **28**
   speciosa 28
Lagunaria patersonii 29, **29**
Lemon 90
   'Eureka' 90
   'Genoa' 90
   'Lisbon' 90
   'Meyer' 90
Lepidozamia species 81
Leucadendron species 63
Leucospermum species 63
Licuala ramsayi 81
Lilac hibiscus 39
Lime 90
Linospadix monostachya 80
Lipstick tree 16
Liriope muscari 144
Litchi chinensis 90
Livistona 80
   australis 80
   mariae 80
Lobster cactus 158
Lobster claw 136, 165
Lollipop plant 56
Loquat 92, **92**
Lucky nut 60
Luculia 56
   grandifolia 56, **56**
   gratissima 56
Lychee 90

Macadamia 93, **93**
   integrifolia 93
   tetraphylla 93
Macnut 93
Macfadyena unguis-cati **109**, 110
Macrozamia 80
   communis 81
   moorei 81
Magnolia 29
   delavayi 29
   grandiflora 29, **29**
   virginiana 30
Majestic palm 73
Malay ginger 132
Malvaviscus arboreus 54
Mandarin 90
Mandevilla 110
   x 'Alice du Pont' 110
   laxa 110, **110**
   sanderi 111
   splendens 111
Mangifera indica 94
Mango 93, 94
Maranta species 130
Marmalade bush 66
Maurandya barclayana 111
Medinilla magnifica 57, **57**
Megaskepasma erythrochlamys 57, **57**
Melaleuca 58
   alternifolia 58
   hypericifolia 58
   thymifolia 58
Melia azedarach 19
Merremia tuberosa 108
Meryta sinclairii **32**, 33
   sinclairii 'Moonlight' 33
Metrosideros 30
   excelsa 30, **30**
   kermadecensis 30
   polymorpha 30
   'Scarlet Pimpernel' 30
   'Springfire' 30
   'Tahiti' 30
Mexican blood flower 106
Mexican fan palm 85
Mexican hand plant 18

Mexican lily 70
Mexican orange blossom 59
Mexican petunia 146
Mexican sage 48
Michelia 30
   champaca 31
   doltsopa 31, **31**
Mickey Mouse plant 61
Miltonia 168
Mina lobata 108
Mock azalea 152
Mock orange 58
Mondo grass 143
Monkeypod 13
Monstera deliciosa **112**, 112
Moonflower 43
Moses-in-the-cradle 148
Mother-in-law's tongue 24
Moth orchid 171
Mountain cabbage tree 22
Mountain pawpaw 89
Murraya 58
   koenigii 59
   paniculata 58, **59**
Musa 94, 141
   ornata 141
   x *paradisiaca* 94
   sumatrana 141
   uranoscopus 141
   velutina 141
Mussaenda 59
   erythrophylla 59, **59**
   frondosa 59
   philippica 59
   'Queen Sirikit' 59
Myoga ginger 149

Naboom 157
Naranjilla 96
Nasturtium bauhinia 15
Natal flame bush 13
Natal plum 45
Natal wedding flower 50
Nelumbo
   lutea 141
   nucifera 141, **142**
Neoregelia 163, **163**
   carolinae 164
   concentrica 164
Nerium oleander 60, **60**
New Zealand cabbage tree 21
New Zealand Christmas tree 30
New Zealand flax 144
Nidularium 165
   fulgens 165
   innocentii 165
Nikau palm 83
Nopalxochia phyllanthoides 157
Norfolk Island hibiscus 29
Norfolk Island palm 83
Norfolk Island pine 13
Normanbya normanbyi 81
Num-num 45
Nymphaea 141
   caerulea 143
   capensis 143
   gigantea
   hybrid **142**
   lotus 143
   mexicana 143

Ochna serrulata **60**, 61
Octopus tree 32
Odontoglossum 168
Oleander 60
Oncidium 168
Ophiopogon 143
   japonicus 143, **143**
   planiscapus 'Nigrescens' 143
Opuntia microdasys 151
   microdasys var. *albispina* 151
   stricta 151
Orange 90
Orange clock vine 120

Orchid tree 15
Orchid shower 114
Orchid trumpet vine 105
Orchid vine 118
Oyster plant 148

Pachycereus 155
Pachystachys lutea 56
Pagoda flower 46
Palm-leaf begonia 128
Panda plant 158
Pandanus 31
   odoratissimus 31
   sanderi 31
   tectorius 31
Pandorea 112
   jasminoides 112
   pandorana 112
Papaya 88
Paphiopedilum hybrid **172**
Parlour palm 76
Parrot's beak 136
Passiflora 95, 112
   antioquiensis 113
   x *caeruleoracemosa* 113
   coccinea **113**
   edulis 95
   laurifolia 113
   quadrangularis 113
   racemosa 113
Passion flower 113
Passionfruit 95, 112
Pate 33
Pawpaw 88, **89**
Peace lily 146
Peacock flower 22, 44
Peacock plant 130
Pedilanthus tithymaloides 157
Pelican flower 100
Pentas lanceolata 55
Pepino 96
Pereskia 158
   aculeata 158
   grandiflora 158
Persea 95
   americana 95
   'Fuerte' 95
   'Hass' 95
   'Sharwil' 95
Persian shield 41
Persimmon **91**, 92
Petrea volubilis 114, **114**
Phalaenopsis Hybrids 172, **172**
Philodendron 114
   bipinnatifidum 115
   erubescens 115
   scandens 115, **115**
Phoenix 81
   canariensis 82, **82**
   dactylifera 82
   reclinata 82, **82**
   roebelinii 82, **82**
Phormium hybrids 144
Physalis 96
   ixocarpa 96
   peruviana 96, **96**
Piccabeen palm 73
Pigtail anthurium 127
Pilosocereus 155
Pindo palm 74
Pineapple 86, **87**, 159
Pineapple lily 134
Pink lacebark 18
Pink rock orchid 169
Pink shower tree 19
Pitcairnia 159
Plumbago 61
   auriculata 61, **61**
   auriculata 'Alba' 61
   auriculata 'Royal Cape' 61
   indica 61
Plumeria 61

obtusa 62
rubra 62
rubra var. *acutifolia* 62, **62**
Podranea species 105
Pohutukawa 30
Poinsettia 50
Polianthes tuberosa **144**, 145
Polka-dot plant 138
Ponytail palm 16
Poor Knights lily 144
Potato vine 117
Powderpuff lillypilly 34
Powderpuff plant 44
Pride of Barbados 44
Pride of Bolivia 36
Protea 62
  cynaroides 63
  nerifolia 63
  'Pink Ice' **62**
  repens 63
  sulphurea 63, **63**
Psidium 96
  cattleianum 97
  guajava 97
Puka 33
Puriri 36
Purple heart 148
Purple passionfruit 95
Purple wreath 114
Puya 159
Pyrostegia venusta **115**, 116
Pygmy palm 82

Queen of flowers 28
Queen of the night 43
Queen palm 84
Queen sago 78
Queen's flower 28
Queen's tears 163
Queen's wreath 114
Queensland black palm 81
Queensland nut 93
Queensland silver wattle 12
Queensland umbrella tree 32
Quisqualis indica 116

Radermachera sinica 35
Rainbow-bark gum 25
Rangoon creeper 116
Ravenala madagascariensis 147, 148
Ravenea rivularis 73
Red angel's trumpet 43
Red bauhinia 15
Red bird of paradise 44
Red-centred hibiscus 39
Red dombeya 48
Red fairy duster 44
Red-flowering gum 25
Red ginger 126
Red ginger lily 136
Red honey myrtle 58
Red ivy 138
Red-leaf philodendron 115
Red passion flower 113
Red silk-cotton tree 20
Red silky oak 51
Red ti 21
Renga renga lily 127
Rhapis 83
  excelsa 83
  humilis 83
Rhipsalis paradoxa 157
Rhodochiton atrosanguineus 111, **111**
Rhododendron 63
  Indica azalea 63
  Vireya types 64, **64**
Rhoeo 148
Rhopalostylis 83
  baueri var. *baueri* 83
  baueri var. *cheesemanii* 83
  sapida 83
Rice-paper plant 66
Rick rack plant 157
Rock orchid 170

Rose apple 34
Rose cactus 158
Rose grape 57
Rosebay 60
Rosella 53
Royal poinciana 22
Ruellia 145
  brittoniana 146
  macrantha 58, **58**
Russelia equisetiformis 65, **65**

Sabal 83
  minor 84
  palmetto 83
Sacred fig 27
Sacred lotus 141
Sago palm 78
Salep 166
Salvia mexicana 'Limelight' 48
Sansevieria trifasciata 24
Saraca 31
  indica 32
  thaipingensis 32
Scadoxus 134
  multiflorus 134
  multiflorus x *katherinae* 134, **134**
  puniceus 134
Scarborough lily 134
Scarlet bottlebrush 18
Scarlet cordia 20
Scarlet leadwort 61
Scented bouvardia 51
Schefflera 32
  actinophylla 32, **32**
  digitata 33
Schizolobium parahybum 33, **33**
Schlumbergera 158
  cultivars and hybrids 158
  truncata 158
Screw pine 31
Sea almond 35
Sedum morganianum 156
Selinicereus 155
Sempervivum 155
Senegal date palm 82
Senna 65
  alata 65, **65**
  corymbosa 65
  didymobotrya 66
Sentry palm 79
Shell ginger 126
Shrimp plant 55
Silk tree 13
Silky oak 53
Silver dollar gum 25
Sky flower 118
Sleeping hibiscus 54
Slender lady palm 83
Slender palm lily 22
Slipper orchid 171
Small-leaved lillypilly 34
Snow bush 47
Snowflake 50
Solandra maxima 117, **117**
Solanum 96, 117
  jasminoides 117
  muricatum 96
  quitoense 96
  rantonnetii 117
  wendlandii **116**, 117
Solenostemon 146
  amboinicus 146
  scutellarioides **145**, 146
Soursop 87
South African bulbs 134
South African coral tree 24
South African wild pear 50
Southern magnolia 29
Southern sweet bay 30
Spanish bayonet 70
Spanish moss 159
Spathiphyllum 146
  cultivars and hybrids 146
  'Mauna Loa' 146

  wallisii 146
Spathodea campanulata 33, **34**
Spider lily 132, 133
Spineless yucca 70
Spiral aloe 154
Spiral ginger 132
Sprekelia formosissima 139
Star fruit 88
Stephanotis 117
  floribunda **117**, 118
Stigmaphyllon ciliatum 118
Strawberry guava **96**, 97
Strelitzia 147
  alba 147
  juncea 148
  nicolai 147, **148**
  reginae 147, **147**
  reginae 'Mandela's Gold' 148
Streptosolen jamesonii 66, **66**
Strobilanthes dyerianus 41
Stromanthe sanguinea 129, 130
Sturt's desert rose 39
Sugar bush 63
Swamp lily 132
Sweetheart vine 115
Syagrus romanzoffiana 84
Syngonium podophyllum 115
Syzygium 34
  jambos 34
  luehmannii 34
  wilsonii 34

Tabebuia 35
  chrysantha 35, **35**
  chrysotricha 35
  heterophylla 35
Tahitian gardenia 51
Tahitian lime 90
Tamarillo 91
Tapeinochilus ananassae 132
Taro 125
Tea bush 47
Tea-tree 58
Tecoma stans 35
Tecomanthe 118
  dendrophila 118, **119**
  hillii 118
  speciosa 118, **119**
Telopea species 149
Terminalia catappa 35
Tetrapanax papyrifer 66, **67**
Thalia dealbata 131
Thevetia peruviana 60
Thunbergia 118
  alata 120
  coccinea 121
  gibsonii 120
  grandiflora **119**, 120
  mysorensis **119**, 121
Thyme honey myrtle 58
Tibouchina 67
  granulosa **68**, 69
  'Jules' 69
  lepidota 'Alstonville' 69
  lepidota 'Edwardsii' 69
  organensis 'Kathleen' 69
  organensis 'Moonstruck' 69
Ti kouka 21
Ti ngahere 21
Tiare 51
Tillandsia 159
Tipuana tipu 36, **36**
Titoki 13
Toddy palm 75
Tomatillo 96
Trachelospermum 121
  asiaticum 121
  jasminoides **120**, 121
Tradescantia 148
  pallida 148
  spathacea 148
Traveller's palm 147, 148
Tree aloe 154
Tree euphorbia 157

Tree philodendron 115
Tree tomato 91
Tree waratah 53
Tropical almond 35
Tuberose 145
Tulip tree 33
Turk's cap 54

Umbrella palm 79

Vallota 134
Vanda 'Miss Agnes Joachim' 172
Vanilla orchid 166
Violet tubeflower 54
Vitex 36
  lucens 36
  negundo 36
  trifolia 36
Vriesea 165
  carinata 165
  carinata 'Mariae' 165
  fosteriana 'Rubra' **164**
  hieroglyphica 165
  splendens 165

Walking-stick palm 80
Waratah 149
Washingtonia 84
  filifera 85
  robusta 85
Wattle 12
Wax ginger 132
Wax plant 107
Weeping bottlebrush 18
Weeping myall 12
White floss-silk tree
White frangipani 60
White ginger lily 135
White hibiscus 53
White sails 146
White sapote 89, **89**
Wild plantain 136
Windmill palm 77
Wine palm 75
Wonga wonga vine 112
Wood rose 108
Worsleya rayneri 139

Xanthorrhoea australis 69, **69**
Xanthosoma 149
  lindenii 149
  violaceum 149
Xanthostemon chrysantha 25
Xeronema callistemon 144, **144**

Yellow bells 35
Yellow granadilla 113
Yellow guava 97
Yellow oleander 60
Yellow pride of Barbados 44
Yesterday-today-and-tomorrow 43

Yucca 69, **70**
  aloifolia 70
  elephantipes 70
  filamentosa 70
  whipplei 70

Zamia 85
  furfuracea 85
  pumila 85
Zantedeschia 147
  aethiopica 147
  aethiopica 'Green Goddess' 147
  elliottiana 147
  hybrid **146**
Zebra plant 40, 130
Zingiber 149
  mioga 149
  officinale 149
  spectabile 149
Zygopetalum 168